G.R. MORRIS

ISBN: 9780615852379

CONTENTS

This night seems as good as any to kill the universe's messiah.

If a human is reading this letter, do the universe a favor and kill yourself, for death is better than the doom that comes for your species.

I'm not going into a diatribe about my past, because to hell with it. None of it matters, and neither do you.

How is life worth living if there is no purpose, no point, no free will?

I stupidly assumed the good guys would win.

Don't be a fool.

Release the preconceived notions of choice. I want you to consider where you live, your parents, your friends, and your emotions.

Consider the events that happen around you, how they sculpt your future.

Reading this right now sparks a certain emotion.

Still think you're in charge of your life? I've got even better news.

People are behind the curtain pulling your strings.

Everything has been predetermined before you were even born.

I don't care what planet you are on, or from what time you've traveled.

I've seen the progress of time. In the end, there was death.

Even now, I have doubts; there are so many grays in the world, so much uncertainty.

Perhaps humanity is weak; it needs to be controlled, because without control, there is chaos.

I have saved the lives of billions, yet none of them know my name.

I am Nightstalker.
A mindless marionette like the rest of you.

This night, I cut my strings.

PART ONE

NIGHT'S MOURNING

And I saw another savior fly in the midst of our fallen brethren, to bring unto them death to all that dwell beyond the earth. He brings destruction to every galaxy. In the end days, I see no forms of life, and no planets remain. So fear humanity and make waste of them. Fear their savior and bring about salvation. And in the last days, their knight shall fall to The Dragon.

—The final doctrine.
The Nullados Prophecy: 24:15

CHAPTER ONE

*"Life contains but two tragedies. One is not to get
your heart's desire; the other is to get it."*

—Socrates

Earth in the distant future...

Kill me! K... k... kill me! Please!" A bed of spinning, white-hot
nails ground into the flesh of the black-scaled alien pinned to
a wall. "It's A Beautiful Morning" by The Rascals roared over
the faint, silvery voice of a girl singing along.

"Please, God, somebody!" The creature looked down and
watched a nail burst through the front of his shoulder.

Small blinking lights from a circuit board shone through an
undulating, black, gelatinous blob gripping its legs around the top
of the alien's head. The organic tool was keeping him alive; but like
a parasitic squid, its transparent legs fluttered with electricity like
individual Tesla coils.

A torrent of voltaic streams crackled through the clear tubes and into the back of his skull; weak light flickered against pink confetti glued to the cracked walls with dried blood—someone had drawn dozens of smiley faces in it with their finger. The room mocked with a hundred heads of grinning china dolls plastered within the gore.

A long-legged silhouette of a skinny, petite girl danced. *"There will be children with robins and flowers."*

"Oh God, oh God!" he cried.

No amount of blood loss would give the creature peace. It was missing every major appendage, and every vital organ was pierced with a white dagger etched with glowing glyphs.

A mischievous, high-pitched giggle echoed in the dark. "Silly Billy. What God allows *this?"* She was poisoned candy, bubbly and childishly sweet.

An angelic female voice boomed, "Stop."

The music muted. She still danced.

"Thanks for spilling your cute little guts." The tip of a pink high-heeled boot broke into the light and kicked the creature's entrails across the gray steel floor.

"How many times must I tell you, *genocide* is not a sport! Wildfire, let him go," the serene voice said.

A soft glow of white wings appeared on the ceiling.

"An angel! Save me!" the creature gurgled.

The girl laughed, the sound dainty and delicate like tingling chimes in a gentle breeze. "No *angel,* darling. One more freak playing a loving god. I like freaks."

The alien watched her thumbnail, painted with a diamond skull and cross pistols made of bones, glide around a single red button in the center of an alien-symbol-covered control module.

"Release him!"

"How can I possibly be expected to handle work on a day like this?"

A disk hovered in the middle of the ceiling. It was angled toward the alien, leaving the rest of the room in near darkness. The tortured creature could barely make out the outlines of a disheveled penthouse apartment and several piles of bodies. Beyond the long row of broken windows, the ash fell like snow through clouds of smoke beneath a pitch-black sky.

The woman's jagged bone tiara caught some of the light. "Hire me, people die. That's the breaks."

"He told you everything he knew four hours ag—"

"Oh, pooh," she giggled. "Will ya *shut up*!? I swear it's always"— Wildfire deepened her voice—"'stop killing so many *people,* don't blow up that city,' and 'it's not polite to *punch* people as a greeting!'"

Another white dagger streamed through the air, stopping in the center of the creature's chest. "So ya think he chose this suffering? He wanted this? *You. Are. Sick.*" Light bounced off Wildfire's smile.

"Mocking me won't make Kevin love you."

The alien's chuckling captor responded to the voice. Two more daggers hit their mark. Now there was almost no more room for another one on its body.

The alien whimpered. "By heavens, help me!"

Wildfire stopped laughing. "Yes . . . save him, Raksasha! Aren't ya all powerful? Aww, the changeling god don't care about you. That's messed up, girlie."

Numerous alien foot soldiers halted at the base of the building where a loud tinkling chorus of music boxes played. Two large pink flashing arrows above the front door illuminated BAD GUYS WELCOME written in dripping alien parts hung on bedazzled spikes.

"Rhinestones?" An armored figure wiped blood from his goggles. "Um . . . we need the guin—I mean scout."

"Yes, sir," a soldier groaned.

Wildfire sniffed the air. "Goody. Your pals will play!" She stepped into the light, inches from her prey's face.

As seen through the curtain of green blood cascading from his forehead, her face was that of a sadistic clown. Half was painted the milky white of a geisha—the other half, the blood red of a killer. Scattered like bright stars in space across the red cheek were tiny black alien symbols speckled like glitter.

On the white cheek, a small human heart was drawn in contrasting blood. The woman smiled, displaying that evil jester grin. Her dainty voice was almost eerie. "Honey, ya buddies are gonna"—she fluttered her blood-drenched eyelashes—"go *ba-booom.*"

A little of the life-giving liquid seeped out of the crimson-filled sockets and flowed down her cheeks. The walls of the room vibrated at the sound of an approaching alien ship.

Several floors beneath Wildfire, the aliens approached.

G.R. MORRIS

Glitter and gunpowder caked on the walls. Hundreds of pink teddy bears were piled in the lobby and fixed the scout with a glassy stare.

"Clear!" The scout yelled.

Dozens of soldiers entered the stairwell and waded through broken pasty doll parts. As the rest of them filed in, each of the bears' eyes lit red.

The alien ship painted Wildfire's room with light.

With what was left of the tortured alien in one hand, she charged, her body bursting through the broken windows.

The copilot lost all color in his face. "Reverse thrust! Reverse thrust!"

Flinching, the pilot gripped the stick, launching a missile.

Wildfire drove her fist through the warhead. The ship's front thrusters ignited.

Too late.

"You forgot your buddy!" Her body ablaze, she landed on top of the ship and slapped the torso of the tortured alien to the cockpit.

"Ahhhh!" The pilot thrust the stick down and dove the ship into the building.

Glass burst, metal crunched metal and Wildfire's skull-and-pistols thumbnail pressed down on the button of the control module. *"Wheeeee!"*

In an instant, the gelatinous device attached to the creature's forehead expanded to the size of a basketball. There was an acidic *pop,* and the building atop a mountain of ash and debris burst like a Roman candle.

Then a crescendo of secondary explosions ripped through its floors, pulling the structure down.

Dropping the detonator, the silhouette of a female figure fell sixty stories, her fall turning into a dive, full of fire and destruction. Flaming multicolored confetti shot from bursting windows, whirling through the sky.

"Merry Christmas!"

No sooner had she pressed that button than came a cacophony of stunning proportions, a ground-shaking storm of detonations, and ten city blocks ignited in churning flames.

The figure spun and, moving like an Olympian, landed on her feet with her arms in the air, welcoming the rubble piling up on her.

Accompanying the snapping of metal and crunch of stone was the prolonged, painful squeal from a group of burning soldiers crushed under the debris.

She was dancing around the destruction, frolicking inside the fire. "Doo-dloo-doo-doo-doo! I'm singing in the pain! Just singing in the pain!"

"Not everyone likes *napalm showers*," Raksasha said. "What if I was still alive?"

Wildfire's hands went to her hips. "Aww . . . why you always killin' my buzz?"

A few hours later...

Nightstalker was alone. Old New York was a skeleton of the city it once was. All the buildings had their guts torn out, leaving scorched bones. Alien corpses buried earth's surface like a shroud. Even the fire that warmed him was dying.

But at least it was quiet, with the sun almost a distant memory.

G.R. MORRIS

Good, he thought. *Sunshine always brings people. And I hate those.*

His ghostly albino skin magnified the claw marks under both of his eyes. He blanketed himself in black.

His long black leather jacket was dirty from remnants of the departed beings he sat in for days. His stringy hair was so dark that not even the firelight could illuminate it. The strands bathed in the hollowed-out robotic skull , which he barely sipped from, savoring the fluid's deep, sugary sting.

His expression was vacuous as he watched the liquid rainbow colors, beyond the human spectrum, change dramatically.

A beautiful feminine voice thundered, "This is not who you are."

Over his shoulder, he saw the shadow of a figure on the large stone wall. The few walls still standing always had some kind of graffiti, and this one was no exception. KILL THE CHANGELING DEVILS was written everywhere.

"If it is all part of a plan, there are no failures." Her melodious voice pushed through his body, and each syllable tingled with bliss.

Dragging his gaze from the fire, Nightstalker looked across the long expanse of the alley. The bright glow spread out like the white wings of an angel, illuminating the far end.

Wings moved like a shadow across the ground, feathers rose off the surface and burst into blood-red cherry blossoms that swirled into cloth. The beautiful chaos stopped, and what was left was a figure walking toward him.

There she was, her glow adding to the flickering firelight. Her long cloak was deep crimson. White hands hung from the sleeves, but no face was in the raised hood. In its place, an intense light surrounding a mass of mirror like energy.

Another hallucination, he thought.

Nightstalker turned around and, raising an elbow, lifted his drink to his lips. He groaned.

Ten feet away from him, she stopped. "My physical body is gone, but I'm here with you." With every alluring word, the energy flickered.

Nightstalker coughed, spitting up some of his drink. He closed his eyes and lowered his head.

"Come back to me." Her perfect voice cracked.

Nightstalker took another sip.

"Please," she muttered.

He ran a hand through his hair. "Shut up. Just shut up."

"Night, I . . ."

"Your voice . . . ," he whimpered, and clenched his eyes.

"Please, I need you." She reached out her hand. "Everyone needs you."

Nightstalker put down his drink and covered his ears.

Raksasha took another step closer. "You cannot ignore me or this future you've made."

"Everything's a choice." He paused. "I do what I w—"

"You're drunk." She took a couple of steps back.

Nightstalker struggled to get to his feet. "Go away!"

He chucked the flawed diamond skull toward the cloaked figure.

The missile fell short. It shattered into brilliant flashing crystal and a splash of liquid color.

Her cloak didn't even rustle.

Nightstalker's face grew livid. Dark steam rose at the creases of his clenched fists and smoldered at the edges of his eyes. Shadows lengthened across the ground and reached out toward the woman.

The garbage pile burning at Nightstalker's back popped, throwing showers of sparks into the air.

G.R. MORRIS

The walls shook. Dust swirled as the ground trembled.

The alley around her exploded into molten rock and steel.

She raised her head at the flaming debris that spiraled in the air.

Shards rained down upon the figure until a cool wind rushed in and dampened them, shrinking them into embers. The shadows receded.

Raksasha's cloak rustled slightly. "I won't be scared away."

"Please," he breathed, stumbling back to his gutter. "I can't do this anymore."

Raksasha walked closer. "Demons are coming to bring hell and ultimate suffering. Have you forgotten?"

Nightstalker squinted at his wavy reflection in her hood. "I've tried the mind purges a hundred times. Guaranteed, my ass."

Her hood lowered. "You're trying to forget me."

He winced at her soothing voice.

Nightstalker turned his head away. His face fell into his hands. "How dare you."

He clenched his teeth until his jaw muscles trembled. "There isn't a second where you don't just pop into my head." He blinked back tears. "So excuse me for numbing my mind with alcohol."

He thought of her when the sun was supposed to be rising in the sky and when he played alien exterminator for credits. Thought of her all day, going about his endless life, watching other lives end. Thought, during his nightly dinner of booze and fake meats, of how her beauty could make him forget about everything he'd done.

She sighed. "Continue on this path, and all life, everything will be nothing. Help Kevin."

"Helping requires me to actually give a damn."

She raised her robed arm to the sky. "Look past the ash clouds and burned sky to this dying universe."

He glanced up. The stars were vanishing. A black mist flickered over his pupils. He could now see beyond the moon, past Mars and to a crumbing Jupiter.

The Darkness spread like a raging river, bloated by the countless planets it devoured. Within its swirling pools of vanishing blood, spaceships stuck to its waves exploded when it churned. The lightless sludge surged forward and swallowed Mars.

He lowered his head back to the fire and shrugged.

Raksasha folded her arms. "Your vision won't go beyond the Darkness, because there is nothing beyond it."

"So?"

"Kevin is the only one who can stop all this. If you don't protect him, there will be nothing."

He sighed. "Again, why should I care? Maybe I want nothing. At least there won't be suffering."

"And no joy," she said.

Nightstalker stared back at her. "I've traveled this empty space," he groaned. "It's dark, it's cold, and life survives only by people preying upon one another. They cause pain by being born and—"

"Complaining about problems does not solve them."

"And they live by inflicting pain, and in pain, they die. Am I to believe your precious humans chose all these wars . . . this suffering?"

"You exaggerate." She folded her arms.

"Do I? I've had it with all your *missions*." He threw his hand in the air. "The grandiose, endless propagation of man doesn't exist." He turned his back to Raksasha. "Your perfect future is gone."

Her voice softened. "It's not over."

He threw a stick into the fire. "I couldn't save you. So, yeah, it's over."

G.R. MORRIS

He threw a stick into the fire. "I couldn't save you. So, yeah, it's over."

"You'll fight because you choose to." She placed her hand on his shoulder and he felt his depression drain away.

"That could change real fast," he said, looking at the nozzle of an energy pistol peeking out from under a damp newspaper. "My body is a *prison*."

"Please. This will be your last trip to the past. Your purpose will be fulfilled."

A light glossed over his eyes and an unnatural glow relieved him of emotional darkness.

You always made me crazy, he thought.

Nightstalker sighed, staring at a pile of alien bodies in the distance. He took a deep breath and got back to his feet. "I know you can't lie. All right, what do I gotta do?"

"Protect Kevin so that he can slay the Dragon. Save humanity."

Nightstalker laughed. "Oh, is that all?" He sighed. "The Timeweb shows every outcome with the Dragon killing everyone—and if I face it, it kills me, too."

"I will open a time flux around your old shopping center in Angels City."

"You've got to be kidding me." Nightstalker moaned. "Am I supposed to believe the Timeweb is wrong?"

The figure placed its luminous hands on its hood. "You have twenty-four hours until the Darkness devours Earth."

Nightstalker stared into the fire. "You might as well feed me to it now."

"My champion is on her way and will assist you."

"I swear one day that girl's gonna put a diaper on a bazooka," he mumbled. "Well, I guess that's it then. I'll just figure out how to stop it, just like that."

The figure floated past him toward the withering flames. Her voice still echoed. "You will."

Nightstalker rolled his eyes. "Fine."

The figure stepped into the fire. Light burst around her, then she was gone. At last, he looked up and saw his growing shadow on the wall. He watched large swirls of light within the flames as the heat from the now-raging fire danced higher and higher.

In the center of the blaze, huge ornate doors appeared, swinging open.

He sighed as a young woman entered the alley , her long ponytail falling like rope over her black leather bodysuit. One hand held a derringer; the other, a double-barreled chrome plasma cannon. And as soon as he saw the familiar face of his large-breasted friend, the doors were gone.

She made a sarcastic pouty face and shook her hourglass hips side to side. "Super Stud needs . . . little me?"

"Shut up, Wildfire." He forced a smile.

She tapped him on the nose with her finger. "Which big baddy are we offing now?"

"The one thing that can't be killed: the Dragon."

Wildfire's eyes widened with excitement and she licked her lips. "Ooooo, neats. I'll sic Sparky on it."

"I doubt your favorite pet gun will do anything."

Extending her lower lip, she pointed at him. "Don't you talk about him like that."

Nightstalker lightly gripped her shoulder, and with a quick smile passed her. "All right, Giggles, follow me."

They stepped down the alley.

The surface of Earth was as dark as ink; its sky was charcoal. Even the steps they took added darkness to the air as their feet brushed through ash.

"It's been years. How's life?" she asked.

"I'm alive," he breathed.

She shrugged her shoulders. "And?"

"That's right. Unfortunately, I'm still here."

"I didn't mean to—"

"What did you expect me to say?"

"You'll get her back." Wildfire reached into her back pocket. "Ya will." She winked.

Wildfire held out a flat, shimmering disk. "Here." She pressed a diamond button in its center.

From the disk, a light illuminated twenty feet in all directions; the soft fluorescent glow revealed every tiny corner and crack. Both of them could see perfectly well without it. This was for something else.

The light bounced off the crumbled walls of a children's toy store. They walked around burned teddy bears and blood-caked plastic balls.

Nightstalker grabbed the disk and began walking. "Oh, thanks for the light. Remind me to get another one of these gooer repellents. Try to keep up."

Crispy alien and human skulls crunched beneath their feet. The whimpers of people dying sounded in the distance. Wildfire's face lit up when she heard the light drum of explosions.

"Do ya *really* have to make all this go away?" She tilted her head.

"We don't have to do anything." He rolled his eyes. "We *choose* to."

The wind was full of toxins; green and purple hues spiraled through the sprinkles of black ash. Nightstalker wiped away some that had collected on his face.

"People suck." He sighed.

Just then, the alien liquor he had been drinking took its toll on his body. Wildfire continued talking, but to him, her words were just noise. He leaned over and placed a hand over his mouth, hoping to avoid throwing up.

"Ya know, last time I bumped into ya, you were just floating around in space lookin' like a *corpse*." Wildfire slapped Nightstalker hard against his spine.

He knew she did it to try to get him to puke. He moved forward a bit but held his own. "I like the peace and quiet." He coughed.

"Why you back? What was all that 'Earth is the universe's outhouse' talk?" Wildfire asked, licking gunpowder off her fingers.

"If feces could take a crap, this would be the place. But, hey, Changeling Ale is the only stuff that gets me drunk." Nightstalker moaned. "This will be my three thousandth mission." He made air quotes with his fingers, "'To save mankind.' Stupid ingrates."

Nightstalker rubbed his eyes. "Every timeline I've traveled ends in some kind of catastrophe, and goodbye humanity."

"So, we just walk?"

"We never have a choice."

Wildfire stepped over an alien corpse. "How's good old Princess *Perfect* anyway?"

"Why must you do that?"

"What?" She smiled slyly, then pushed her lips out and sarcastically pouted. "Poor, poor baby. Seeing your dead one *true* love. You can't hold her, or squeeze her, or give her sweet, sweet *kisses*."

G.R. MORRIS

Nightstalker shook his head. "Somewhere, I thought the good guys would win."

"Should've known better, Mr. Nightstalker. Mr. Serial Killer."

"I should have never told that reporter in 1985 my name."

Wildfire patted the top of his head like he was a dog. "Oh, poor baby, it'll be all right."

"You're the only one who can make me smile since she's been gone. I'm glad Raksasha picked you."

"Yeaaah." She tossed a bullet in her mouth. "Your games are fun fun fun. Oh, hey, I toasted the Blood Syndicate. I squashed a ton of baddies trying to kill ya."

"You know I don't care, right?"

"Just sayin'." The bullet crunched between her teeth.

The two entered a desolate plain of destruction, littered with the ashes of hundreds of warriors killed in battle.

As Nightstalker looked at the ground, memories twisted in his head, one after the other. He stopped, and stood staring at the blackened remains of the once-mighty warriors.

Wildfire stopped to look back at her halted comrade. "Beautiful, huh?"

Nightstalker leaned down and picked up a helmet full of laser holes. "I'm sure he didn't wake up one day and say, 'All of this living business is overrated. I hope I get shot in the face.' Everything is a choice? " He dropped the helmet, and they continued walking.

Wildfire never walked, she sashayed; daintily swinging her arms and swaying her hips, the whole world was her runway.

Wildfire took a deep breath and soaked it in. "Ahhh, the smell of death. Lovely. Lovely."

The two of them moved through Times Square, a place once crowded and full of life. Now the city was mostly rolling hills of garbage and death. Fragments of buildings were piled with rotting corpses; many were holding various weapons.

"Remember how the changelings crashed their ships on Earth?"

Wildfire giggled. "Like I'd forget. You kept trying to stop them, over and over and over and over and over," Wildfire was skipping, "and over and over and over—"

Nightstalker lightly shoved her.

"They can blow me." Wildfire made an oral sex gesture.

Nightstalker smiled. "We've got to stop them. *Again.*"

Their travel came to an abrupt halt. Gravel and ash rumbled beneath their feet as a twelve-story alien beast obstructed their path.

The monstrosity resembled a demonic caterpillar; its gaping, sharklike mouth was devouring everything in its way.

Wildfire raised her guns. *"Ooh, ooh!"*

"Bad, crazy girl. *Bad!"* Nightstalker placed his hand on the gun and pushed down. "They're saprotrophs," he yelled over the sound of crunching metal. "They only eat the dead. *Unless you attack them!"*

Wildfire made a pouty face as she put her guns away.

"But I—"

"Didn't you *just* slaughter several armies of aliens?" Nightstalker asked.

"Pfft! Yeah, like ten minutes ago! A girl's gotta kill. Come on, when are we gonna start shootin' people!?"

Nightstalker grabbed her hand. "These things travel in packs. I don't have time right now to fight hordes of giant alien monsters just because of your addiction. We go around." He pulled her behind him.

Wildfire ripped her hand away. "I'm coming."

Nightstalker sighed. "I am so sick of being the universe's babysitter." He pushed a door that opened to a demolished football stadium. "Through here."

"Should I kill the next living thing I see?" Wildfire mumbled.

"What was that?"

"Nothin'," she said with a wide, yet seductive, manic grin. "Just negotiatin' with the voices in my head."

The sports arena was leveled. The stands were nothing but ash. A few surrounding walls were upright, held together by luck. Just like everywhere else, alien carcasses were piled in all directions.

"I think the people who died in the explosion were the lucky ones. I mean, the swarms of aliens just don't stop."

"Did the changelings do all this?" Wildfire said.

"This isn't their fault; it's mine. I'm sorry this is turning into a speech."

She pinched his butt. "It's cools."

He pushed her hand away. "Humans are crazy! They're always finding new ways to off themselves."

Wildfire giggled. "Let 'em die. Sounds good to me."

Nightstalker hopped over a puddle of boiling chemicals. "So, the changeling god wants me to stop her own people. *Again.* I never get tired of her saying they're just misguided. They've been killing people and swapping them with fakes since the species started."

"Ya want to marry a ghost!" Wildfire started kissing the air. "Oh, how sweet, doing all this because ya *looove* her."

"You go on ahead," he continued. "It's your turn to get supplies. Raksasha is opening a door to a different timeline. We're meeting where we always meet."

Wildfire's face lit up. "The old supermarket where Los Angeles used to be?"

Nightstalker nodded. "Don't spend all day on a mountain of weapons. We've got about twenty-four hours until the Darkness absorbs Earth ."

"And no," he made gun gestures, "You can't just *bang bang* that away too. While you're inspecting supplies, I'll stop by and get some breakfast and wait for you there."

"Just eat *my* food."

"I'm sorry, *pain* is not a flavor."

Wildfire smiled. "I'm taking the light disk. They got one there I betcha."

"They do." He turned around. "And keep the body count down. We don't have forever."

"So we play with the Dragon," she yelled, rubbing her hands together, "and that's it?"

"No, he said as he was walking away, "we kill *Kevin*."

CHAPTER TWO

*"One soweth and another reapeth is a verity
that applies to evil as well as good."*

—George Eliot

Ten minutes later...

Dawn struggled through charcoal-black, apocalyptic clouds. Old New York trembled. Dirty, blood-caked windows rattled in their frames. Skulls littered the ground, crumbling to dust, covering any green that once peeked through the old carnage. In some houses, one could hear echoes of voices from people who once lived there.

The tremor would have registered 6.8 on the Richter scale, but no one was alive on the surface to care.

Except for one man, who walked among brittle corpses that turned to powder, then swirled into the air.

Nightstalker wiped the dried gore from his face. *It never fails. I always get some of this crap in my mouth*, he thought.

The pungent metallic scent of blood blended with the nauseating, sweet, putrid, steak-y perfume of burned flesh and clung to his nostrils. The smell so rich and thick that he could taste it anyway.

He stepped on a manhole cover. A pillar of light rolled under his feet. The illumination revealed dozens of jagged claws reaching for him, dripping black blood.

Nightstalker noticed. He rolled his eyes.

"Welcome, human. Estimated time of survival for your species in this city: two hours, three minutes, five seconds."

A bar of energy shot up to his waist and solidified into shimmering metal. As he gripped the glowing bar, a clear dome moved over him, and he was inside a transparent pod. He dropped through the ground.

He descended past remains of soldiers buried in the earth. He continued through a red glow from eyes of robotic sentries policing the sector. The deep crackle of the sea of running power tubes sounded through the crust. The elevator burst through a mass of cobwebs into the vast underground metropolis.

The earth was one giant ant farm. There were thousands of tunnels in every direction. Some with hovering signs depicting roads. Some were advertisements flashing some kind of product. There were small tunnels for foot traffic, medium ones for hover cars, and large air pockets for businesses.

It was a hodgepodge of multicultural alien symbols, scrolling LED words on sides of buildings.

The two most common holographic ads that hovered like ghosts were scrolling text and images accompanied by rotating voices in multiple alien languages. *Hungry? Try the new FTF model Series 12! THE FIREGUT! It works so well, you'll FIRE the old one!*

They were everywhere. You couldn't go about your day without walking through at least a dozen ads. *Buy this, you idiot!*

Eww! Still breathing that old toxic air? Do your loved ones keep nagging you that they're dying? Old converters leave you smelling like foot and ass. Well, you, too, can join in the millions of other happy customers who have already upgraded their air converters. Stop those annoying complaints with the new Death Delayer Five Thousand! We're all going to die, but we might as well do it with pure air. This advertisement was brought to you by pants. Pants!

The man in the smoke-black leather jacket stopped in front of a reflective wall and three-foot-high bright yellow text blinked ONE MOMENT, PLEASE . . .

Text swam through the wall, along with holograms of food and prices spinning above them.

Human entrance completed. Please enjoy your stay.

A wooden door materialized, and as soon as he entered the diner he could hear customers complaining.

Nightstalker's disgust was written all over his face the moment he walked in. *Freaks.* A pile of slime with spikes formed a mouth and began chewing a plate of eggs—plate and all. The creature pulsated when it breathed, leaving wet spots everywhere in its booth.

Another biped appeared human, except for its head. There wasn't a place on its skull that didn't have an eyeball. It was a mass of pupils and a mouth. But that wasn't the alien that he found the most disgusting.

One of them seemed human enough, except for its green skin and its face. It was just one giant eye. *Gross.* He watched the alien bring a fork to its eye and began chewing with it.

Nightstalker, head cocked back with his thumbs in his belt, swaggered up to the bar and waved over a waitress.

"This is for the mess," he said, dropping a small pile of credits on the counter.

"What mess?"

He took a seat in one of the floating booths. It was like sitting on a cloud. The cushions were comprised of rotating energy that changed shape to accommodate the size and frame of each customer.

He heard the grumble of a creature sitting behind him that quickly turned into yelling in an alien tongue.

"You apes have some nerve showing your ugly faces in this sector."

Nightstalker sat looking down at the holographic menu embedded in the clear hovering table. He pressed his finger on pancakes and a three-dimensional image rotated a foot above the surface; a hologram so vivid he could smell the butter and syrup.

The creature behind him was humanlike, inasmuch as he was another biped. His skin was composed of red, flaky scales. Spikes protruded everywhere on his overly muscular physique; his head sprouted demonic ram horns.

The spike-covered customer slammed his fists on the table.

"I *refuse* to eat next to a *human!*" He stood up.

Nightstalker, still with his back to him in the next booth, smiled. "I am as far from human as you are from a bath."

The horned alien took a step toward Nightstalker's booth then froze, suddenly immobilized. His eyes widened, and his legs began to tremble.

"Sit . . . down," Nightstalker lightly waved his hand, as if brushing him away.

The humanoid's body slammed back into its seat.

"*I'll feast on your intestines for this!*"

Nightstalker sighed, and a dark, snakelike cloud swirled in his eyes. "No, you won't." As soon as he spoke that last word, the man's head popped, leaving green sludge and red cranial goo on the ceiling and walls of his booth.

The waitress behind the counter gasped, covered her mouth, and almost dropped the credits.

"I believe that should cover the damages. I'm ready to order now."

Nightstalker took a deep breath of the semi cleaned air and heard chatter from the bar. An alien humanoid with skin like leather scratched at his red, cancerous sores. "You ever think we'll make it back to the surface?"

The glimmering, slender silver robot put down his glass of oils. "We don't much care for organics, and we don't like your kind poking around where it doesn't belong. There are already too many of you bio pukes up there trying to terraform."

"Asshole."

A waitress walked up to the two of them. "Be thankful that you're still alive and that the last wars didn't overly damage our city here. Besides, it's only been twenty years since the last war; give it time."

Looking past the cold steel counter to the warmth of the kitchen, Nightstalker stared at the flames growing on a grill. He noticed the white, pillar-like robot with twelve different arms spinning, making several dishes at once. *How the hell am I going to beat a monster that by all accounts is omnipotent?*

He allowed every bite to stew in his mouth. His eyes focused on his food as if he were entranced by it. *This may be my last meal,* he thought.

Finishing his first plateful of scrambled eggs, he pressed the images of a tall stack of pancakes and more chocolate milk.

Two six-foot-tall Philodorians entered the cafe. "Oh, honey, take a pic of me in front of this FTF machine!"

Their skin, like chalky bones, shot dust in the air when they moved and spoke. The tourist paid its credit and bit down on the sandwich.

A group of patrons roared in laughter. The Philodorian blankly stared and blinked its vertical slit eyes.

"Hey, idiot," a patron screamed. "FTF stands for Feces to Food!"

"What!?" the Philodorian spit chunks. "This used to be poo?"

Someone patted the Philodorian on the shoulder. "Yep. That's how we solved the waste and food problem!"

By the time Nightstalker ordered his fifth breakfast, he was the topic of conversation in the kitchen. "A human? I didn't think there were any of them left! Wow . . . he's a beautiful specimen . . . just look at him!" one girl said.

The other female employees found an excuse to pass by his booth.

Here we go again—more girls trying to get me to hit on them. Nope. Not gonna happen.

His waitress was a giggly blonde named Emily.

"You must be a Series 100 model. I thought all of them died off years ago," Emily said, placing her card reader on his table.

He looked up at her and smiled. "I'm no hyper-engineered Cyber-Clone, but I'll play along."

She giggled self-consciously, but her blue eyes fixed on his. "You must be pretty brave to be around here, lookin' like a human and all."

He smirked. "Maybe I'm just dumb."

She stood beside the booth, one hip against the edge of the table, leaning forward, not so subtly letting him know she might be available. "It's been a while since we've seen one of you guys come in here, and I don't think I've ever seen one so handsome." She winked.

Still smiling, he pictured himself taking hold of her, dominating her and pulling her hair just the way she wanted.

Then he pictured the face of the woman who haunted him, who he could never get over, no matter how hard he tried. She stared at him speculatively. "You must have trained in the Great War."

Nightstalker nodded and removed his jacket to reveal the muscles bulging through his black T-shirt.

She tapped his forearm with one finger. "I guess being the Series 100 lets you eat as much as you want, and it turns into muscle."

"That's the idea," he said. "Replicated metabolism."

"Huh?"

"I burn up a lot of calories running away from everything." He nodded.

She laughed.

He took another bite. "Like a frightened Skingerthrog," he said through a mouthful of pancake.

"No way. I bet there's nothing that could scare you."

She was attractive, about thirty years old, ten years older than he looked.

Yet another woman I can sleep with. Oh well.

She would need a little wooing, just enough so she could convince herself that he had swept her off her feet, playing Romeo to her Juliet, and had tumbled her into bed against her will. Not my type, he told himself.

She leaned close to his face, brushing the tips of her fingers across the top of his hand. That was when he saw the faded bar code under her left eye.

Android. They're making them better each year. It almost convinced me this time.

He left her a good tip, paid his credit slip using his fake bar coded ID at the door, picked up a light disk, and stepped outside.

There was a three-foot-tall, bright-yellow-skinned frog-like man in a green tuxedo waiting on a holobench. It was taking pictures with an image pad.

Nightstalker walked up to it and sat down. "Forever the tourist, I see. I figured something would have offed you by now."

"I'm too fast for 'em." The frog's skin undulated with every croak. "I've two profitable miscreants located in se—"

"Got my ticket?"

"Always business with you," it said, extending its tiny webbed palm.

He held a coin showing a picture of Earth and a series of numbers—coordinates to a specific location.

"Ahem." Nightstalker cleared his throat.

The frog turned the coin over in its palm. The other side was an embedded live video showing piles of debris and shop signs. "Why would anyone want to go there? Absolutely dreadful old place."

Nightstalker snatched the coin from its hand and began walking away.

"Don't you want to hear about my adventures?"

"I'd rather die," he said. He shoved the coin onto a rock face and twisted it with his thumb. The coin exploded into speckles of color that bled into the wall. The rocks crumbled and parted, revealing a passage with glowing stairs leading up to the surface. The hot, dry, polluted air hit him like a burning pillow smashed against his face.

Noxious gasses poured out of the hole. It was that smell that reminded the living to get to safety, to hide underground. Or in a few minutes, your lungs would ignite, your eyes would bleed and, if you were lucky, you would die immediately rather than in the hours it took most people.

A shiny black basketball-size sphere zoomed next to him. It opened a red, pulsing, horizontal slit across its center. "Citizen! Close that gate immediately or—"

A brief explosion. Nightstalker lowered his fist. Neither his eyes nor his head turned to acknowledge it.

The light disk clicked on. He stepped into the wasteland and took a deep breath to let the toxins fill his lungs. The smell was close to that of rotten meats coated in paint and bleach.

The smell of home. Can't say I'll miss it.

Light from the disk reflected on pieces of broken glass, bouncing the glare to tile-covered heaps covered in swarms of inky gelatinous blobs with teeth. They scattered like cockroaches and sunk into the ashy road.

"Wildfire should be here soon with those supplies," he mumbled. He was his own best company.

He walked to the shopping center and stopped in a corner of the large lot in the shade of broken metal and rubber that he thought used to be parts of a crashed commercial airliner. *Need to stay away from the stores. Too many gooers there.*

He climbed down into a hole in the rubble and pulled down a flattened alien husk he had used for a door. *Welcome to first class.*

He stretched out on cushions from the seats that had been duct-taped together. The giant breakfast like a boulder in his belly, he mocked fate. *Nap time. Did I choose to sleep through Earth's death? Let's find out.*

An hour later, Nightstalker woke from his nightmare. He was sweating and shaking; half his body burning and the other freezing at the same time. He hugged a seat cushion with one arm and punched the air with the other. At first, he didn't know where he was. He sat up and felt the metal wall with one hand, squinting while his eyes adjusted to total darkness, and gradually orienting himself. Upon realizing he was in his hole, he relaxed and sank back into his mattress.

Tall, thin, inhuman silhouettes stood in the corners and stared. They threw their arms up and stretched them across the ceiling. He watched as their claws, like stalactites, fluttered toward him.

Nightstalker rubbed his eyes and blinked. They vanished.

Hallucination?

He lifted the alien-skin door and sat for a minute until his eyes adjusted to the light. Wildfire and her light disk were getting closer. He thought about seeing his true love again. He remembered her silky hair, her flawless skin, her perfect body, and how happy she made him.

Maybe I can save her this time.

He pondered what he was going to do in the past and its relevance to his other missions. And then it hit him.

There is only one constant in every timeline. It's me.

Green-scaled hands with long, cracked, crimson claws moved over flat-screens flashing with multiple layers of alien symbols. The image of Nightstalker climbing out of the plane wreckage appeared on a monitor.

"So, this even records what people think?" Jason's voice echoed in the background.

A deep reptilian voice bounced through the cavernous room. "Please calculate the probability of this future."

"Based on current timeline location of this machine probability . . . 99.6753 percent," a feminine robotic voice replied.

"And the Dragon?"

"Probability of—"

"How many times are you going to check this?"

"Shut up, Jason."

The computer voice continued. "Probability of the Dragon timeline and the end all life: 99.9994 percent."

"Sounds like we're making progress," Jason said with a chuckle. "Do you really think Kevin is the guy we're looking for?"

"I will not let the thousands of years of my plan fail. The changelings must be stopped," the reptile said.

PART TWO

KNIGHT'S DAY

"There is a Trinity of Choice. You can believe you live your life like a broken leaf, tossed about by the winds of chance or forced by Mother Nature's cruel vision. Or you can believe you are the captain of your own ship; you decide where the winds will take you. Whatever it is you choose to believe, it's up to you to make up your own mind."

—Raksasha

CHAPTER THREE

*"There is a storm gathering in a kingdom beyond the heavens.
It shall deliver upon the Earth a dragon, a false Savior. The
day shall come, one planet against all others. This will be the
sign of the end. But in the day of our Lord there comes a knight
bearing the name of Kevin. After the great cataclysm of fire,
this knight shall slay the dragon to bring about a great change
and everlasting peace to the future of all non-human life."*

—The log of Ellodion: Time observer.

Changeling notation: 161:12

December 24, 1975

Go ahead… hit me. Hit me." William was leaning down,
an inch from Kevin's face. Kevin felt the spittle that flew
through William's yellow teeth. He smelled the tobacco on
his breath; however, he remained silent and his body still.

He waited.

William raised his head, his beer belly brushing against Kevin's
nose. "You little puke. You don't have the guts."

His mother was veiled in grief. Watching her son being berated once again, she melted into her scuffed brown leather chair. Her face dropped into the well of her hands.

She cries every day, Kevin thought, watching William throw down the empty beer bottle. Glass scattered everywhere on the kitchen floor.

"Clean that up!" he yelled, pointing at Kevin.

Kevin stood still. "No."

"No?" William smiled. "So the little boy gets some courage. It's about damn time. Let's see how courageous you are when I take your disobedience out on your mother!"

William walked over to where Sara was sitting in the living room and grasped her wrist, pulling her to her feet.

Kevin raised an arm and knelt down. "Stop! I'll do it. Just . . . just don't hurt her."

"Please do what your father says," Sara sobbed.

William shoved her toward an open door. "Bitch! To your room!"

Kevin's mother stared at the group of men in suits in the corner who were watching the family scuffle, their arms folded. Kevin's eyes narrowed and, gritting his teeth, he gripped a piece of glass. Blood trickled down his wrist.

His stepfather grinned. "What are you gonna do, tough guy? Why don't you try calling the cops on me again? There's the phone."

William picked up the rotary phone and threw it at Kevin's knees. "Go ahead; I'd enjoy hearing them laughing at you again."

William had let himself go. Just five years ago, he had a six-pack, but now most people would say he had an entire brewery distributor. His excessive eating, tobacco chewing, and beer drinking had diminished his health over the years.

Even his prickly blond buzzed flattop was now overgrown, clumping over his shoulders.

Kevin's black hair was down to his shoulders, and had the disheveled look that came from rarely being cut or combed. The hair helped conceal the deep, thin vertical scar under his left eye. From his sharply contrasting pale white face, it was obvious he rarely saw the sun. He was covered in bruises.

He was toned and had the body of an Olympic gymnast, complete with washboard abs. He was of average height for a child of sixteen years, but he was muscular beneath his ill-fitting white T-shirt and baggy blue jeans.

Will was drunk. And he made the mistake of turning his back.

Still gripping the glass, Kevin struck his stepfather in a wild fury and laid open a small cut on the man's neck. On the next swipe, though, he slashed air as the drunken man moved back.

"You have no technique," William said. "Have I taught you nothing?" He swatted the glass from Kevin's hand.

Kevin briefly closed his eyes and stepped back. He remembered his stepfather's words: Anger is the enemy of the mind; it pollutes your focus. Kevin lightly touched his facial scar, recalling the knife William had used the last time Kevin stood his ground.

Filling his lungs with air, Kevin took a fighting stance and put up his hands like a boxer.

William stuck out his chin and leaned down. "All right, kid, let's see what you got."

William jerked his head back. Kevin struck air. He followed with a left hook. William knocked it away with an open palm. In the same fluid motion, Kevin hurled his left heel into a kidney.

"Predictable." Kevin smiled, watching his stepfather stumble back.

William regained his footing and raised his fists.

Kevin's attack was precise, calculated. He'd been sparring with him for years. *I finally hit him!*

William was no longer the unbeatable, untouchable, inhuman monster of his nightmares.

Yet the fight ended with William holding both of Kevin's arms against his back and pinning him face down against the carpet. Kevin looked to the group of men standing at the front door and wondered for the millionth time, *What kind of bodyguards let a kid get beat up all the time?*

After an open-handed smack to the head, William pulled him off the ground. "Enough fun for tonight." He kicked him in the butt. "Go to your room; you have school tomorrow."

He blew it off like this attack meant nothing. I don't get it. Was it because I hit him? Maybe I can make it past the suits. He looked out the garage window. He could see his guards smoking cigarettes.

Kevin gripped the metal handle of his sliding steel door. *Hmm. Better to wait for school.*

A large white backpack dangled on a coat hanger against the black brick wall. Large white Christmas lights covered the ceiling; small ones striped along the walls. Kevin hit the switch, and they all flickered, dimly.

Kevin stepped back into the well-lit hallway. Taking a deep breath, he paused and exhaled slowly. He thrust his arm inside and snatched the backpack. "You ain't getting me."

Kneeling down, he pulled out his armament. He strapped on kneepads, elbow pads, and a headband, and slung two belts across his chest; all of them embedded with glow sticks.

Kevin felt the scream hit his ears and dropped the bag.

"I haven't heard that door close!" It was William.

I bet I could hear those feet stomp a mile away.

Kevin pulled out a flashlight and put the backpack on its hanger. "The lights are going out again!"

"Again?" William slid a cardboard box across the floor, stopping right in front of Kevin. "What a sad piece of work." He shook his head and turned around. "Being scared of the dark at your age."

Staring at the flickering lights, Kevin twisted his flashlight in both hands and mumbled, "I'm not scared of the dark."

"What!?"

"Nothing."

Kevin opened the box and took an armful of replacement lights. *Just twelve steps, just twelve.*

Kevin felt the wood creak beneath his polished black combat boots. He looked down at his flashlight. *Please hold it together, Mr. Bulb.*

Kevin always stepped down his stairs at an angle, imagining if something were to grab his ankles at least he wouldn't fall flat on his face.

He reached the bottom, and even with all the lights covering his body, Kevin's pulse raced.

He rushed to the four generators at the edge of the room. The flashlight quivered in his hand as he dropped the pile of lights. His breathing heavy but shallow, Kevin plugged the lights in and switched on the power.

The walls were metallic gray and as thick as a vault with air being cycled through a singular vent in the basement's ceiling.

"Just another night in the hellbox," Kevin mumbled.

Twenty minutes later . . .

"He's your son! He's sixteen, for God's sake! Tell him to grow some balls and stop being a freak!" Although William yelled at Kevin's mother every night, the emotional sting hurt him the same each time.

In his room, every day was Christmas. Kevin managed to replace the bulbs that were mounted several rows deep on every wall and the ceiling. There were lights stacked upon lights, daisy-chained together. Not only was there a multitude of fire hazards, but the room was a sauna.

There were eight gas-powered generators, four on opposing sides, which accompanied piles of lamps both propane and electrical. He remembered William screaming, "Stop wasting my money on this crap!" And his mom always coming to his defense. "He keeps dreaming about the world being swallowed by darkness. He thinks he's preparing for a doomsday. If he feels safer with them, then I don't see a problem. It's his allowance; let him do what he wants with it."

There were boxes of books everywhere. Some were even hidden under his bed. Papers were haphazardly taped to the floor, bedposts, and a dresser. The papers were notes, many of them covering hundreds of religious, scientific, and philosophy books.

Kevin sat at his desk, the only place not cluttered by the notes. "Well, this is just garbage, too," he said, sliding a religious book into a large trash can.

The screams continued, and Kevin picked up the Bible.

"I don't want any of this. I've read you over a hundred times. It seems the more I do, the more I can't imagine that all of this is true. You just seem so fake." Kevin paused. "Look at me. I'm talking to a book."

There was a ten-inch black-and-white TV at the end of the room. The local news was on. *"Up to 155,000 fleeing refugees were killed or abducted on the road to Tuy Hoa. Sources estimated 165,000 South Vietnamese died in the re-education camps. The number of Vietnamese boat people who died is estimated at 400,000."*

"The deaths continue to rise, and a military spokesman had this to say. 'The United States government will not be held responsible for these heinous acts. We had to pull out. It was the right thing to do.'"

Kevin threw the Bible across the room and it smacked against the television, turning it off. Now the screams of his parents were coming in clearer.

"How can you be real when you let all of this happen?" Kevin yelled at the ceiling. Wiping away tears, Kevin began pacing and looked down. "Even in your book, there's genocide, slavery . . ." He shook his head. "What the hell?"

He immediately headed to his desk and shoved in a pair of earplugs. It merely muffled the screaming, as it did every night. "I'll bet Ma Kent was never treated like that, was she, Clark?" he said, picking up a copy of *Superman.*

Kevin sat with his face buried in his comics for a little over an hour and began to get sleepy. *Oh, great, I forgot to do my workout!* He looked at some Velcro weights on his desk. *Oh, well, I hit him today. I'll give him a black eye tomorrow.* He took out his steel, black-and-white embossed Superman emblem from his back pocket and put it on his dresser.

Almost the moment Kevin's head hit his pillow, the screaming stopped. A few minutes after Kevin closed his eyes, Sara opened his door. She stepped into his room in her black nightgown and fleecy slippers. In one hand she had a bottle and in the other a Ziploc bag. She placed the bottle on his dresser and tapped the Superman emblem. "I'm glad you love the birthday present I gave you, but do you ever leave the house without it?"

"Nope. My lucky charm."

"What are you still doing up?" She pressed her fingers into the bag, sifting through a pile of pills.

There were blue ones for taking the pain away, clear ones for anxiety, and white ones for helping her sleep. After throwing several of them in her mouth, she picked up her bottle of brandy and washed them down, not stopping until it was half-empty. Kevin, staring at the bottle, shook his head. "I wish you wouldn't . . ."

She smiled. "They help mommy cope."

Although she was now forty, her face was still wrinkle-free, but had a soulless look, showing no trace of how its owner had lived her life in agony. "We all have our issues. Speaking of which, that's why I'm down here. Your father wants me to talk to you about your problem again."

Kevin sat up. "I'm not scared of the dark. It's what's in it that bothers me."

"It's just the dark, honey. There's nothing to be afraid of," she said, stepping around boxes of light bulbs and batteries. "You know, when you were a baby, the night-light broke, and William wouldn't let me put in a new one."

She sat down on his bed. "You screamed and screamed your little lungs out until I found you asleep on the windowsill. I don't know how a two-year-old finds his way out of his crib and over the kitchen counter. But there you were, laying in the moonlight. Such a very determined little boy."

"I don't know, Mom. It just feels like there's something out there. Like a bunch of things are watching me. Some nights, I swear I can hear footsteps and breathing. Speaking of being watched—I guess he's asleep?"

"He's passed out, drunk." Sara looked around his room. "You fixed up your lighting in record time. But I wish you'd be more organized and neater."

"Superheroes are too busy saving the world to worry about being tidy," he smiled.

"So you're Savior Kevin now?" she asked, standing up.

"I'm not cut out for that, but superpowers are cool."

Sara walked over to the Bible and picked it up. She noticed all the religious books stacked in the garbage. "Please, a little more respect."

"The more I read those things, the more I think it's all a bunch of lies."

"You'll come along, sweetheart," she said, putting the Bible on the counter.

Kevin leaned back against his pillow and stared at the ceiling lights. "You've been feeding me this idea that I'm supposed to be a savior of the human race, and that this supernatural god is dependent on that?" Kevin breathed. "I'm sorry, but it's like you're asking me to believe in Santa Claus or unicorns."

Sara began picking up his papers and straightening up his room. "You sound like your father."

"Don't call him that!"

"Sorry."

"It's ironic that this God made me with all these emotions. There's nothing that I care about more than freedom and justice. Not just for myself, but for other people. Yet in the Bible, he's cruel and unjust. I need more evidence."

"Your father—I mean your real one—was an angel, remember?"

"So you say." *My family is nuts.*

Sara shook her head and stacked the Bible back with the rest of his books neatly on his desk. "What kinds of issues are you having?"

"Issues!? Let's start with the one that I have about being locked in here!"

Sara quickly turned around. "It's for your protection."

"I'm sorry. That was a low blow. I'm just sick of not being free.

You have me reading all this information, and all it's done is generate more questions. I'm sorry; I just don't buy this idea you've been feeding me that I'm the savior of the universe. I want to know the real reason we are all here. I just need to know the truth."

Kevin raised his arm and began counting his fingers. "For starters, if God is the alpha and omega, then who created him? Why is he the only one who doesn't need a creator? And, most importantly, how can he allow all this suffering? It seems to me that he either doesn't care or is incapable of doing anything to help. Both options lead me to think that this person does not exist."

"Well, honey, I have something to say about this, as this was told to me by your father. And I mean your real father," she said, taking a seat on his bed. "What he told me was, 'Just remember everything happens for a reason. We're all connected, special, and have purpose.'" Sara began to wrap her arm around him.

Kevin gently pushed it away. "What? That's it!?"

Sara paused and began to whisper. "I shouldn't be telling you this, but in the next few days, every single one of your doubts will be laid to rest. Every one of your questions will be answered."

"Okay. I'm listening."

Sara went quiet.

Kevin sighed. "Another one of those cryptic prophecies that you can't tell me about?"

She nodded and looked deep into her son's eyes. She placed her forehead against his and hugged him. For a moment, his mother's gentleness brought him ease.

"What if I fail? What if I discover I'm not special? What if I turn out to be a horrible person? Can't I just be normal? Do you think anyone, ANYONE, would like the entire weight of the multiverse on their shoulders?"

Sara squeezed him tighter. "You will be the savior. It's not a matter of if—you will be. It's just a matter of time."

Sara stood up and walked to his dresser. "Oh my God, it's a good thing Will hasn't seen this." She picked up a pill bottle marked phenothiazine. It was an antipsychotic. They were next to the pills to treat his claustrophobia.

"These are to help you. You don't want to see those crazy monsters anymore, do you? Where have you been putting the rest?"

Kevin sat up on his bed. "I chucked them out the bus window."

Sara put the bottle down. "They didn't catch you?"

"That's why that bottle is still sitting there. I don't even bother trying to hide anything anymore. He finds out everything, eventually."

"He's just trying to keep us safe." She walked over to his bed and sat back down.

Kevin reached under his bed. "I'm going to get us out of this, somehow."

Sara put her hand on Kevin's arm. "No need for your first aid kit tonight, just some minor bruising. I got a pack of peas in the freezer."

Kevin fluffed up his pillow and leaned back against it. "Why don't you just leave him?"

Sara paused, and her voice softened. "Everything happens for a reason; even the smallest little detail. I wish I could tell you more."

Kevin lowered his head into his hands. "Ugh. It's not that I don't believe in all of this. It's just that I have doubts, is all."

"And you should. The doubts are what allow you free will."

Sara smoothed her hand through his long black hair. "You're special, and not just to me. You have great things ahead of you."

Kevin rolled his eyes and shook his head. "You mean like all these bruises? I can't believe you let him get away with this."

His mother pressed down lightly on his nose. "We seem to talk about your bruises every day. Don't worry. It's almost over."

Kevin's eyes grew wide. *Wait! There's no way she knows I'm making my escape tomorrow. No way.*

"It's getting late," she said, pulling on the bedcover.

Kevin laid his head on his pillow and slid the blanket over his head.

She pulled it down.

"I know you're too old for this, but I can't help it. I love you." She kissed his forehead.

"I love you, too."

She waved her hand to him as she closed the door. "Nighty night."

Kevin forced his eyes closed . . . and then came the dream.

Directly over a spectacular jungle, the sun bounced light off shimmering emerald greens and sparkling waters. Tigers were off in the distance, walking peacefully through meadows with rabbits, deer, and elephants. Birds with large majestic colorful wings fluttered away like groups of multicolored leaves blowing in the wind.

Standing in a cool breeze, Kevin could feel the sprinkles of water on his face. There was something special about this place. Looking down, he watched the bruises on his arms disappear. The chirping of the birds and the chorus of animals were like music over the rushing waters.

Closing his eyes, Kevin deeply inhaled the aroma of tropical fruit with a hint of cotton candy. *This is just a dream,* Kevin thought. *Just a dream.* He opened his eyes.

"I know you're behind the waterfall. Just come out already," Kevin said, stepping onto the rocks. Even those seemed pure, almost artificial. "Why am I having this same dream?" Kevin said under his breath. "I mean, at least ten times this year. Come on."

He looked into the stream. It was like a living rainbow passing by. A multitude of brightly colored fish seemed to dance below him. He stared into the waterfall. Behind it, he saw a blurred vision of a woman in a brown cloak. She seduced his ears with a whisper more enchanting than any siren's song: "Find me."

Kevin looked up into the cloudless sky. "What does this mean!" he yelled.

The dream was over.

CHAPTER FOUR

"Truly, it is in darkness that one finds the light, so when
we are in sorrow, then this light is nearest of all to us."

—Meister Eckhart

December 24, 1975

Nearing midnight, a dense collection of black clouds moved beneath the moon and over the Knights' residence. The cold, obscuring darkness brought with it a murder of crows moving over the horizon like a fluttering blanket.

A man was heading home, jogging under the streetlamps. He kept inside their light like it was a protective shield. Turning around to the sound of birds, he saw the bulbs behind him burst. His jog turned into a sprint.

Kevin lived on a street where the developers liked one floor plan so much that they stuck with it for the entire neighborhood. Every house had a small white picket fence to match its bone-colored walls.

In addition to the Porsche that was in the garage, there was a Lamborghini and a Ferrari in the driveway.

Inside the house, William was typing away on his keyboard. He sat in what he called his "special secret room." Its entrance was hidden by a bookcase in the master bedroom and was used for surveillance and communication. Three of the four walls were covered with CRT monitors. They held rotating displays showing different areas of the house and several dozen feet beyond the property. The one wall that wasn't crowded with monitors held a desk, one small embedded screen, and several piles of wires connected to a speaker and keyboard.

William was looking at the screen and typing in a digital chat session.

Will: No, he should be asleep by now.

Robert: His eyes are closed, and he's lying down, but no, he's not asleep. He had that dream again. Like I said, he's going to escape, and you're going to have to let him.

Will: What? They'll rip him apart!

Robert: Stop questioning me.

Will: When are you going to let me use the Skyviewer?

Robert: Never sounds good. The Darkness is trying again.

Will: Is it stupid?

Robert: They are persistent.

Will: How long do we have till the Halo fields burn out?

Robert: They can be turned off, but never breached or broken.

Will: Why do they even bother?

Robert: It's a victim of its own nature. Darkness will always attack the light, even if it knows it will fail. Instead of asking me about my tech, you better be making sure that Kevin doesn't leave the field.

Will: He won't. But, wait a second. What about giving me another portable one, you know, just in case Kevin takes off and we need one with a longer range?

Robert: Ten feet for the portable one should be enough. There were only three Halos pulled and constructed when the Garden of Eden was dismantled. You have two of the three. The largest one is here with us protecting the changelings' entire population. And, no, we cannot just build another one. We've tried for thousands of years. Other alien civilizations have tried and failed. It's a problem with the power output. Kevin will be invisible to the HPA and the Coven as long as you keep him within the boundaries.

Will: So it's true, then. There are some things only a god can do.

During their chat, William periodically turned around to watch evil make its way toward their home.

A jogger found himself being chased by a dark shadow that exploded all the street lamps and dimmed all lights from every house.

———————◆———————

Got to get to my car; outrun it. Breathing heavily, he reached into his pocket with shaking hands. Running past the Knights' house, he noticed the shadow had moved on, yet their porch light remained bright. *Come on, door, open!* An oozing, dark steam was rising from the pavement surrounding his car.

The inky phantasm formed ghostly, skeletal fingers that scraped over his sneakers. He slammed the door shut and put the key in the ignition. His little white Volkswagen Beetle was dead.

On the verge of hyperventilating, his eyes darted around, looking for another means of escape.

He noticed the branches of the olive tree in his front yard rustling from an unholy dark wind. The leaves fluttered from green into velvet black and crumbled into dust. Like the ash off the end of a cigarette, the tree was gone.

He watched as a viscous slime as dark as tar clung to the automobile like slugs rising up the windows. The yellow of urine soaked through the white of his sweatpants.

Without him trying to turn the key in the ignition, the car started. Squeezing the steering wheel, he threw the car into reverse and hit the gas.

The crows were too fast, spiraling together in a massing whirlwind just above the roof.

The second the car moved out of the driveway, an explosion of black goo splattered over it.

The entire vehicle was now encased in a blob of dark, fluctuating sludge. The jogger could see his breath. Before his next inhalation, ice crackled, painting the inside of the car and gluing his hands to the steering wheel.

"I . . . can't . . . breathe! God, save me!" As he struggled for the last seconds of oxygen, he knew his life was over. His eyes closed. The goo vanished. It was gone faster than it had come. The ice remained, but all the air returned.

Like breaking the water's surface after a great plunge into an ocean, he took a deep breath. As he opened his lungs, his mouth gaping, the goo exploded from the air vents, forcing itself down his throat and nostrils like a wild serpent. He screamed as a dark mist rolled over his eyes.

The ice melted from his hands, and the cold was gone.

But so was his mind.

William noticed a flash of words go across his screen.

Robert: You better do something about that.

Will: I'm already on it.

A group of six men in black suits rushed out from the sides of Kevin's house, drawing Uzis from their jackets.

Just as the man in the car floored the gas pedal, the shower of bullets started. Hundreds of the metal projectiles passed through his convulsing body. Brains and black goo spattered in the rear window.

The car kept going, the momentum crashing the vehicle into William's precious Lamborghini.

"Oh, great!" he yelled.

Robert: You can always buy another one.

Will: I've been meaning to ask. How is it that this card you gave me produces limitless funds?

Robert: Does it matter?

Will: Guess not.

The man in the car, whose body was barely holding together, thrust open the door. Dark goo plopped and boiled, turning to ash at its feet.

"Yoooou will join us!" he gurgled. The air filled with the scent of body odor, feces, burned flesh, and sulfur.

The men in suits lowered their weapons. "Wow, these things stink."

The walking corpse took its next step toward them. It stopped, and no part moved even a millimeter farther as it collapsed, gliding down an invisible wall.

The body smacked against pavement. Beams of radiance burst from every wound. Every pore expelled a myriad of colors, displaying a brilliant light show.

The corpse sparkled into nothing.

The men in the suits smiled. "I love it when that happens," one of them said.

The popping of glass and clear plastic caused Kevin's eyes to open. The bulbs were bursting.

He tried turning on the flashlight he had next to his pillow.

It was dead.

Kevin watched the ones that weren't exploding flicker, and his heart began beating faster; a cold chill like dead fingers tapped his spine, and he lowered his head into the shadows under his bed.

The flickering stopped. He was in total darkness.

"Oh, dammit," Kevin said. Swallowing through a lump in his throat and shaking, he slid out a small metal box, which was full of his glow sticks and more flashlights.

The pile of glow sticks had lost their illumination. He switched on one of the flashlights.

When he raised his head, the bloody face of a little blonde girl smiled at him a foot away from his nose. She was clutching a headless doll made of stitched flesh. Before he could scream, the light went back on.

The girl was gone, as if the light's full glare had banished her. "Well, that's nice." Kevin shook his head and looked at the table where his pills were.

Quickly shuffling through the metal box and pushing aside a pile of batteries, he grabbed another flashlight and clutched it to his chest. It wasn't until he turned it on that his shallow breathing stopped.

"That's it. I'm out of here."

G.R. MORRIS

CHAPTER FIVE

"Before demanding proof, define it; then differentiate it from facts and evidence. When realizing none are objective truth, demand for proof disappears."

—Nullados

December 24, 1975

That makes the fourth person who has just…walked by. What makes you think this boy will be the one who helps her?" Jason asked.

His voice resonated around a giant screen displaying an alley. Scrolling alien symbols at the top of the screen changed rapidly when the camera zoomed in on a woman crouched under a rusty fire escape. This broken, dirty virgin woke up screaming. She clutched her chest, knocking off the newspapers that provided shelter from the rain.

"Because he's Kevin," a reptilian voice replied.

The agonizing December cold showed in each erratic breath she took. Another immaculate conception was about to take place. This time it would be on Christmas Day.

Kevin, jogging nearby, turned his head toward the pregnant woman. He stopped.

Kevin, jogging nearby, turned his head toward the pregnant woman. He stopped.

Her lips moved, but no sound came out. Something more than her pregnancy, more than the blood on her face and stomach inspired the kid to assist her. This gut feeling came like a dull headache, boring like lasers into his brain.

"Oh my God, has nobody helped you? This world is cruel. Believe me, I know. Here"—the boy bent down with a grunt and threw her arm over his shoulders—"let me help you."

Supporting her brutalized body after his workout would mean the ten miles to his home would be a struggle.

"Sorry," Kevin said. "I don't trust anyone. Even hospitals are death traps."

"Keep watching Kevin if you want. I have to step out. Lots of work to do," the reptile said.

"Damn it, Robert." Jason laughed. "You smug bastard. I hate that you're always right."

A few hours later...

"Murderer!" Popovich shouted.

"Prick." Kevin Knight's eyes peeked through the unkempt hair that drooped down to his shoulders. He was sitting on a bed, covers drawn up. "Jingle Bell Rock" was playing through the speakers and echoed through the building. The jail's smell of mildew, mixed with burned coffee and doughnuts, almost overpowered the scent of pine that came from the heavily decorated Christmas tree just beyond the bars.

No other convict occupied the cell with him; police passed light to other cells, leaving him in the dark. Kevin was sitting in a jail cell with the light of a single interrogation lamp that the cop turned toward him and burned into his retinas. It stood on top of a small white plastic table in front of the bed.

Kevin bathed in the light and smiled.

The cop gritted his teeth. "I could punch your face, and it'd be the word of a killer against mine."

Kevin looked up at him, and some of the strands of his hair moved away, revealing a black eye.

"I'm going to find whoever did that to you and buy that man a beer." The cop smiled.

Kevin raised his middle finger.

The cop punched the bedpost. "Where's the woman?"

"You don't have to yell. I'm right here."

"You're hiding something. I'm going to find out what it is, or you're gonna be spending the rest of your holidays with me and my boys here."

"You were there; you saw them put her in the ambulance!"

"I had that ambulance tailed. Not one officer has reported back!"

"Don't look at me. Maybe those cops are stupid, like you."

The guard switched off the light. "I hope you get a good lawyer, 'cause I'm gonna make sure the judge throws the book at you." He unlocked the door and stepped out.

"Yeah, and I hope you die fast, 'cause I'm gonna make sure I bash my fist in your skull," Kevin whispered to himself.

The police officer slammed the cell door shut, nearly knocking off the wreath. "What was that?"

"Merry Christmas." Kevin smiled and turned the light back on. "'That's the jingle bell rock.'"

Kevin's claustrophobia reminded him to stand up, inhale deeply and grip the cell bars. He glared at the officer moving down the hallway. The officer passed a man dressed all in black—black suit, black shirt, and black tie—black all the way down to his shiny, black shoes. It all matched his greasy, slicked-back hair and dark black oval sunglasses. He unlocked the cell door and took a seat at the interrogation table.

He dimmed the light. "I've been assigned to your case; I'll be your lawyer," he said through his overly whitened teeth—the kind of teeth that seemed to be twice the size of any that Kevin had ever seen. The man's voice was deep and scratchy; he seemed almost alien. "You want to tell me the story about how you got here?"

This is stupid. Aliens don't exist, Kevin thought.

Kevin looked down at the table. "It's not my story, particularly. I don't have one."

The lawyer smiled. "You're here because you shot and killed your father," he said, placing a black briefcase on the desk. The man shuffled through papers and continued. "It says here you're claiming that there was a woman, a pregnant woman, you were protecting. Where is she now?"

"Don't know."

"Come now, I can't help you unless you level with me."

"So you want me to repeat myself too? Listen, I told you. I don't know," Kevin said, turning away.

"All right. From the top: your statement says you randomly found her lying in a gutter. What compels a sixteen-year-old boy to bring a homeless woman into his house?"

"Call it a gut feeling."

"Those gut feelings can get you into trouble." The man pushed the briefcase to the side. "Your prints are on the gun. There's even a video of you shooting your father in the head. But you know what?

I'm the best there is. I can still prove your innocence."

Kevin furrowed his brow. "But I shot him. I'm not pleading innocent. I know what I did. I fully admit to it. I shot the bastard. My stepfather had it coming. Oh, he had it coming since the day I was born. Truth is, I did it, and there's no way you can prove I didn't."

The lawyer touched his face. It was full of scars. It appeared as if the man had been in a knife fight. Several knife fights. *Or perhaps,* Kevin thought, *he just enjoys making out with running lawnmowers.*

"You see, Kevin, proof is subjective." He threw a newspaper down on the table. The headline stated, "Three Hundred Inmates on Death Row Recently Found Innocent Due to DNA Testing."

"Right there. They were all proven guilty, but they were truly innocent. Or were they? Everything is about convincing a jury, and it's convincing them to believe whatever I choose. Proof is drawing a conclusion, and that conclusion isn't always drawn from truth; they just have to believe it is. Proof is evidence when the mind is compelled to accept the evidence as true. Unbiased is not equal to objective. Even if proof was unbiased it would still not be objective. That which exists, exists objectively, irrespective of a mind's interpretation or bias." The lawyer rubbed his hands together. "I have certain . . . let's just call them methods and connections, which allow me to put evidence in the right places and right times."

Kevin folded his arms. "Really."

The lawyer rolled his wrist. "With the right number of naive and crazy jurors, I can convict anyone of being a unicorn, although we haven't tried it yet. Evidence does not speak, it does not tell you it's true; even if it did, people would misinterpret it. So you see, Kevin, I don't need your statements. I'm here to gather information to see if it might be useful to us." He reached across the table and placed a small audio recording device in front of him. "So please tell us everything, and from the beginning."

Kevin looked around his cell, looked at the strange man and the exit door. "How do I even know I can trust you?"

The man smiled—a full smile of horse teeth. "You don't. Choose to run and you'll make it past two guards; but if you run through that door, the third man who meets you will shoot you. Once in the arm and then in the head. He's not going to try to kill you; he's just been drinking spiked eggnog all day, and the fat man has been a poor shot his whole career. I won't try to stop you."

"How do you know that?"

"I know you're not going to run. Also, in thirty minutes and five seconds from . . . now," he tapped the table with his finger, "someone is going to take you away from me. So please sit down ."

"I'll stand."

The toothy man raised an eyebrow.

Kevin looked at the soft red cushion on the chair; he'd been training all night. "My legs are tired. I choose to sit."

"Choose? No. Try compelled."

"What?" Kevin said, pulling the chair out.

The lawyer pointed at the recorder. "Talk."

Kevin told his story.

"I'd been running. I was lost. It was already dusk. I had been weight-training earlier that day and I was just exhausted."

"So why not just take her to a hospital?"

"Because every single time I go to one, someone knocks me out or tries to kill me. No thanks."

The lawyer smiled. "So, is that the only place?"

"If you guys are so smart, then why don't you tell me why, like, I'm always being hunted?"

"What makes you think we would tell you that?"

"So why not just take her to a hospital?"

"Because every single time I go to one, someone knocks me out or tries to kill me. No thanks."

The lawyer smiled. "So, is that the only place?"

"If you guys are so smart, then why don't you tell me why, like, I'm always being hunted?"

"What makes you think we would tell you that?"

"So you lived with a monster," the lawyer smirked. "I can relate. Moving on, what else led you to shoot him?"

Kevin leaned back in his chair and looked at the ceiling. "It was everything. The way he made me catalog all my actions: the times I took out the trash, the time I went to the bathroom and—"

"That explains the room with the monitors."

"Yeah," Kevin squinted. "Just how much did he have on those tapes of us? Me and my mom, I mean."

The man in black tilted his head. "No. Please continue."

Kevin shook his head and sighed. "I thought my mom married my stepdad for money. She said my real dad was murdered before I was born. I get nightmares all the time. Usually it's just William killing my real dad over and over again."

"You snapped one day and blew his head off?"

Kevin yawned and leaned back in his chair. "You aren't listening."

"You mind telling me why this paperwork says you were born in Mexico, and then this other one says San Diego?"

Kevin shrugged his shoulders. "For a while, we lived in Mexico; that's where my parents met. William was stationed there as a sergeant in the army. I guess that's where he was taught how to be a controlling asshole."

The man clicked a pen and began writing something down on a notepad. "So I'm sure a kid like you rebelled at some point."

"It didn't do any good. My mom said I was training the day I started walking. She said he made baby arm and leg Velcro weights for me to wear. So here I was, a baby walking around getting buff, I guess. It didn't really work out so well since I was, you know, a baby." Kevin looked down. "He beat her even back then, usually after he drank."

"When he couldn't find the remote control, it was my fault. When he couldn't decide what pair of pants to wear, it was my fault. And when he couldn't find me, it was my mother's fault."

"Why didn't you do anything then?"

"I did. I was the family doctor for a while; the wounds my mom and I suffered were pretty severe. They forced me to learn martial arts, and I started sparring at five years old. I pretty much know them all."

"How often did you move?" he asked, tapping his pen.

"The longest we were in one place was a few years. Will always said it was because of his job. Of course, that was a lie. Mom said it was because I was special. She kept saying"—Kevin began talking with a high-pitched voice—"'You're special, Kevin. You're going to be the savior.'"

"I'm assuming you didn't believe her." He wrote furiously on his pad.

"Um, duh. It was kind of strange, though, since everything she told me has come true. Especially when I go against the plan."

"Why not call the cops?"

"That's what I said. At least the first time," Kevin continued. "But I've had run-ins with the cops several times, and each time they've been trying to kill me."

The lawyer tapped a finger on the table. "So you must feel safe right here, right now."

"Well, that's why I'm spilling the beans. I figure at any moment I'll be dead anyway."

The man in black looked up at the clock. "Okay, fast forward to today."

Kevin nodded. "It was awesome. I was so motivated after I hit him that I pushed myself and ran even farther. I lost focus, though, and went off track. And then I found her. So I took her home where my medical kit was so I could fix her myself. I thought I could hide her from Will and his cameras, but then she started screaming."

The lawyer leaned forward. "Did the woman tell you who she was?"

Kevin paused, looked at the man and back at the door. "Her tongue was torn out. But it seemed like my mom knew her somehow."

"And?" The lawyer tapped his pen on the recorder.

"Okay, well, when Will came in, my mom wasn't about to let him touch her. For the first time in their relationship, my mother put her foot down. But Will was drunk. She got the worst beating I've ever seen." Kevin swallowed, pushing down the lump in his throat. "I wasn't about to let him shoot the stranger."

The lawyer just stared blankly at him and turned off the recorder.

The man broke the silence. "The doctors said she suffered from severe lacerations, head trauma, and massive contusions . The police said that they could not find any evidence that Will was the killer. Your statement says that you managed to get the gun away from him and shoot him. Because, as you said, he got his gun out and was going to shoot the homeless woman. So you shot him."

There were tears forming in Kevin's eyes when he slammed his fists on the table. He stood up. "Of course I shot him. He killed my mom! Of course there isn't going to be any evidence that he did it. It's all on me! They're gonna blame me for both of their deaths."

Kevin looked down and noticed the top of the newspaper. It was thirty years in the future. "What the—"

"Well, you're definitely the right guy." The man stood up and opened his briefcase. "I hate to be the bearer of even more bad news."

He took out a pistol and pressed his shiny black-gloved finger on Kevin's lips. "Shhh. Yell, and your rescuers die."

He continued screwing on a gun silencer. "It shouldn't come as a surprise, but I'm here to end your life."

CHAPTER SIX

*"For humanity is the holy people of the light; Raksasha,
our god, has chosen us to be their protectors. For out of
all the species in every world, they are the ones whom
can save it. Truly it is then if humanity goes, so shall
the universe, so shall the changelings. I see no other
important act than to ensure their continued existence."*

—The log of Ellodion: Time observer.

Changeling notation: 181:12

December 24, 1975, a few hours earlier

T he holiday night brought gently frosted rain. Puddles of water
along the roads reflected the city's festive lights and its cloud-
filled sky.

Numerous cars passed over the roads and splashed water against
the sidewalk, managing to irritate the nearby homeless. A gusty wind
brought trash, pushing through its alleys, rolling it along the ground
like tumbleweeds.

This was a part of the city that even prostitutes kept clear of. It was an area referred to as a "poor man's outhouse."

Directly under the filth and scum lived a subculture of beings whose job it was to protect mankind.

It was a busy day for death in Los Angeles. Many people died from natural causes, of course, and these deaths were not required by procedure to come under the Human Protection Agency's probing eyes. However, the Changeling Investigation Department (CID) had nine others with which to deal.

Two traffic fatalities occurred: one involved a man who shape-shifted into a woman seconds after death; the other found a man's body partially morphed into glass. Two other men, dead from gunshot wounds, had no traces of blood in or around their bodies.

One child changed the color of its skin and then was beaten to death by a mean-tempered, drunken father. A woman was shifting and simply drowned in her own skin. Two young men committed suicide by cutting off their flesh while trying to stop their erratic shape-changing.

Then there was Kevin.

Kevin wasn't dead—at least, not yet—and not if Robert had anything to say about it. And Robert definitely had something to say about it.

Robert's job was to be the all-seeing eye. He had worked in CID's main office, five hundred miles under Los Angeles, for more than two hundred years. It was always dark, and the temperature ran at 350 degrees; that was the way he liked it. His wasn't your average cubicle: its walls were steel, the floor and ceiling were titanium, and the door was a waterfall of shimmering gold energy that spewed from the ceiling.

Patriotic music played through the speaker system; it was the changelings' anthem. He could see dozens of his workers lowering their heads, raising their arms, and speaking the Shifters' Pledge in unison.

The alien in the cell next to him rolled his eyes. "I'll never understand this language. Are they saying 'freedom is oppression' and 'control is prosperity'?"

———◆———

"I know this is your first day here, but you're just going to have to get used to it," Robert said, propping up his brown-strapped boots on his desk.

Peering through a window to the office across from him, the man in the large-brimmed, white leather cowboy hat started sharpening his fangs. "Are we the only ones here who aren't shifters?"

"Racist." Robert grinned.

The cowboy continued to push a thin metal file over his teeth. "I don't like the idea that I could be talking to my boss when I'm thinking I'm talking to you."

"Those intensive energy scans you pass through in every room won't let that happen . . . unless, of course, the council hacks the HPA security system. And our bosses have better things to do than try to hack the system I designed just to screw with us. That'd be something I would do. Besides, the shifters—the aliens who stole changeling technology to shape-shift—have nearly been wiped out." Light bounced off the alien cowboy's deep red face, and sounds of a video played in the background. "We're told the changelings are good, incapable of doing anything wrong." Robert said.

The cowboy paused the video. "Nothing wrong, huh? Then what's the deal with that mess in the center of the barracks?"

Robert nodded. "Yes. The stairs, the doors that go nowhere, and a stationary elevator. I thought it was a joke until I consulted the builder. It was a nonbeliever who said to me, 'Since life has no purpose, neither should this building.'"

"That's insane," the cowboy said.

"I asked him if he built the foundation the same way."

The cowboy chuckled, and the video continued. "Thousands of years ago, our race was perfect. There was no crime; everyone was equal. We were harmonious, loving, and lived to evolve technologically. But we were naive to the evils of the universe and paid for it. The slavers invaded. They absorbed all our efforts. They stole our technology. More than half our population was wiped out, and the rest of us escaped to a nearby galaxy. The brutality of it all opened our eyes, and it was then we realized we needed tools to defend ourselves."

The video stopped again. "Is all of this true?" the cowboy asked.

Robert just chewed on his unlit cigar and nodded.

The voice-over continued. "In our efforts to protect ourselves, we polluted our world and escaped deep beneath the planet Earth. We had to watch the slavers use our own technology to enslave the large lizards and wipe out all the wondrous life on the surface. For this reason, in the next couple of weeks, you will learn the policies of the HPA and how humanity must be controlled."

Robert, overhearing the video, shook his head in disgust.

"We welcome our alien brothers," the video explained, "but many of them do not welcome us. We walk among the humans. It is our responsibility to protect the people from themselves. Humanity must be disarmed. Their guns are just the beginning. We know what's best for them. We are superior. United as one mind, one purpose. We will save lives. Restrictions must be enforced and technology limited."

Robert tapped a claw on the separating force field window. "Hey, Maddox! Since you're my replacement, you should know what you're getting into."

The face of the alien in the room across from him turned as white as his hat. "How did you know?"

"I don't want to brag, but I pretty much know everything."

"I'm sorry that—"

"You will be the head of the recording process, which monitors everything. There is nothing that isn't being watched and scrutinized."

Robert pressed a button on his console, and a holographic image of an atom appeared, hovering in front of the cowboy's face. "These are Ellodion chips. Yes, named after the creator of the Timeweb. They are as intangible as that hologram in front of you."

The alien cowboy squinted his red, marbled eyes. "People who want to hide something are the ones who are doing something that needs to be hidden."

"I wonder if I was as brainwashed as you when I started."

Robert stood up and, snapping his claws together, created a spark and lit his thick, black cigar. "The chips make up a network called the Skyviewer. Just like everything changelings create, the chips have the ability to change shape. So even if you were to somehow see at the subatomic level, they mask themselves. They exist in the air you breathe, the food you eat, and in every grain of sand and salt in the ocean."

"Aren't you concerned about the head of the HPA?"

"I told you . . . I know everything. I saw this very conversation over a hundred years ago. They're filtered."

Robert placed his hand on a metal box under his Hoverseat. "Being the head of CID is a pretty big job. Even with the diamond walkers and your thousands of staff, you'll find that you have to exterminate humans every now and then."

Light passed over his claw, and the box opened. Inside were guns, clothing, and packets of tools.

"Changelings believe it is more important to keep the existence of all alien life a secret, even if it means humans die. And if even more must die so that the majority survives, so be it. For most of my life, I agreed with them."

Placing baseball-size metal orbs in the pockets of his trench coat, Robert sighed. "There are very few nonshifters here in this underground metropolis. As good as they appear to be, please keep in mind that they believe the ends justify the means."

"They don't?"

Robert spit out his cigar. "I was going to let you discover this for yourself."

Walking back to his console, he placed his claw down onto a small rectangle full of needles that began drawing his blood. "Beta, delta, four, twelve, six, nine . . ." He continued speaking a series of numbers and letters for five minutes.

A narrow beam of light passed over his body, and Robert shook his head. "From the beginning, and even today, every major political leader is a shifter, a walker, or a changeling."

"But the head of the HPA is a human. So they're basically ruled by a human, which keeps them unbiased," the cowboy said.

"Please," Robert said. "Even CID was originally created to keep the changelings honest and moral. The last five hundred years, it's been about monitoring the control and following orders."

The hologram of the Skyviewer chips changed to an image of a man standing on a platform.

"What is this?" the cowboy asked.

"The birth of the Coven."

The old man in the hologram had tears in his eyes; a bright spotlight above him was nearly blinding. "As a human and as a Jew, I implore you to stop this madness!"

Three voices spoke in unison and boomed around him. "The continuance of the human species is more important than your religion or a few lives."

"A few lives? A few!? You people created Hitler! I beg you, not only for myself but for humanity, please reprogram him. This one, Walker!"

"Calm yourself, or you will be held in contempt."

"I find contempt in everything you do to us."

"There is no requirement for us to explain the good we are doing. Not to you."

The voices hushed as the man fell to his knees and whimpered. The platform beneath his feet began to split open. "You, you would kill me!?" He turned around and took off running.

His face smacked against a cylinder of invisible blue energy that now surrounded him. "You monsters!" His sweat turned to steam and rose off the boils forming on his skin.

"You'll pay for this!" His body burst into flames.

A demonic voice whispered into the room. "Edwaaarrd . . ."

A dark, boiling, inky patch appeared below his feet.

"Ahhhh! You will suffer!" Flailing his arms, he dropped toward Earth's core.

The hologram vanished. "Was that—?"

"Edward Blackthorne. Yes," Robert said.

"Wait a second. All of the reports say he's still alive," the cowboy said.

"Rumor has it he made a deal, and he's back for revenge."

"Bullshit."

Robert smiled. "You know, it makes you think. There was a vast improvement in technology and medicine that was a direct result of World War II and the holocaust."

Maddox shrugged. "So?"

"So maybe the Timeweb's insistence on causing it was right. Maybe it was necessary."

"Crazy old man."

Robert coughed. "Says the guy who believes in consequentialism. Our sacred prophet the Timeweb was programmed to believe that too."

Maddox mumbled inaudibly, rolled his eyes and nodded.

Another hologram appeared in front of Maddox's face; this one nearly filled his entire two-hundred-square-foot office.

"More of your propaganda?" he said, as the images moved through him.

Like a video camera, the hologram panned over vast rolling hills coated in spheres. From above, the hills looked like giant packages covered in supersize bubble wrap.

And then the camera zoomed in.

"This isn't just a zombie paradise; it's an example of the dark place where the changelings have gone."

There were billions of brains like heads of lettuce growing out of a garden of wired technology.

"What is this?" Maddox asked.

"The average human brain can process 36.8 petaflops of data per second; once genetically enhanced, they range to about 50.4 per second. There are exactly two brains for every man, woman, and child on Earth. Still, even with all this processing power, it only increases the probability matrix around six percent. But it's all in the name of seeing all possible futures, saving mankind from extinction and apparently protecting them from themselves."

"Why not just get more?"

"That's not the right question," Robert said.

The camera panned over a brain stem inside a container filled with gelatinous fluid. It began to follow the black tube that ran into a main line. The camera sped up, moving over the vast terrain of pipes. There it was, an immense supercomputer: a skyscraper of technology fifty miles wide and fifty miles tall.

It was a giant, fluctuating square of circuitry and wires coated in countless screens that were changing shape and size.

Maddox folded his arms and leaned back in his chair.

"This is the Timeweb, and as you know, its main program is the Skyviewer. Its computational power is immeasurable because it's constantly growing. This is due to the other timelines—the other Timewebs—that it's networked to. Those brains are from people who couldn't be controlled. They were replaced by walkers."

"Our employers aren't monsters. You're wasting your time. You honestly think this is gonna make me go against them?"

Robert blew smoke into the air, which formed the shape of daggers. "Real control is influencing someone to the point that he believes his choices are his own. It's a miracle what you can get away with when you misinterpret religious doctrine."

Maddox laughed. "Okay, tough guy, why not just start offing the changelings one by one?"

Robert sighed. "You aren't listening. The changelings aren't evil; they're being brainwashed by the head of the HPA and the council."

A bell rang throughout the underground facility.

Robert knew the sound was coming from his sleeping quarters. He was being paged by the HPA. Whenever they called CID, it was guaranteed someone would answer.

Robert ran through the steel halls, the energy door, and into his room. An image of a white hood, a blurred-out face, and captioned text floated above him. Robert recognized it as the head of the HPA.

"Report to Providence immediately!"

A snap of fingers echoed in the halls.

Robert appeared in a living coliseum; twisting fleshy vines transformed into Gothic stone pillars, the arches swelled, and the architecture constantly changed in design.

At its edge, a thousand gray stone steps leading to the diamond throne, was the head of the HPA in his white cloak, drinking from a crystal chalice.

As soon as Robert appeared, thousands of changeling spectators got to their feet and cheered. Thousands more booed.

Fifty-foot-tall titans slammed their black-diamond staves into the ground. The sound exploded, knocking the fervor from the crowd.

"Silence! This is judgment!" the HPA leader's voice boomed.

The four titans standing at each corner like robust kings grunted in unison. They were adorned in precious furs, jewels, and crystalline crowns. Their skin was faded gray, which matched the garb of the council and most of the décor. Their flat faces were scrolling marquees showing one word: QUIET.

Robert looked to the sky; thousands of hexagons encasing the coliseum were showing images of his life, both past and future. He shrugged his shoulders and looked down at the long crease in the metal floor below his feet.

"Blackthorne . . . I'm coming for you," he mumbled.

"You know why you are here," the HPA leader said.

"Of course," Robert smiled.

The HPA leader leaned back. "Council, you have the floor."

The council was comprised of shadowy humanoids with dozens of plugs like umbilical cords connected to machinery. They swam in murky, gray goo, cradled by six transparent orbs mounted on a network of wires that bookended the stairs.

All six spoke as one. "The acts you have been involved with are in direct violation of the changeling code. You are accused of treason." Their sound was mechanical.

At the base of the steps was an inscription: *ELLODION IS TRUST; ELLODION IS THE WAY OF PROSPERITY.*

Robert ground his fangs at those words. "You bastards spit on his grave with this," he mumbled.

The council's voice boomed. "You will speak up in the presence of the almighty!"

Robert unfolded his arms and pulled out his cigar.

"No smoking in front of our lord!"

Without hesitation, he lit it with a claw and blew a smoke ring in the air. Thousands of spectators voiced their opinions in a roar.

"Disgraceful!" one of them said.

Robert pointed his cigar up the stairs. "What you are doing to humanity is immoral."

"Your morality is yours," the council said. "There are no absolutes."

"You absolutely sure about that?" Robert smirked. Hundreds of people in the crowd snickered. The titans gripped their staves.

"What is true for you may not be true for others."

Robert shook his head. "Is that true for everyone?"

There was silence for a moment while the council looked at one another. "Reality itself is merely subjective," they said, looking back at him.

Robert turned his back to them, took a puff on his cigar, and looked at the crowd. "What do you think I've been doing for the past two thousand years? Wasting my time? I swear, if that were true that would make my job impossible."

He pointed at the sky to the images of his life. "I've been looking for the one timeline, the one that will inevitably occur. Whether you believe Kevin is the destroyer of all life or whether you believe he is the savior, those beliefs are independent of what is going to happen in the end." Robert turned back around and glared at the council members. "There is only one possible outcome, only one prophecy that will come true, and only one truth. It's the stupid timeline you've been manipulating since you got here!"

The head of the HPA spoke. "That's enough. People die every day, whether we have a hand in it or not. We do what must be done. Humans die; deal with it. You can't save them all."

"I'm not trying to," Robert said. "But I'm not the one putting them in chains and slaughtering billions."

"Enough! Given all that you have done for us in your past, I will be lenient. We know that your final job will be to train Kevin and prepare him for his mission. However, we all question your loyalty to the changeling cause. We've seen the choices you've made throughout your life. It's time for you to be replaced. Your reports say that this Kevin is the one foretold in the prophecy. Are they correct?"

"I believe he is. Yes," Robert said, looking up at the throne.

Voices echoed in the room as roars of conversation bounced off the walls.

"*With that kind of past, there is no way he's the right guy.*"

"*The stupid machine must be broken; there's no way he's the one.*"

"*This is ludicrous! There's no proof that this religion is true, and now these idiots say this loser, this nobody, is their king and savior?*"

"*This is mass delusion. They will believe all kinds of dogma that comes out of that ancient box.*"

The figure in the white hood slammed down his fist.

"Silence! Never question the Timeweb!" Then he pointed at Robert. "I do, however, question your interpretation of it."

"My interpretation of it," Robert continued, "does not change what's been happening. Nor does my interpretation have anything to do with what will happen."

"Ellodion said he would come from a normal life. This Kevin is about as normal as a square circle. You must be mistaken."

Robert, narrowing his eyes, flipped him off. "Why do you talk down to me as if I don't know what I'm doing?"

"You will *not* speak to me this way! I lead this government. *I* do."

Another voice echoed from one of the orbs. "Careful. You speak to the ruler of the world. We know how some of the people here feel about you, but you better watch your tongue, servant."

Robert chewed on his cigar and glared at the collection of jelly-filled orbs before him.

"How do you plan to reach him?" the HPA leader asked, calming himself.

"I have someone on the police force keeping him secure until I arrive." Robert paused and took the cigar from his mouth. "Why? Why must I continue to slaughter them? These strange feelings I have, the humans call it remorse, are beginning to—"

The cloaked man interrupted. "You are dismissed."

Nothing more was said, and with another snap, Robert appeared back in his cubicle, sitting in his chair.

All the spectators had vanished.

A screen appeared, floating in the center of the dome, right in front of the HPA leader's eyes. Robert was being watched. A cold silence fell over the meeting, icing over their tongues.

"Good. Now that he's gone we can get down to the business at hand."

An orb full of dark clouds and boiling, inky mucilaginous fluid appeared where Robert had stood, and floated toward the stairs.

"You have your orders. I expect you to take care of him and leave nothing that can be traced back to me."

A dark, shadowy figure in the orb nodded its head.

It vanished in a charcoaled puff of smoke, and as the air began to clear, the council spoke. "He's the head minister. My lord, can we control him?"

"We control everything."

PART THREE

SINS OF THE FATHER

"Therefore, just as sin came into the world through one man, and death through sin, and so death spread to all men because all sinned."

—Romans 5:12

CHAPTER SEVEN

*"If the means were not objectively bad, one would not
need the ends to justify them. Do not mistake motive for
goodness or backwards rationale for righteousness."*

—Raksasha

Sunday, April 6, 1958

There was an air of peace and calming elegance about Jason's
New York penthouse. The place spoke of money squandered
and wealth astutely applied. Sitting atop the eighteenth-century
Tuft table was an ice bucket containing a bottle of Dom Pérignon. At
the foot of the bed was a case of Chateau Lafite 1787. The comforting
scent of cinnamon in coffee wafted in from the kitchen.

Technology not of its time was scattered everywhere; the 175-
inch flat-screen plasma television was just turning on. *"Welcome back.
For those just joining us, we've been talking about the escalating war in
Vietnam. We go now to Defense Secretary Robert McNamara describing
yesterday's raid."*

Evidence that the Easter holiday had just passed was everywhere. Neatly stacked by the door were three-foot-tall solid-gold bunnies and gift baskets loaded with diamonds cut in the shape of eggs.

Jason heard a beautiful voice every morning. It was as if sound itself made love to his ears. "Time to wake up, honey!"

A pair of D-cup breasts pressed into his face. He took in her scent. "Ahhh." The aroma filled his lungs as he stared at the mounds rising on either side of his nose. "Too bad none of this is real," he mumbled. *"What am I doing? Jessica has been dead for years."*

The angular face of the blonde Greek goddess looked down inquisitively. "What?"

He looked into her eyes. "Do you love me?"

His lingerie-model wife reached over his side of the bed and turned off the alarm. "Of course I do."

Jason slid out of bed and walked in his boxers to the ten-foot-tall, gold-framed picture windows. Placing his hands against the glass, Jason lowered his head, clenched his eyes, and sighed. "I miss you so much, Jess."

His wife slipped into her red lace bra and walked up behind him, placing a hand on his back. "What's wrong?"

Opening his tear-filled eyes, Jason looked down at the swarms of people with a heavy heart. "Do you think it can love?" he mumbled.

The Odhert residence was more than one room with a view: six bedrooms, a sauna, an indoor pool and a personal gym, all with impressive overlooks of Central Park. The twenty-story building peered down upon the swelling tide of business with pompous disdain.

The sun was powerful enough by 8:00 a.m. to make morning dew on the pavement lift like wisps of smoke, creating a heavenly green glow against the trees.

His wife took a step back. "What are you talking about?"

Jason stared through her and tuned out. Soon he was aware of only the deep, raspy voice that embodied the sound of thousands of years of accumulated knowledge.

This voice inside his head answered him. "By every human definition . . . it loves the same as you do. You're the one who wanted her back."

Jason turned away from his wife. "I don't know. Not like this."

The reptilian voice echoed in his skull again, the same one that had been with him for twenty years.

"It's her memories. She bleeds the same, she feels the same, she reacts exactly the way she would if she were still alive. By nearly every aspect, it's still her."

"But it's not. That son of a bitch took her from me."

———————◆———————

Turning around, he looked at her feet—those small, cute, perfectly pedicured little toes and those legs—those shapely calves and toned legs. Her stomach—oh, how he loved her abs. She worked on them every morning. Most of all, he loved her face. Not just how thin her nose was, how high her cheekbones were, or even how her teeth never seemed to stain no matter how much coffee she drank.

None of that was ever as pleasing as looking into the eyes of someone who was as much in love with him as he was in love with her.

She grabbed her white cotton blouse from the floor, and her blue eyes widened. "Honey, you're starting to scare me. What's wrong?"

He looked at the ceiling. "I've been married to this thing for ten years. It seems so wrong to just destroy it. I mean, I feel terrible."

"Today is the day you get revenge. The portal is right out the window this time. You have sixty seconds," the voice said.

Jason walked over to the black oak nightstand and opened the drawer. "Hey! Where are my shades?"

"Your visor was always meant for the savior. Fortunately, I've prepared a more permanent solution. Make haste. They are already tracing this line."

"Ten, thirty-four, beta-trio-six. Engage!" he yelled, pulling out a large black marble.

For a second, the walls of the room flickered as if someone were adjusting television reception to reality itself. His wife's face abruptly locked in an expressionless gaze, and she sank to her knees.

As he raised the orb to an inch away from his right eye, his wife took a meditative position, sitting cross legged and pressing her hands together. Concave markings in the shape of fingerprints embedded in the small sphere were glowing. Jason pressed his thumb into the indentations, and the sphere popped open, revealing a thin, translucent, fluid disk.

"I had it modified to synch with your DNA. So it should work ."

The object inside of the orb sprouted eight thin, metallic legs.

"Wait, should?!"

"Twenty seconds."

The device propelled itself out from the sphere and onto his open eye socket. Jason's head jerked back as the spider coiled its limbs deep behind his eyeball and positioned itself over the pupil. He heard sloshing as the tentacles stirred through his skull. He felt them growing, moving behind his eye, and burrowing into his brain.

Then came the pain; the scorching reminder that said this was no dream. The spider dug its teeth into his cornea, and it was as if the devil's pitchfork had struck his skull. The scream was unavoidable.

"Ahhhh!!"

"Eighteen. Oh, stop being such a big baby."

A robotic voice vibrated in his socket. "Skyviewer isolated. Firewalls and encryption enabled."

The ball slid off his face and clunked to the floor. Removing his palm from his blinking, tear-filled eye, he saw the truth.

Reality was a white lie. The flat-screen television, the golden bunnies, the wine, the table, the bed, even the Persian carpeting—all of it was a deception. None of it was real. Everything, including the walls, was made of strings of layered, flowing energy. Even his wife was a fraud.

Her body was a series of energy streams, and within them billions of electrical balls coated in spinning symbols piled one atop the other. Her skin, a shell, was a thin membrane of light connected to energy webbing out from a river of luminescence.

At the center of her chest hovered a crystal that had facets of a diamond . A circulatory system plugged into the crystal, connecting all the energy streams.

Balls of light passed through the crystal, which, like a human heart, directed them into the energy currents. As condensed as the streams were, she was as transparent as the entire room and everything in it.

Her big, sensual lips were nothing more than hundreds of small threads of energy shaped into a human form. She spoke. "Deletion of twenty-four hours of memories . . . successful."

"Eleven."

Following the current of light orbs through the room, he saw they originated far beneath him.

The matrix flowed down through the floor and past all the people living in the building. The other humans slept on beds that were not beds. They were walking on floors that were not floors and even taking showers with water that was not water.

Peering down past his feet, beyond the layered levels of light, he saw most of the people in the building were like him—human. Only a half dozen of the diamond walkers were passing themselves off as mortals.

Then he turned around and stepped up to the window.

"Ten."

He pressed his hand to the glass and watched the transparent waterfall of light bounce off his fingertips. His hand was still lying to him. There was cold in the material; the texture was smooth.

"Nine."

He could still sense the slight burning pressure in his eyes when he observed New York City's morning streets.

"Eight."

Across the entire metropolis and the rest of the world were other buildings, people, and even trees made of light. More than half the world was an alien construct, an artificial existence mixed with reality. Even many of the real buildings were stained in alien graffiti of glowing crimson symbols.

"Seven."

A bird of pulsing light dived down out of the sky.

Someday you'll all know the truth. He watched a woman jog with a pack of glimmering Dobermans.

"Six."

Off in the distance was a passenger plane, and at the base of the engine was another diamond. The gem acted as the plane's heart, extending out into a circulatory system, much like his wife.

Every person aboard the luminous vessel was human, except the pilot. "Oh, God, that's an accident waiting to happen."

I hope they've encrypted the pilot better than my wife. If he dies, of a heart attack what's that mean for the destiny of the crew?

"Five."

He backhanded the tinted window, throwing glass toward the street.

"Four."

As soon as his bare feet touched the windowsill, the shards merged together like mercury. There he was, a man in only his boxers on a Sunday morning, looking like he was going to commit suicide.

"Three."

He looked down at the fluctuating puddle below him. Inside the rippling waves, he could see another room. Jason suddenly thrust himself headfirst off the building.

"Two."

He splashed into the small, hovering pool.

"One."

The portal vanished. Jason landed submerged in an indoor spa, and there was that voice again. "Cutting it a little close this time, don't you think?"

Jason's head broke the surface. "Oh, I always make it." He smiled. "How about you keep the door open a little longer than sixty seconds?"

"We've been through this. It's just too risky. Any longer and they'll trace the portal's origin. Unless you want to start making them?"

"Point taken."

The small room had giant computer terminals to his left, and to his right he saw a fifty-inch mirror, a desk, and a black chair with keyboards embedded in its arms.

"Activate EVE," Jason said, getting out of the spa.

The computer terminals opened hundreds of small slots. Microchips with legs of wire poured out, collecting into large piles on the floor. The mechanical mess began taking the form of feet.

Jason worked with a special division of the CIA: the Central Intelligence Special Services, or CISS, sometimes referred to as "Sissys." They worked in conjunction with the FBI and handled paranormal cases and anything that was beyond what even the CIA should know.

As far as the public was concerned, this group did not exist. All inquiries about this group were quickly put to rest, with either a laughter curtain or a series of in-depth tasks to prove its nonexistence. No one who stupidly decided to leak information about them lived for very long.

"The time has come, Jason. The day I said you would have to fight against your employer," the reptilian voice said.

Jason looked into the mirror at all the battle scars covering his pectoral muscles. He was proud of his entire physique—his toned abs, his broad shoulders—but everywhere he looked there was some kind of blade mark or healed bullet wound.

Half of the mirror filled with computer images of weapons and boxes of text.

"Hmm . . . new weapon shipments came in today. Good timing."

Jason walked over to a black phone on his desk.

"Time to check in," he said, pressing a large red button.

"Good morning, Agent Black. I will connect you to Jon in Special Services."

Jason walked to a closet. "Thank you, Darla."

"Late, as usual," a voice said through the small speaker.

"Hey! I show eight o'clock on the nose!"

"Eight-oh-one."

Jason smiled and pulled out a pair of camouflage jeans. "What do you got for me?"

The voice softened. "This is very serious. Your partner, Alex Knight, has been dealt the skull card. He's currently vacationing in Hawaii and is unquestionably the most dangerous man in the world. Capture is not an option. This is coming straight from the HPA. Word is he's been playing both sides from the beginning. He's been selling the United States' secrets to all of America's enemies: Iran, Russia, China, everyone—including the Coven. Jessica, bring up his background."

Shaking his head, Jason zipped up his pants. A sound like metal raindrops fell in the background as circuitry piled onto legs and a torso took shape.

Over the phone's speaker, there was also the sound of computer keys clicking. "Alex Knight was recruited into the division in 1938. He was off the charts in every test, from aptitude to supernatural physical capabilities for fieldwork. His last assignment was in Hanoi, where he was to eliminate changeling rebels assisting the Viet Cong."

Jason headed back to his desk and scribbled a note on paper. It read, I'm not surprised, but why didn't you tell me my partner was a double agent?

The reptilian voice in his mind responded. "I tell you what you need to know and when you need to know it. And stop flipping me off."

Jason pulled out a lighter and set the paper on fire; he continued to listen to the call.

"You really need to fix your mute button," Robert said. Jason rolled his eyes.

"One year into his mission," Jessica said, "he racked up over five hundred kills in World War II. Several years later, he recruited over half of the highest-ranked people who currently work in this division—including Jason, code name Agent Black.

"Every procedure we have, every protocol we follow, is because of this man. Before him, aliens looked at us as a nuisance. Now, we're a threat. It's thanks to him that humans have a voice with the changelings.

"Five years into the war, Knight was suspected of selling secrets to the Russians, but it was never proven. He's also allegedly responsible for the murder of twenty other agents. Two years ago, he disappeared.

"Knight is a wanted man in every state and every country on the globe. His last known sighting was with his pregnant wife in Hawaii. We have to assume that he wants to be found because, unlike us, this man does not make mistakes. We already have several teams moving in on him."

"Am I reading this report correctly, Jessica?" Jon asked. "We're calling in every member of the division, and we're involving local support?"

"Yes. This is Alex Knight."

"Agent Black, we know how close you are to this case, but you are our best man," Jon said. "You basically lived with the man for twenty years. You know him better than any of us. I know what he did to you, but I can't think of anyone I would trust more to do this job."

"Thank you, sir." Jason pulled on his black T-shirt.

"What about the wife?"

"Try not to kill her. We need to bring her in for questioning."

"Give me an hour. Agent Black, out," Jason said, pressing down the red button.

The microchips were forming behind him and had now stacked to create a female robotic figure. Pink fluid began spreading over the circuitry. As it thickened, it gave the appearance of skin.

As he rolled a finger down across the glass, the selection screen scrolled to different weapon types. "Hey, Robbie, which of these should I take with me?" he asked.

Jason could hear Robert's voice in his head again. "I left your birthday gift in your left desk drawer."

He picked up out of his drawer a large diamond in the shape of an orthorhombic crystal. "Wow, a Stadium-class DRR!"

Jason couldn't help grinning at the sight of his new toy. This Diamond Reality Replicator crystal held enough power to produce a large stadium with everyone and everything in it. It was more than enough to construct an army of diamond walker assassins.

Jason placed the rhombic diamond prism in a black circular holding base on his desk.

"You are going to need a larger pocket army this time," Robert said.

Jason's fingers moved expertly over his keyboard.

"Okay. Fifty walkers should do it. I should be able to increase their durability. Yes . . . ," he mumbled to himself. "Okay, I'll take out their capacity to speak. I'll make them a bit more agile. Now, just to make sure the reincarnation is set at fifty percent damage."

A sexy female voice with a British accent echoed behind him.

"Good morning, Master. Query: Please clarify operational parameters."

His black leather chair swiveled around, and he saw the inhuman beauty. Her blonde hair moved as if tousled by wind. However, there were no open windows and no breeze in the warehouse. Her large simulated breasts were covered by a thin gray bodysuit so tight it clung to her pale skin like paint. She could almost pass as human until you looked into her eyes. The whites were blue, and the pupils were black moving cogs; behind them, numerous gears were turning.

Jason smiled. "Prepare two Throg SMG 40s and a bunch of clips for both. I need piercing and detonation rounds."

When she spoke, her voice had a hint of electronic static. "Processing request." She walked toward the stacks of boxes in the corner.

Robert's voice vibrated in Jason's mind. "Jason."

"Yes?"

"I can't say I blame you for wanting to get back at the changelings. If not for me, they would've had you pushing papers for the CIA and dying at seventy-two of a heart attack. I freed you from their influence. But if you are going to continue to enjoy the real world, and my gifts, I'm going to have to ask you for one thing."

"What's that, sir?"

"To trust in me. "

"I will. I mean, of course I do."

Jason paced and glanced at a chair, a bookshelf, and even his gray cat. They were all fakes. "Makes you think, doesn't it, boss?"

"No."

"You cut the changelings' strings on my mind, and now I'm being led around by circumstance—and by you. All you did was move me from one puppet master to another. What makes me different from any humanoid diamond walker? I mean, except for the fact that they are put there to replace the humans that the changelings killed."

"Will you be able to handle this?"

"I've been preparing for this moment for years, and I told you then that I could do it."

"You know what I mean."

"Will I be able to kill the last angel: my friend, my partner for twenty years? I thought you knew how everything was going to happen; I mean, don't you?"

Robert's deep reptilian laugh crackled in Jason's mind. "I also know what I'm supposed to say and do so that things go the way I want."

"He was an angel. All my friends and my wife are gone because of him. I've spent the last ten years looking for justice. Their minds," he breathed, "replicated in an artificial shell. I can't wait to put him down."

"You know, he butchered her when he was still light so you'd have the balls to kill him now."

Jason let out a slight laugh. "He's always pulling my strings. Fine. Let him."

"Your limiting beliefs are the only things that bind you. Now, step back and get ready for the jump."

CHAPTER EIGHT

*"Death, therefore, the most awful of evils, is nothing
to us, seeing that, when we are, death is not come,
and, when death is come, we are not."*

—Epicurus

Monday, April 6, 1958, 11:55 a.m.

The island of Hawaii was a perpetual balance of pain and pleasure; a metaphor of the equilibrium of life itself, the good and the bad. The bright, scorching sun nearly burned the skin, until it was cooled by the humid breeze moving over clear waters. For a moment, tranquil peace surrounded the five-star hotel in Keolu Hills.

The twenty-story hotel, located at the bottom of a hill, was surrounded by other tall buildings, except for the south wing, which held fantastic views of the beach.

Sara Knight traced the words "I LUV U" into the humidity covered window. She smiled, rubbing her pregnant belly.

Alex pulled his long black hair into a ponytail. "Our son will have your good and my evil."

He sat down on the white waterbed. "They're coming. If something happens to me, I need you to know you're going to hear some horrible things about me." He lowered his voice and added, "Some of them are true. But everything I did, I did for our son. It was the only way."

Sara rolled her fingers through her dirty-blonde hair. "Honey, you're starting to scare me. What did you do?"

"I—"

Whirr! Whirr! Whirr!

An alarm screamed from the oak dresser. Alex pressed his hand in the center of the mirror mounted just above it. "Kevin, the savior."

As he spoke the password, dozens of screens appeared within the reflective surface and displayed a holographic console full of buttons. Alex's fingers sped over the keyboard. "What? This is earlier than I expected. Oh, well."

Alex looked into his monitors. On one of the screens, helicopters were flying grid patterns over the building. Heavily armed men dressed in black dropped from ropes. Another one showed crowds of soldiers massing by the dozens on foot at the base of the building until over a hundred swarmed the place.

Alex heard everything through his speakers. "Alpha squad in place!" one of them yelled into his headset. The last member of Alpha squad's feet touched the roof.

Alex held out his hand. "It's time to leave." Sara placed her palm against his. A dark cloud enveloped them, and in an instant, they were gone.

An abandoned warehouse. Tokyo, Japan...

A dark cloud in the center of a stack of cargo containers quickly dispersed and vanished, leaving behind the standing figures of Alex and Sara.

Someone was already there, standing behind them on top of a container. "Hello, partner," Jason said.

Alex shook his head. "How the—oh, Robert! You future-peeking bastard!"

"That's right," Jason said. "He's my new partner, so you can forget about running."

Alex pulled his wife behind him. "I'm not running from you. You can't beat me."

He turned around, looking deep into Sara's eyes. "Go!" he said, pointing to the far corner of the warehouse.

Jason watched as she scurried off. "If I didn't know better, I'd swear you actually still love her."

"I'll never forget the reasons I chose to darken my heart."

Jason jumped down and stood a few feet from Alex. "You're a monster."

"There's a monster in all of us. I just let mine out. You know that voice that tells you to do bad things?" Alex smiled. "Yeah, I just listen to it now."

"Did it tell you to murder my wife, my friends, my family!?"

Alex raised a fist in front of his face, and pockets of darkness swirled around it. "You don't understand the power of evil; it was the only way . . . I had no choice."

Jason folded his arms. "You have forgotten your training. *Everything* is a choice."

"You think you're free being Robert's puppet? He never told you the truth about angels."

"I don't want to hear it."

"We can't procreate. Whose idea do you think it was for me to clip my wings by choosing the darkness and becoming mortal so that this savior would be born?"

Jason narrowed his eyes.

Alex took a step back. "Let me ask you something. You think you have a chance against me?"

Jason smiled. "Robert has shown me this very moment unfolding in a dozen different ways, and in every single one, I beat you."

Alex laughed. "He obviously hasn't told you yet of the anomaly. He's not always right, you know."

Jason looked up. "What is he talking about?"

The reptile did not answer.

"Not speaking, is he? Not surprising, after all; I guess he wouldn't, since 'Tomorrow's End' was my theory . . . Okay, this is boring," Alex said, raising both arms. "You can't possibly beat me one on one, even with your prep time."

"I brought help," Jason said, gripping the side of his utility belt.

He launched the laser wire into the roof. Flying into the air, he pulled an Uzi from its holster with one arm and began spraying gunfire at Alex. With the other, he reached into a leather pouch.

Alex dodged by bursting into a dark cloud, changing position all over the room, steadily moving closer to Jason. Jason curled a diamond prism like a curveball out of a pitcher's hand. Spinning, the rhombic projectile drilled through concrete and moved deep into the ground.

Dark fingers solidified like a ghost around Jason's throat. Jason felt Alex's superhuman grip as he was slammed to the pavement.

The impact caused concrete and plaster to explode around his body, and his Uzi bounced away.

"It's over," Alex said, pulling his left arm back.

Jason struggled to pry Alex's fingers from his throat.

Fifty flat, glowing circles began growing on the walls and on the floor. Diamond prisms of light dispersed into the room. The colorful light glinted off Jason's eyes and reflected in the smoking, liquid black evil that flowed over Alex's arm.

Jason grunted, his grip weakening, "You haven't won." He saw the tips of samurai swords coalesce from the base of the circles of light. Jason's arms began to quiver. But he smiled.

Spiraling blood cells fluttered in and out of Alex's skin. As his fist plunged down, a gauntlet of jagged spikes made of darkness formed.

The strike stopped.

Jason watched the hairs of his eyelash split by the shadowy blades.

Alex looked up at a stack of bullets that had frozen in time an inch from his face, and a glimmering katana hovered at his throat.

That was enough to force Jason's attacker to jump off him.

"Stadium-class diamond walkers. I'm impressed," Alex said.

Crowds of ninjas and heavily armed military soldiers all dressed in black materialized out of the circles and took cover behind the containers.

Alex turned around. "You're just delaying the inevitable." He raised his arms, and six of the cargo containers lifted in the air. He thrust his arms forward, and the large projectiles rolled, crashing into the men. The canisters shattered, throwing boxes and debris along with human parts. Their bodies crushed into blood spatter against the walls.

That accounted for only a little over a dozen walkers. They were replaced by energy sprites that materialized above glowing circles in the ground and assumed human form.

The remaining walkers shot at Alex. Their bullets collected in a cloud of massing darkness.

Alex answered by hurling the bullets back. The walkers jumped and rolled out of the way.

Jason charged and reached into his utility belt.

Alex clenched his fist. He closed his eyes, and as shadow steamed out from them, fissures split open in the walls and the floor. Within the growing cracks, phantasmal blobs darker than ink sculpted themselves into vines.

Jason stopped on his heels. "Crap," he said, and jerked out a flickering blue diamond, shattering it against his chest.

Reflective particles swarmed around Jason and formed a transparent glowing white shell. The tentacles sprang from the broken floor, twisting around dozens of Jason's soldiers.

Bones crunched and screams gurgled as they were wrung like wet towels. The tentacles chucked their mangled bodies, and they smacked against the ceiling. The dark snakes coiled three feet from Jason's body. Jason shrugged and charged through the bleak congestion.

Alex opened his eyes to the point of a blade. The ninjas were still coming. He slapped it from his face and dodged three more katana slashes in succession.

Then the mutilated carcasses struck the ground. The demonic tubules latched on to Jason's field, and the dark fumes surrounding them thinned. Squeezing like pythons, their spikes dug deep lines and spewed sparks. They turned into spears, and struck again and again, dozens of times and more. They splattered against the shield but left only fading holes.

Jason was upon him then. He leaped from the stygian cloud, executing three separate actions before he reached his mark. First, he put on a pair of black sunglasses.

Next, he pitched a crystal orb, which exploded in a blinding luminance that limned the room in glowing white. The tentacles burst into vapor, and the fissures vanished. Alex felt the stinging glare and shielded his eyes.

Then, Jason drew another crystal from his belt; it extended into a shimmering white sword. Alex's arm was coated in hardened darkness and shadowy scales. Jason's sword struck Alex's palm, and he crumpled the blade like paper. Before Jason could land, Alex spun back and viciously kicked through the diamond shell into his gut, catapulting him thirty feet.

Jason smashed into stone. He watched Alex turn away from him and, with his darkness claws, cut through three of his men per second.

Jason landed next to his Uzi and picked it up. He pressed a button on its side. It now displayed flashing LED detonation rounds. He pulled another Uzi from its holster.

"Your toys are running out of energy," Alex said, with his back still turned to Jason.

Jason raised his other gun, flicked a switch, and began unloading fire that collected in a dark cloud an inch from Alex's back.

Alex turned around. "Standard bullets? Shit!" The concentrated collection of mini-explosions boomed through Alex's body, smashing him against the brick wall.

Alex was more than stunned. It was taxing to breathe and a chore to move. Blinking through the falling rubble and dust-filled air, Alex saw a blurred vision of Jason raising both his guns. Alex could not move away; the impact had drained his strength.

Jason flicked both switches of his guns to piercing rounds. "Abracadabra this."

Streams of gunfire moved through Alex's convulsing body. Burning cloth added smoke over the splattering of black blood.

The gunfire stopped when he was nothing more than a steaming pile of gore.

Sara screamed as Jason walked up to her. "Alex! Noooooo! My God!"

Sara was crying in her hands. Jason leaned down and held out his hand. "I'm here to protect your unborn son."

The reptile spoke again. "Take her to her new husband. I will prepare her for mind alteration. The birth of the savior is almost upon us."

"You want to explain what Alex said?"

"My actions do not require explanation. As I said, you have to trust me."

"I never believed in your religion or your messiah; the only thing I care about is freeing humanity and stopping the changelings."

"There is only one way to prevent the annihilation of all life in the universe."

"How?"

"Kevin."

PART FOUR

ESCAPING CHRISTMAS EVIL

"Whether or not you look both ways before crossing the street, life is about the discovery, experience, and understanding of that choice. The choice you have already made, before you think you've made it. If you closed your eyes and walked out blind and got hit by a car, part of you needed that experience and that understanding, or you wouldn't have made that choice. Personally, I believe few people need that experience, which is why we look both ways. There is no such thing as failure, only feedback."

—Nullados Log, Page 1

CHAPTER NINE

*"Those who 'abjure' violence can do so only because
others are committing violence on their behalf."*

—George Orwell

December 24, 1975

O n Christmas Eve, the San Diego jail was relatively empty—
some two-bit thieves, some drivers who had one too many…
and then there was sixteen-year-old Kevin. However, it wasn't
until he arrived that the building was suddenly under the protection
of the local ATF and SWAT.

Something in the late-evening darkness was coming for him, and
not even a small army was going to stop it. An attempted murder of
the jail's newest inmate was about to take place. The man in the black
suit had just entered his cell, and Kevin was telling his story.

Behind the three-story jail, snakeskin fingers and cracked crimson nails clacked on a small, flat digital screen. The surrounding lights turned off. The scaly digits glided over shifting symbols and floating holographic numbers. All interconnecting telephone wires sizzled and snapped.

A guard named Bill—an obese family man with two kids—patrolled the outside area. As he rounded the corner of the building and entered the alley, his journey abruptly ended. His rotund body popped; his flesh sparked and streamed into a spray of bright shattering plasma, illuminating the transparent energy wall. He wouldn't be going home to his kids, and neither would anyone else who decided to play detective.

Inside the building, Greg, the front desk security guard, furiously pounded on his desk. "Oh! What the hell? Every single one?" All the embedded monitors had turned to snow. "Santa Claus Is Coming to Town" buzzed on the speakers.

Near the front doors, the SWAT members began laughing. "Rough night?" one said.

"Why the hell are you guys here?" Greg asked.

"Just following orders."

"Great," Greg said. "Hey, George, I'm not getting any signal to the cameras down here. Come and take a look, will ya?" He released a button on the handheld receiver attached to his belt.

"Ugh. Haven't you figured out how to not break things? I'm on my way," George replied.

At the entrance, two men armed with M16s and blanketed in Kevlar stood at either side of the revolving door. "Is there a problem?" one of them asked.

Before the man at the front desk could answer, darkness swallowed the room as all the lights went out. The man scrambled, his shaking hands searching through pens, papers, and office supplies in the front desk drawer.

The moment his quivering fingers felt the shaft of a flashlight, a deep, scratchy voice whispered in his ear.

"You're not going to want to see what's out there." He raised his hand from the drawer. "And you're especially not going to want to see"—glowing reptilian eyes that dripped and bubbled crimson ooze appeared before him—"me."

Stumbling from his chair, his pants soaked with urine, Greg made his way toward the only light source that came from outside. Something stopped him at the entrance. His feet and scalding shins noticed the revolving doors had been melted into a shallow puddle. Under the strain of burning agony, he barreled over.

The instant he opened his mouth to scream, his head left his body.

As the skull descended, a barrage of piercing claws slashed, ripping clumps of flesh from Greg's convulsing body, pulverizing it into a red mist.

"Greg? Hellooo! Do I need to go back for a bulb?"

"Oh, great, now the power's out. Merry Christmas to me," George mumbled, opening a door.

For a brief moment, light cut into the room. It came from a flashlight shining on five bloodied digits, extended by five-inch nails, spread out to reveal a circular device embedded in its palm. The instrument, held by a thin black wiry glove, opened, showing six shining rows of metallic teeth.

George saw the weapon, but it was too late. The mouth of the small orb opened; the arm moved back and then thrust forward, throwing several rows of energy in the form of transparent glowing nets.

The webbing branched out several hundred feet, passing through him and into fifteen more victims in two rooms and a hallway behind him.

The fervent webbing passed through its last victim, the unearthly arm yanked back, and the teeth of the device began grinding and drawing the net back into its aperture. Each strand of energy bound itself to the victims' veins, passing through nonorganic matter, tearing all the life-giving vessels from their hosts.

Strings of human plasma exploded through the rooms and shot back into the device.

Metallic teeth clanged and slurped on the spaghetti strands of blood.

George's body fell to the ground. Before his last vein was stripped from his eyes, he saw one final image. After withdrawing the device, its other eerie hand threw an object that resembled a chrome baseball toward the ceiling. Before the weapon shot through the first-floor ceiling, it had already targeted organic life on the second and third floors.

As it reached the middle of the second floor, circular holes opened, encompassing the entire sphere. The ball spun in a blur, spitting thousands of lasers per second through the walls and cutting down its targets. It breached the roof, splattering the remaining flesh until it was steaming blood. It was back in his scaly hand almost as soon as it left.

There was still light in the building, but a misty darkness made its way from the entrance, room by room.

A curious SWAT leader noticed the lights going out. He pressed the communicator against his face. "On the roof!" he called out at the top of his voice. "Check in, dammit. Check in! Floor two! Beta, Delta squads, check in now!"

Silence. An icy trickle ran down his spine. He stared at darkness and the blood collecting at the bottom of the door. His heart quickened; he still heard nothing from the floors above.

"Soldiers, report!" he shouted out, not caring who should answer him.

He heard no answer. His heart thundered against his ribs. Someone had turned up the music. "It's Beginning to Look a Lot like Christmas" blared.

He could see his face reflected in a large police badge mounted on the door. The bloody glowing eyes of a hellion hovered behind him. His quivering hand moved up for his pistol. He felt the wetness in his palms squish against his holster.

As he turned around, the lights went down.

"Ahhhh!" His screams were brief.

In the adjoining hallway from the main entrance, the thunder of rubber soles on the floor made its way toward the commotion. The SMG Forend WeaponLights attached to the M4s and M16s illuminated the chief's demise. A rain of blood formed a pool of crimson. His body was thrashing into the ceiling over and over again in rapid succession.

But they saw no attacker.

The first group of four SWAT members knelt, slamming their ballistic shields into the ground. Placing Uzis through the gunports, they blindly opened fire into the hallway. Taking cover behind them, a row of four more men added streams of AK-47 bullets into the flashing blaze.

"Ahhh! Ahhh! It's a monster! Ahhh!" one of them screamed.

Each of them managed to unload almost an entire clip, only to be hit by the same projectiles they expelled. Bullets first hit the very holes from which they came, knocking weapons and flashlights from hands, then flattened into Kevlar and steel.

It was then that a single flashlight illuminated something, something more horrifying than any of them could imagine.

There was a faint tremor in their voices. "What—what is that?"

Their bodies lifted a few feet from the ground, impelled by a force beyond physics and reason.

With that same force of will, their bodies crashed, colliding as if smashed together in an invisible vise. Bones shattered, armor crumbled, and what were once twenty men was now a single ball of metal and blood-dripping flesh.

Meanwhile, as the darkness was making its way toward Kevin's cell . . .

The man in the black suit finished screwing on the silencer and slid in his clip.

Before Kevin could even take his first step, the man in black obstructed his exit. The shine of fluorescent light glimmered off his teeth as joy splashed across his face. The man in black pressed the barrel of the gun against Kevin's forehead.

"Do you think you chose to die, right here, right now?" He paused, sliding the nose of the gun to Kevin's temple.

Kevin remained motionless, his throat turgid with fear. As beads of sweat collected on his brow, he swallowed and closed his eyes.

"Hmm. How delicious. I'm about to convince billions that their religion is a lie, just by pulling this trigger. Goodbye, God."

Click! Click! Click! Click!

The gun was fully loaded, but no bullet left the chamber.

"Noooooo! That's impossible!" His grip loosened in disbelief. After swatting the gun away, Kevin's fists shot out like lasers, hitting their marks with absolute precision.

His knuckles landed on the man's throat, a left palm struck his chest, and he followed through with a right haymaker.

The man didn't flinch. There were no signs that he had been hit, except for Kevin's fist imprinted on his face.

Kevin backed against the wall, rubbing his knuckles. *This is what punching a steel door must feel like.*

"Try to fight me all you want, but we both know how this is going to end," the man said, pinching his cheek and smoothing out his skin.

"Ouch. What the heck is going on? You a robot or something?" Perhaps more likely, Kevin thought, a victim of some kind of horrible fire with metal face implants. Maybe there was a plastic surgeon on drugs; still, not even wrinkly old grandma skin hung and moved like his did.

The lawyer stepped toward Kevin. "It's hopeless, boy, you . . ." He paused as he heard sounds of gunfire and screams coming as a deluge against the walls of the complex.

A few moments earlier . . .

A single room allowed access to the containment area.

Moments after Officer Popovich left Kevin's cell and closed the door behind him, he took his seat. The cop knocked over his desk for cover. It sounded like entire clips were being unloaded at once.

Kneeling behind his desk, he reached for his revolver. He heard the barrage in the next room: fellow officers' screams coupled with the blare. An explosion of blood and bits of flesh splattered against the wall mere inches over his head. Five or six shots had passed since he hit the floor. The gunfire stopped.

He heard someone saying, "Jesus, Jesus, oh, oh, God!"

Seconds later, those sobs turned to gurgling, then died. The officer remained crouched behind the desk, watching the wall above him.

"All those soldiers," he mumbled. "We're being invaded!"

From the next room, he heard another man screaming in terror. "Ahhh! Ahhh! A m-m-monster! Ahhh!"

The next room was less than ten feet away.

Emerging from the screams was a sound of snapping and crumbling bones, then silence.

He tried to swallow through a lump in his throat. "Invaded . . . by aliens?"

The cop heard only his own heavy breathing and the drumming of his heart against his chest. His eyes moved to see something rolling past his right knee, stopping at the wall. It was his partner's head. His gaping eyes and bright red face were frozen in the expression he wore at death. Blood streamed down his chin, spurting from his neck—a crimson trail that led to the next room.

Popovich clutched his gun as if the cold steel was his savior. "This isn't happening, no fucking way!" he said, grabbing hold of the table. He pushed it against the open hallway, blocking the entrance, and backed against the wall.

Something moved into the doorway, a shadowy figure with giant, muscular arms. It was so tall it had to duck to get through the opening. Popovich raised his gun.

The beast rushed at him. The desk exploded, sending splintering wood in all directions.

"Take this, you—you—hallucination!" Popovich pulled the trigger.

The figure vanished, but not before the bullet struck. It left behind a floating, dark-blue wound. When the shadowy form reappeared, it was bleeding from the shoulder. The liquid spilled down its hairy, beastlike arm to a scaly hand with five-inch claws.

Before he could get another shot off, and before he could even blink, the gun was knocked from his hand.

He watched in terror as the bullet hole instantly sealed itself. The creature's blood remained as only speckles on its hand, and it was there that the officer saw his gun.

The creature lifted the weapon in its palm as if showing it to him. The gun crumbled to pieces, along with it any hopes Popovich had of fighting back.

The beast grabbed him and lifted him off the floor.

The creature's hand grew so large it overlapped the officer's entire upper torso. Pinning him against the wall with its claws, its five fingers held him against the corner. Its long pinky speared through his left shoulder as easily as water, and its thumb squeezed down on his throat.

Popovich screamed in agony as the creature twitched its pinky inside the wound.

"Where is he? Where's Kevin?" spoke a deep, scratchy, reptilian voice. The wide-eyed cop turned his head to his right, toward the cellblock hallway.

"Thanks," it said. The hand squeezed, popping the cop's upper torso into red jelly. The man's head twirled to the ground shortly after his legs and stomach, leaving behind a mess of human parts.

Kevin heard the disturbance outside.

The man in black finished smoothing out his skin and adjusted his glasses. "Right on time."

Kevin got as much distance from the horse-toothed man as he could in the ten-by-ten-foot cell.

The gunfire and noise stopped. Kevin could do nothing but wait. He thought about fighting back, but then looked down at his bruised knuckles.

His attacker grasped him by his arms, thrusting his body hard against the wall. "I can smell your soul!"

Kevin heard the sound of clacking bones and snapping joints as the square teeth began to move apart. The lawyer's mouth gaped, elongating over Kevin's entire head, and a misty cloud of darkness billowed from deep in his throat.

Kevin's squirming was futile. The cloud entered his nose, his eyes, and his mouth.

For a moment, Kevin stood still, blinking with charcoaled eyes.

Kevin's body dropped to the floor.

———————◄►———————

A few minutes later . . .

"Merry Christmas, hero," a deep, snakelike voice uttered from above.

Kevin woke to see a six-foot-tall figure with a dark complexion and long brown hair, dressed in an all-black suit that was torn and tattered. Each strand of hair seemed to have a mind of its own and moved like a serpent. Hanging from the ceiling by his feet, he folded his arms in a figure X, his pose reminiscent of a vampire.

Another crazy man in a costume? This just isn't my day, Kevin thought. The man's face screamed experience and intellect. He had shallow, thin cheeks and a long, narrow nose. When the man spoke, his lengthy jowls revealed that he had two tongues. One tongue was human; the other split like a reptile's. The size of his jaw was more than adequate to accommodate both. The tongue wasn't the thing that Kevin took most notice of; it was his strange hair that seemed to grow and shrink at random. Dark black sunglasses dangled from his shirt pocket, and Kevin saw why he carried them.

Dark red snake eyes. "Groovy costume."

The man leaped down from the ceiling and landed squarely in front of Kevin's face. Looking into Kevin's eyes, he extended his scaly fingers. "This is where you take my hand."

Kevin backed away.

The man smiled, his mouth full of large, green, sharp teeth, and turned around. "Follow me. Don't make me force you."

The cell bars began to bend. He walked through the large oval opening in the bars, waving for Kevin to follow.

Superpowers? Kevin thought, Better do what the monster says. He followed the man through the cellblock door and into Popovich's office.

"What the hell happened?" Kevin asked as they stepped over human entrails.

"A quick change of plans required me to kill them. Don't worry; the cleanup crews will take care of the mess."

As they entered each room, Kevin saw piles of body parts that were once police officers lying about in every direction.

"Oh my God." Kevin's eyes widened. "You did this?" he asked, cupping a hand over his mouth.

Blood was splattered on every wall, and he could make out at least one person's brain in each room.

"Oh, come on, you big baby," the man replied.

Each door they passed seemed to open by itself, several feet before the man reached it. As they walked toward the outside doors, he noticed more and more holes in the walls. Kevin assumed that either the cops were terrible shots or they couldn't see what they were shooting at. Kevin had no idea what was happening, but he had no reason to go home, now that there was no one to go home to.

They reached the double doors that led outside. A large green Hummer, the engine still running, was stopped just in front of the police station. They drove away on empty early morning streets. After they'd gone a few blocks, Kevin's stomach growled.

Before words reached his lips, the man spoke. "Let's get all the questions you're going to ask out of the way. My name is Robert. No, I'm not going to kill you. I wouldn't be able to kill you if I tried. You're not supposed to die now; I don't believe it's even hours or days from now, either . . . and, no, you're not dreaming."

Kevin opened his mouth to speak, but Robert interrupted. "I've been looking after you my whole life. Everyone's been waiting for you. But you won't find a bigger fan than me."

Robert paused for a moment. He was staring at Kevin. "Sorry. It's just I'm so excited to finally meet you. Please ask away."

"You're nuttier than a Snickers bar," Kevin breathed. "But, hey, so far you haven't stuck a gun in my face, so that's a good start. I think the most important question right now is, where are we going?"

"To a place where eyes cannot see and ears cannot hear," Robert replied.

"Oo . . . kay."

Kevin touched his eyes and ran a finger around his lips, remembering the man in black. "I'm a little freaked out. A guy came to visit me right before you came in to"—Kevin made air quotes with his fingers—"'rescue' me. What happened to him?"

"They are ministers of darkness, a proxy of evil. I felt his presence when I arrived. Just before I made it to your room, it was gone."

"It did something to me."

"I know. I know everything. Yes. Everything. Anyway, you are the prophesized one. You're the hero. It's up to you how you deal with it."

Kevin dropped his face in his hands. "Oh God, not this again. I can leap small kittens in a single bound, but I don't think that qualifies me to go world-saving."

Robert slammed on the brakes. Kevin's body smashed against the dashboard and then fell back into his seat. Other than having the wind knocked out of him, Kevin was unscathed.

"Look," Robert said. "We were driving a hundred miles an hour, and you were not wearing your seat belt. Why aren't you hurt?"

Surprised, Kevin answered, "Luck?"

Robert shrugged. "Some call it luck when a pilot has a heart attack, the plane crashes, and everyone dies except for one man. We call it choice."

Robert pushed on the gas pedal. Kevin looked outside his tinted window at the other cars they were passing.

"So if I jump out of the car right now and fall out into oncoming traffic, somehow I'll live?"

Kevin snapped on his seat belt.

Robert pressed a button and unlocked the passenger door. "Go ahead. Just because it's not your time to go, doesn't mean you won't be unharmed. You won't jump out because you've already chosen not to."

"So I'll just sit here and let the world take care of itself."

"Everything has its purpose—even doubt. It's doubt and ignorance that sometimes cause people to act. But for you, it'll be the willingness to fight." Robert looked in the rearview mirror. "Ask yourself: What do you want?"

Kevin folded his arms "I want a normal life. I want to be free."

"A person's identity grows. It's almost impossible to know who you are because it's always changing. If you don't know who you are, how can you know what you want?"

Kevin stared blankly.

"Sometimes," Robert breathed, "when people get what they want, they realize it wasn't what they wanted at all."

"You aren't gonna try and convince me a god exists, are you?"

"People refer to their gullibility as past tense even though they were sure they were right. How do you know you are right about what you think you know when you were sure you were right before? How do you know you are not being gullible now?"

"Evidence," Kevin said.

Robert smiled. "Since you had evidence before and you were wrong, what good is evidence now?"

Kevin rubbed his head. "This is making my head hurt."

There came a bellowing reptilian growl that Kevin figured must have been Robert laughing. "Most people have to experience the fullness of life in order to understand its meaning. The key is you will either choose to accept what I will show you or reject it."

Kevin looked at him inquisitively. "You mean to tell me that you know the meaning of life?"

"Of course. And you will, too. I am your protector, your teacher, and your guide. You have many questions, and they will all be answered. There are many things you must learn, including the secrets of the universe."

"Fantastic. I've been broken out of prison by an alien . . . named Bob."

CHAPTER TEN

"Give light, and the darkness will disappear of itself."

—Desiderius Erasmus

December 24, 1975

On the bleak late-December night of Kevin's escape, while children nestled in their beds waiting for Santa, countless lives rarely seen by human eyes waited for their god to be born. Nearing the hour of Robert's macabre massacre, the virgin whom Kevin had protected was moments away from giving birth to perfection.

"Did ya see that?" A man pointed down the dimly lit alley.

"Not this crap again. You need help."

Two figures adorned in white hospital garb stood by a bus stop lighting cigarettes. As cars drove by, the faces of screaming, clawing demons were reflected in the windows.

"Tell me you see that!" His breath stalled.

Thunder rumbled.

The other man stared with wide eyes. "That's strange." His cigarette smoke was moving downward, sucked into the cracks of the pavement.

"I've been working with you for too long; now I'm going crazy."

Several booms of thunder exploded around them, and large droplets of water fell from the sky, dousing their cancer sticks.

Engulfed by the heavy rain, they threw down their cigarettes and hurried toward a twelve-story, ivory-colored hospital building. Even with the torrential shower, the sky was clear; there were no stars and no clouds. The dimness of the night was illuminated by the division of light and dark, a convulsion caused by the collision of good and evil.

The image of the moon appeared as if it was cut evenly down the center; luminous and effervescent on one side, the other obscured in somber shadow.

It was as if half the sky was blanketed in a thin sheet of dark tar, with the moon in the center and its light peeking through the other side. It was odd enough to draw crowds of people outside into the rain to stare and point at the sky.

All of the clocks on the street stopped.

The smell of sulfur saturated the air. The first man in hospital garb wrinkled his nose.

"Wow, did you crap your pants?" he said. "It's burning my eyes."

"I thought that was you," the other man said, coughing.

Something gurgled in the drainpipes.

Sprouting from the earth came a slithering of pure darkness. A thickening, flat, shadowy mass void of any light pushed its way through cracks. It bubbled from soil, turning grass to dust, and gushed into the basement of the building.

Under the light of the first-quarter moon, two rusted, bulky steel doors eased open and an ambulance roared in the background.

Hearing the alarm, the doctors moved faster out of the rain. Running into the emergency room, they noticed soaked EMTs struggling to keep a woman secured on her gurney.

"Get this woman prepped and see if you can get that blasted X-ray machine working!" one of them yelled.

Meanwhile, two experienced doctors had just come on shift and were stepping out of a white Mercedes. The wind whined through the alleys and into the covered parking garage. It brought with it a hint of a growl.

Dr. Travis Mildred was a small, gentle-looking man; five six with a stout nose, short blond hair, and a thick beard, which he stroked while talking to his female partner. "Wow, that's some bizarre storm."

They headed toward the hospital.

Looking out from the shade of the multilevel parking garage, Travis squinted when he saw the rain turn clumpy and red as it slid down the windows of a building across the street.

His head darted to Jill. "Are you seeing this!?"

"Yeah, I'm glad we have our own parking spot now," she said, pointing to the other cars. "Looks like they were right. The entire staff is working overtime tonight. I don't think I've ever seen the lot so full."

"When I was called to come in to work on my day off, I knew something was up," Travis said.

Before his partner could answer, a voice echoed through the lot from a speaker next to the elevator. "Travis, this is David. I've got a twenty-something pregnant woman here in the ER with three gunshot wounds to the abdomen. She's alert, but her vital signs are dropping, and there are no exit wounds. It's a miracle, but the baby's vitals seem stable.

"We couldn't get an X-ray because both machines are down, probably from whatever it is that's screwing with the building's lights. The bullet wounds look like something big, maybe a .50 caliber."

"Bring her to the OR," Travis replied through the speakerphone. "We'll open her up and see what's going on. Jill and I will meet you there."

"Okay, she's on her way. We'll have about a unit of blood out of her before you see her."

Then the voice was gone.

Jill's head was down, and she was smoothing out the rain from her brown hair. "Still not sleeping well?"

Travis nervously looked back at the building across the street. The blood was gone, but dozens of pairs of red glowing eyes were staring at him. He quickly turned his head away and asked, "Ever think some days that you're going crazy?" He pressed the button for the fourth floor.

Jill smiled. "Get some more REM sleep, maybe a glass of warm milk before bed."

"The last couple of days I've been feeling like I've been being watched and followed," Travis said as they stepped into the elevator.

"Don't tell me that you're starting to believe in ghosts," Jill said. "I wonder what the commotion is all about. I think I saw every ambulance out there."

A group of shadowy faces with blind, white, bloodshot eyes washed over the wall in front of them. They appeared in a blink and were gone as fast as they came.

The light in the elevator flickered out, the conveyance stopped, and the steel box creaked. Something scratched at the walls: three tall, bony, inhuman shadows stood behind them. Travis caught one in the corner of his dilating eye.

His heart dropped.

The delay was brief; the light was restored, the shadows were gone, and they continued on their way.

"Um . . ." Travis breathed. "So . . . you were saying?"

"It's just . . . we've lost over thirty patients this week. I wonder if we're doing any good."

The two of them exited the elevator and hurried down the hall. Blood trickled down the walls. Steaming gore bubbled and sizzled on the ceiling.

Then the lights flashed, and everything was normal.

Certain his mind was playing tricks on him, Travis shook his head. "Even if we save a single life and lose a hundred, that one life is worth it." Travis finished drying his hands and snapped on his gloves. "Okay, what's with all the lights? Is the power going out?"

"Weird," Jill said, tapping on the fluorescent tubes above the sink.

"That's my last glass of wine," Travis mumbled.

Much like the arcane, halved moonlight, every light source in the building, every flashlight, and every bulb had been burned out or darkened on one side, divided evenly down the center.

"This is the craziest brownout I've ever seen." Travis pulled his surgical mask around his ears.

The storm howled around the building.

The gurney drivers ran the body though the pneumatic double doors, shouting, "Sedate her!" Their voices could barely be heard above her moans of pain and fear.

Two of the rain-drenched EMTs pinned her down; a syringe pierced her arm. The soaked men hovered above her, hands wet, yet no drops fell on her; the rainwater evaporated inches above her body.

"Check this out!" An EMT shook his hair above the victim.

The water disintegrated

Travis stood by the woman, pulled down on one arm and took her temperature while Jill looked for a vein to administer an IV. This Jane Doe had veins thinner than an infant: threadlike and deep under the skin.

"Get me a new thermometer!" Travis yelled.

The EMT, struggling to keep her down, clenched his jaw. "Go ahead, try another one. It's only the seventh one we've checked."

"You telling me that this woman is running a temp of twenty degrees?" Travis replied.

"Okay, got another one!" the assistant said, plugging in another IV.

Finally, they managed to inject her with ten milligrams of ampicillin, paracetamol, phenobarbital and a maximum dose of morphine sulfate for labor pains.

The woman was now unconscious, either from the pain or from the analgesics, but what the EMTs were surprised by were their now-dry hands. In spite of her clothes being torn and her body being bruised, her amber hair was full of life. There was no strand out of place and no split ends, and it appeared to move on its own.

There was a brief peace between the rain and the sound of the wind whistling through the open ER doors.

They stood there witnessing something alien.

"She's . . . she's not real," one EMT said, gaping and staring.

Her face was remarkable; a modeling agent's wet dream. The right side of it was quite stunning, a young woman's face with high cheekbones, smooth and silky.

Jill looked down as she pushed the gurney down the hall. "Who could do this to something so beautiful?"

Where the features of her right side were like a sculpture of a Greek goddess, those on the left were knotted and broken.

Travis shone a penlight into her pupils. "God help this woman."

Blood showed in the white of her eye, and the flesh around the socket was purple with shades of black. Her left ear was as thick as cancer, already violet bruised, faded into yellow. Which was far different from her other ear, which appeared long and thin, almost similar to the mythical elf—a half inch pointed at the top.

"Pointed ears?" He chuckled. "What kind of person gets their ears pointed like this? I'm betting these cost a pretty penny . . . they feel . . . real."

Travis rubbed a hand over his facial hair as he could see no scarring from any kind of plastic surgery.

She had all the disfiguring marks of a victim involved in a massive fight. Bruising on her knuckles and foreign skin under her fingernails added to this evidence. But there was one piece that didn't add up: her tongue was torn out.

The operation began . . .

The doctors tore the woman's blood-splotched pants off and cut her panties from her thighs. They examined her abdomen for a second time: three bullet holes just above her belly button. The diagnosis was correct.

"Entrance wounds . . . but no exits? The bullets must still be inside. Let's get that baby out of there," Travis said.

One nurse snapped cardiac monitor wires to Jane Doe's chest and wrapped a blood pressure cuff around her arm, while another slipped a plastic tube down her throat and into her windpipe. Her vital signs had been slipping at the outset; the lab techs had come down to surgery and were now cross-matching blood for transfusion.

A fine red mist of blood came from two of the bullet holes.

"Damn!" the respiratory technician said. "What's that?"

Upon leaving the wounds, the blood was thinner than water. As it made its way down her body, it changed in density, thickening and shifting in a rainbow of colors.

The wave of the bouncing, beeping, green line on the monitor fluttered.

Flatlined.

As the straight line moved across the monitor, the darkness made its way from the basement like water pouring into a glass, flooding through hallways and up the stairs, hunting. The supernatural shadow dispersed through every crack, and in its wake, bulbs burst and fluorescent lights exploded on the floors below the operating room.

"Clear!" a nurse cautioned as the sounds of a flatline continued.

The patient's head jostled with the rhythm of the paddles' shock fibrillating her body.

"One, two, three. Clear!" Jill shouted. The body shook, but the green line remained flat. Jill pressed the metal of the pads on the patient's skin for another try. The paddles recoiled from her chest and vaulted into the air. Jill could only watch as the machine surged in a bloom of electricity and erupted in a shower of sparks.

Perplexed by the small geyser of fluid coming out of the patient's mouth, Jill realized that it was, in fact, the mixture of chemicals, including the IV fluid, they had administered earlier. Upon exiting her mouth, the chemicals immediately dissolved.

Sounds of an argument penetrated from the next room. "What do you mean the blood isn't real? You must have botched the test."

"I'm telling you that it's not A, B, AB or O. It's not any fucking letter at all! You know what? Fine! It's FU negative!

"What's going on out there? Someone call security!" a nurse cried.

Jill slammed her hands down on the sparking defibrillator. "They've obviously been called. Stay focused!"

Jill stood and stared, perplexed, as she noticed the patient had not dilated at all, yet showed all other signs of being in labor.

Travis locked eyes with Jill. "Just do the drill. Just go through the motions," Travis said, picking up a scalpel.

Just before his scalpel pierced flesh, her skin began to change pigment, mimicking the composition and reflective finish of the instrument.

A whisper of hellish moans entered the room. Travis looked up nervously. "What was that?"

"What was what?" Jill asked.

Travis took a deep breath and turned back to the operation.

A scar materialized, running up her stomach, past her belly button and ending at the middle of her ribs. The scar began to flutter, spreading open with small strings of flesh popping apart, revealing the baby cradled in her organs. There was no sign of the bullets or internal damage.

Travis looked back up to the other nurses. They all shrugged their shoulders. Behind them, he could see a palpitating shadow on the wall behind the four doctors observing the birth.

Slowly growing from the shadow, bony twelve-inch fingers reached out and draped over their heads. No time for even a whimper. Digging into eye sockets and throats, the bony digits expelled vital fluids. Pulled by their skulls, their bodies were torn from the light, yanked into the deathly blackness.

"Oo . . . kay . . . just my imagination. Just my imagination," Travis mumbled.

"What?" Jill asked.

"Nothing."

Peering into the birthing mouth of her abdomen, Travis pointed at the organs in disbelief. "I, uh, I don't know what that is, or that, or that. I guess that's a liver, but it's not supposed to be there. And if she's dead, why are her organs moving around?"

The Jane Doe began to glow. Like an orchestra tuning up before a performance, her body brightened at every passing millisecond.

Spiraling dark clouds mixed with bubbling opaque goo poured out from the walls toward the birthing god.

Reacting to the commotion, Travis turned his head for a brief second. Looking back, he saw the baby had sprouted upward, six inches from the open womb, surrounded by the mother's fleshy tendrils and cupped in an organic basket.

Ignoring the rest of the living, the zealous coalesced into snakelike tentacles of vile death. The bubbling spears shot from the corners of the room.

Like waves of water crashing against rock, the tentacles of darkness splattered against a luminous field a foot from the surgical table.

The radiant child opened her eyes.

She erupted in a brilliant burst of light, bathing the entire room in her glory and eliminating any trace of shadow.

Just as quickly as it had come, the light diminished, retreating into the newborn baby. The living cradle supporting her was losing strength. The last vestiges of life were leaving the mother. Slowly and gently lowering the infant toward the open womb, the cradle finally came to rest securely inside the mother's belly.

All signs of the dark evil had been expelled; purged from every corner of the building. Outside, the torrential rains stopped. The lights, the bulbs, and even the moon had all returned to normal.

G.R. MORRIS

Travis was at a loss for words, as was everyone else. "This obviously isn't a survivable injury," he said. "Unless anyone has any other ideas, I'm going to call it."

Normally Travis liked to give the rest of the team a chance to speak up before ending any resuscitation.

Nurses seemed to recognize the futility of doomed efforts, and messing around with a hopeless alien was beyond pointless. They stood around in awe and for a moment were at a loss for words. There was silence.

Travis looked at the clock on the wall. "Time of death: 23:59. And I guess time of birth is midnight, exactly. We got a Christmas Day birth."

He stripped off his gloves. "Good job, everybody. This, uh, woman was dead when she hit our table."

Travis stared at the child. "Someone please get a camera down here. We need a Polaroid of this thing."

"That won't be necessary," Jill said, pointing a gun at Travis.

Confused, he looked to the other nurses for help. They just smiled.

"What? What's going on?" Travis stroked his beard and swallowed.

As Jill got closer, her face fluttered, and her body shrank. "I'm sorry, Travis. I'm replacing you. This is the way it's got to be. You've seen too much."

Travis looked at Jill; she was now five six with a stout nose, short blond hair, and a thick beard. In every way, she looked and sounded like Travis, all the way down to his doctor's coat and his sneakers.

"I know what you're thinking," his mirror replied. "You want to know what we did with Jill. Well, I'll tell you. I've always been this Jill person. You've known me for a decade."

"That really isn't that long for us. It's like six months your time. Let me tell you," he said, tapping his finger to Travis's chest, "pretending to be that stupid bitch for a decade was hell."

"If you're one of them," Travis said, pointing to the child, "why didn't you help me save the mother? Surely, you know more about this biology than I do."

"She's not one of us." The other nurses morphed into security guards. "She gives birth like one of us, but she's not one of us. I don't know what she is."

One of the nurses, now a security guard, looked at Travis's doppelganger. "What are you doing? What are you, some kind of evil mastermind telling the hero all your plans before you kill him? Get on with it."

It giggled. "You're right."

The gun fired, and the original Travis fell to the ground, a bullet between the eyes.

12:01 a.m. . . .

The doppelganger's gloved hands picked up the newborn girl.

"Where's Dada?" the infant spoke.

The doppelganger took the baby and wrapped it in a white blanket, cradling it in his arms. His voice changed to an old woman's.

"I'm going to be spending a lot of time with you, my little child."

"I'm curious, when are you going to shift into Conover?" a guard asked.

The voice shifted back into Travis. "My vacation ends next week, but I think I'll be coming back early. I'll make the change after I drop the baby off as Travis."

"What about Robert? Did you speak to him?"

"It's hospital policy to deliver any unparented newborns directly to the local orphanage, not to mention Robert said our orders are to comply with it," the doppelganger replied. "He's going to help us dispose of some of the people here in this hospital after he kills Kevin."

"What about the child? Isn't she our lord and savior?"

"If you believe the Timeweb and our boss, then yes. According to the main three religions, there is the human savior, Kevin, there is the changeling savior, Daren, and the rest of the galaxy believes in the Dragon. Personally, I don't believe in any of it. The orphanage is the only place the Timeweb shows that she will be safe from harm."

"What about the anomaly? Should we trust an imperfect system?" the guard asked.

Travis's doppelganger began walking toward the door. "You don't trust a system that's been tried and true for over five billion years?"

"But it rebooted itself, and the virus code is still there."

"Stop spreading rumors. Besides, we have our orders." He turned around, pointed at them, and gritted his teeth.

"Nobody in this building lives. Nobody."

PART FIVE

LIGHT'S PROGENY

"For all mortals, birth is suffering, aging is suffering, sickness is suffering."

—Buddha

October 15, 1976
Foster File #55148362
Name: Daren (unlisted)   Date of Arrival: December 25, 1975
Hair: Platinum blonde   Eyes: Blue   Sex: Female
Race: Caucasian   Age: Estimated 3 years old

Notes: Daren is exquisite; we have something of a child prodigy on our hands. We're assuming she came from the hospital. She came with a note that gave strict instructions to keep her actions classified. There were also a series of numbers: 0, 1, 1, 2, 3, 5, 8, 13, 21, 34, and so on. It was later explained to me that it's known as the "Fibonacci sequence"; we found the child scratching them into the side of the plastic container she was brought in.

A few days later, the rest of the counselors and I went to the nearby hospital to investigate further. They claimed that they had no births on record the day of her arrival.

The day we got her, one of the clerks at the hospital examined Daren. Based on her appearance, she suggested that she was only a day old, but due to her ability to walk, read, and talk, that was impossible.

We didn't bother bringing up the odd numbers she was writing down. No one would believe us. Anyway, we have all decided to give her an age based on her looks.

In only the past couple of years, she has grown from looking like a three-year-old girl to a youth in her late teens.

She's a perfect kid: never curses, never wets the bed, and always does what she's told with amazing results. But this has not stopped the constant teasing about her unusual growth.

From day to day, people come in, see her picture, and want to adopt her, but she's consistently missing. When they leave, she shows up from out of nowhere.

The staff denies any knowledge about these incidents, and all information has been inconclusive. Whether or not they are involved with her disappearances is currently under investigation. Diversity classes have been scheduled.

Blissful Havens Orphanage: *Dr. Edward Blackthorne*

End of log entry

CHAPTER ELEVEN

"It may be hard for an egg to turn into a bird: it would be a jolly sight harder for it to learn to fly while remaining an egg. We are like eggs at present. And you cannot go on indefinitely being just an ordinary, decent egg. We must be hatched or go bad."

—C. S. Lewis

September 11, 1976

The Blissful Havens Orphanage, at the edge of the city, consisted of two large buildings: one was two stories, fronting the street; the other six-stories, set back on the grounds. This orphanage was unique, once home to thousands of the criminally insane. Long ago, the place mysteriously burned down, but not everything was destroyed. The cells were still intact, and some of the supplies and beds were still available for reuse. Once it was repainted and rebuilt, only people on the inside would remember its horrid history.

The orphanage itself was in the second building.

The office in front was where adoptive parents came to select and meet children.

Where the buildings split stood a huge stone cross, ten feet tall, surrounded by an iron fence with spiked railings extending up toward the sky. For the most part, the institution lived its own life: distinct and separate.

Daren's classroom was clouded with chalk; its dust was in the air, and sticks of it were on the floor, ironically, almost always more there than on the blackboard.

The elderly counselor brought the smell of mothballs into the room with her. A hint of fresh paper and pencil shavings mixed with the scent of mildew. The children were dressed in clothing that looked to be hand-me-downs.

"Children, please be seated," said the old woman.

The soggy, balding, red-carpeted floor was soon packed with children. The seventy-year-old woman looked down at them from behind her cracked and dusty oak desk. Although the desk was colorfully designed with mischief, the old woman didn't seem to care.

"Today is your first day of preschool. Is everyone ready to watch *Fuzzy Wuzzy Explores the Wonders of History?*"

"Mommy!" cried a child who seemed to have soaked himself.

Daren always added her two cents to almost every incident. "Bobby, please don't cry. Go to the lavatory and freshen up, and this time sanitize your hands with the soap. It's much more hygienic."

The kids stared in silence as their classmate spoke like a grownup for the first time. Just as the kids stared, so did the teacher.

Bobby was escorted out of the room to be cleaned up by one of the faculty nurses. The old woman gave Daren a startled look and continued showing the film.

"Huh huh huh, hee hee hee . . . Look at me, I'm a happy bunny!" said the giant purple rabbit, looking in a book.

"Kids, I was just reading about the fandashmabulous, neat-o torpedo past; about our first groovy president! Yeaaay!"

Daren looked at the book that the rabbit was holding and began to comment. "Oh, good. George Washington."

The teacher looked at the interrupting child in disbelief.

"How do you know that, honey?" The teacher shifted her eyes like a mouse.

"I read the history book that I found in the library," Daren said. She held up the seven-hundred-page biography of the president.

"College-level reading material?" the teacher sighed over the echo of giggles. "You couldn't have read this!"

Daren hunched over to look shorter. "But I did, Miss Jackson. I read it last night before dinner."

Miss Conover, marooned at the far end of the room under a decaying doorway, thinned her lips and pointed down the dingy corridor.

Miss Jackson hung her head like a beaten dog and nodded.

"I don't know why you chose now to start lying, but this will put you in the confining room." Without hesitation, the teacher grabbed Daren's left arm, pulling her off the floor.

Daren pleaded as the old woman dragged her down the hallway. "Nooo! I didn't do anything wrong!"

"That's enough!" the woman interrupted. "Fibbing will just get you into more trouble! Now, you'll stay in here until you can learn to stop telling lies!"

The old woman dropped Daren's arm and left. The steel door screeched across the floor. The slam reverberated down the cobweb-filled hall.

Daren's shoulders collapsed and she rested her chin in her palm. *Fifth time this week. Wow.* Daren surveyed the room. *I wonder whether anyone else has been here.*

The walls were like white padded pillows with numerous tears in the lining and strange dark stains from past victims. The bed mirrored the walls, as did the floor and ceiling.

"I guess that's what I get for sharing my thoughts," she mumbled.

Better keep those under wraps unless I want to keep going in here. Daren gripped the sides of her tattered gray rags and noticed a rip along both sides.

"Great," she said. "They just got me new clothes a few hours ago."

She walked over to the bed, reached under the padding and pulled out a piece of loose spring. Placing her back to the wall, she cut into the wall right above her head with the slightly sharp edge.

Daren stepped forward and turned around, comparing the new scratched line to the dozens below it. "Wow. Two inches in just a day. What's happening to me?"

She placed a hand on her chest. "Uh-oh. Those are coming in already."

It was an hour before she was released.

October 13, 1976

One night, Daren began a little adventure on her own. The other children were unconscious, cocooned in their sleeping bags. She quietly pushed open the door and peeked to her left.

She glanced down the hall. *Good. They're asleep*, she thought, looking at the edge of a computer near the front desk, thirty feet away at the corner of an adjacent hallway.

Stepping out into the hall, Daren heard a door opening from one of the counselor's rooms behind her. *That's where they keep the coffee.*

Wait a second, that's around the corner . . . just how did I know that? Daren's face began to get moist and discolored. In a panic, she raced to get under the clerk's desk.

If she sees me, I'm going to get thrown back in the sanitarium, or worse—what could be worse than that? Daren's fear and desire to hide was already causing her shape-shifting genetics to take over.

She could feel the counselor approach. Daren's heart slammed against her chest, her face remained misshapen, and she was staring instinctively through her mind's eye at the clerk's photograph placed securely above her.

After a few seconds, Daren recognized the counselor's worn cotton loafers walking past one of the desk's chipped legs. With her heart racing, Daren's head pounded. Looking down at her hands, she saw they were bigger, wrinkled, and painted with red fingernail polish. Her throat felt odd, and her skin was fluttering like a fluid blanket as her face changed shape. Acting on pure instinct, she stood up.

"The kids are all asleep, I made sure of that. Anyway, I'm going to bed and you should, too; you have an early morning shift, you know," Daren said.

Just what the heck was that? She just heard Conover's shrill, nasally high-pitched voice.

"All right. I just didn't know you were still up, Mrs. Conover," the counselor explained. Daren smiled, and the other counselor turned and walked away.

Oh my God. Oh God! Daren knocked papers from the desk, rushing to the nearest bathroom to look in the mirror.

What's happening to me? Not only had she sounded like the counselor, but she resembled her perfectly.

Not only was her face different, she was wearing the same clothes Mrs. Conover wore in the photo.

Pressing her fingers into her cheeks, Daren knelt, trembling, against the cracked tiled floor.

A few moments later . . .

Stand up, Daren, stand up! She pulled herself up by the counter. She looked in the mirror, and Mrs. Conover's reflection was still looking back at her.

She ran a finger over the four hairy warts on her cheek and pushed them back into her skin. They flattened and disappeared.

She looked up at her thick unibrow. *Poor lady, she sure is hideous. Perhaps that's why she's so mean to everyone.*

Quickly composing herself, she returned to the computer.

Although she had never learned to type, her fingers flew expertly over the keys, mimicking Mrs. Conover's skills as an experienced data entry professional.

Why, this is handy. Within seconds, Daren changed the schedules for the foster visits. She submitted her name into the database so that she would be next in line for consideration for adoption.

She heard the older kids in the room down the hall talking. It was the posh squad. "Did you take my ruby red lipstick, Rachel?"

Daren rolled her eyes. *Makeup. Gross.*

"You know, that's the second time we've asked that bitch Daren to join us. She thinks she's too good for us. The nerve!"

"Easy for her to be against makeup. She's perfect."

Daren made her way back to the children's sleeping area. Just before she turned the corner, she stopped. As if running into an invisible wall, she was immobilized.

Almost instantly, her skin fluttered, her body blurred, and she was back to four feet tall. What were once loafers and hospital garb became worn gray cotton pajamas and bare feet.

Daren, while returning to her bed, wasn't careful enough to go unseen. She was caught tiptoeing across the tiled floor.

One of her classmates was awake, staring through a hole in the roof.

"Where'd ya go?"

"Shhh . . . don't wake Joey. I've had enough of Conover today."

"Ooo, sorry," he whispered.

"I had to change," she smiled.

The blond boy, Thomas Bane, was staring at her.

"Speaking of change. Wow. Daren, I just can't get over how fast you've grown. You look about as old as me now. I think you actually look a bit older since yesterday."

"Great. At this rate, I'll look like Conover in no time."

Tom lay back down on his mattress. "You'll be fine. I actually think the process is slowing down."

"I overheard the preppy sisters gossiping about me again."

"Why exactly do you hate makeup anyways?" Tom asked.

"There's already too many masks people wear on the inside to be going around wearing a mask on the outside."

Tom focused through a hole in the ceiling to the stars. "Ya know, when you look up there, it makes you wonder where it all came from . . . I mean, like, do you believe there's a God?"

He's sweet, Daren thought. *He's the only one who doesn't look at me strangely.* Daren paused and thought about this simple concept. It was as if something deep within her woke up for a moment and was speaking through her.

"Tom. I know we can't call for a pizza, but maybe two large pies with our names on them will show up on our beds eventually."

"What?"

"If something as complicated as a universe can appear, surely something as simple as a pizza will show up in no time," she smiled. "Time and chance alone create nothing. Calling, like praying, would at least be a mechanism."

Tom displayed his toothy smile. "You're weird, Daren. But that's why I like you. What do you think about life on other planets?"

"Tom, as you look at those stars, those beautiful twinkling lights, it stirs the imagination, conjuring endless stories. Be at peace with the knowledge that although there is life on other planets, your life's purpose is not among them. Each one of us here, sleeping on our dirty mattresses, has a purpose in life; there is a reason we are all here. Life is a journey of discovery, finding out our reason for being, and fulfilling that purpose."

Daren flinched as she heard the padded tap of footsteps make their way toward the room.

The voice that had controlled her lips left immediately. *What did I just say? I guess I'll figure that out later.*

Pulling her covers up to her shoulders, Daren closed her eyes. Lying there, trying to sleep, she wondered about her own purpose in the world.

Moments before she fell into slumber, she concluded that she had some kind of higher purpose. There was a warm feeling that she constantly tried to ignore. It was a feeling of self-righteousness, as if she were meant for something infinitely grand.

Daren, unconscious, smiled.

CHAPTER TWELVE

"There is in every true woman's heart, a spark of heavenly fire,
which lies dormant in the broad daylight of prosperity, but which
kindles up and beams and blazes in the dark hour of adversity."

—Washington Irving

October 14, 1976, 6:00 a.m.

The cold cold gray doors opened as if someone kicked them. "Rise and shine!" the counselor yelled. The other children started whining as they always did, but Daren was up in an instant.

The counselor began stomping her feet down the long path in the middle of the mattresses. "Someone messed with our computer last night," she said. She paused at Daren and narrowed her eyes.

Daren could taste the scent of burned coffee seeping through the woman's loose dentures.

Conover smiled. Daren's eyes widened.

"And I know who it was!" claimed the furious counselor, moving her gaze to Tom.

"I didn't do it! I swear!" protested the fifteen-year-old boy.

"Liar!" she said, pointing her broken red fingernail at him.

The sanitarium was once used to process the underage crazies from San Diego's gutters, who were occasionally dumped at the orphanage by the county authorities. Its deterioration came with urine and feces mixed with rubble and trash, so when punishment was needed beyond just a "time-out" in the confinement room, this was where it happened. Daren saw this place in her visions, and her kind heart forced her to intervene.

"Mrs. Conover, it was me. I did it," Daren announced.

"My sweet, sweet, little Daren. Always the protector." She cackled sarcastically. "We all know you could not have done this—not the perfect little girl." Conover snapped her fingers, and two other counselors who stood at the entrance to the sleeping area proceeded to Tom's bed.

"But I can't let you take him. He didn't do it. He's innocent!" Daren argued.

"Since you love helping people, you can join him," the counselor said, snapping her fingers again.

Conover's underlings pulled both Daren and Tom by their arms out of the room.

As they were led down the hallway, Daren whispered an apology. "Tom, I will make sure you get out of this. Don't worry; leave everything to me. Besides, this was all my fault."

Conover walked behind them with her arms folded and her chin down.

They reached the end of the hallway and steel doors opened, revealing a room flooded with the smell of human waste. The counselors paused and turned around to look at Conover. Raising a hand in the air, she cupped her fingers forward in a brushing motion.

The counselors nodded in unison and shoved the two kids into the room.

They fell to the trash-covered ground, skidding across soggy papers and sewage. Abruptly stopping at a pile of rocks, they turned around.

"I want this place clean in two hours!" demanded the cruel counselor. She slammed the door behind her.

Tom immediately got up and lowered his hand to her.

Daren smiled as he helped her up. "*Such a cheeseball*," she giggled. *But I kind of like it.*

Daren and Tom stood in the deafening silence and the stew of waste. From somewhere above, a faint light filtered through a dingy lunette window.

I never knew this stuff could be so gross, Daren thought. The air was cold and damp. As in her visions, the room was filled with piles of garbage and stank of urine and human defecation.

Daren broke the silence. "What does she expect us to clean with?" she asked.

"I don't think she expects us to clean anything. No one has ever tried. Wait." Tom pointed out two scrub brushes and dishwashing liquid among the rubble. "What? Those weren't there a second ago, but I guess, those." In the stale murkiness, Daren found the most secluded and darkest area in the room.

"Go over there, Tom. I'll take care of this mess," Daren said, pointing to the far corner behind some rubble. Besides her physical appearance of being eighteen, there was a very special air about this six-year-old girl. When she commanded anyone, if they listened and obeyed, it brought a great feeling of warmth in their chest.

Tom walked behind the large mass of filth and stepped into shadows.

"I'll tell you when I'm done."

Daren paced across the floor. *Gee, I feel like I can do something about this mess easily, but what?* she asked herself. Her body flowed with the similar odd feeling as when she impersonated the clerk.

Seconds later, Daren's arms and legs began to quiver. Darting to the sink, she filled the bucket with water, added some Pine-Sol and threw the scrub brushes in. Time seemed to stand still around her. She marveled at her speed.

She grasped the brushes. Their grimy wetness splashed soap in her face.

"Gross!" she gagged. After wiping her eyes, she noticed her arms were lighting the room.

Glowing in the darkness, Daren threw herself into the task at hand, and with the speed of what could only be explained as lightning, she began cleaning the floor and walls.

Small balls of light, like sprites, emanated from her body and spread throughout the sanitarium. Streaming into pockets of filth, they began to pop away the sewage in a wondrous array of color. As she worked faster and faster, her glow intensified proportionally until the room was filled with a blinding white light, cresting just as the last pile of debris was cleared away.

Just as Tom was about to see what Daren was up to, a brilliant flash of light filled the room. As his eyesight returned to normal, he noticed the rubble he was standing behind had vanished.

"Amazing!" yelled Tom. The sanitarium sparkled, and his face lit up when he saw the reflective floor. The smell of urine and human waste was now replaced with pine and soap.

The rubble had somehow disappeared, and the ceiling was open to the now-shining sunlight from the once-hidden window above. Daren stood in the middle of the room beside a bucket of clear water.

"Looks like we're done," she said, laughing.

"Wow, I guess so. But how did we do it?"

"Never mind; you don't want to know."

"Then what do we do now?"

"This," she replied, pulling out a board resembling a chess game. "Again, don't ask."

The two hours flew by with Daren the victor, when she chose to be. Then the door opened, and the counselor responded to the clean room by fainting.

The two children joined hands, skipped over the unconscious counselor, and made their way back to their room.

2:00 AM

The storm of whispers involving the crazy clean condition of the sanitarium died down. Hours after the children were supposed to be sleeping, Daren was awake, sleeping on the opposite side of the room from Tom.

Tom, after witnessing the crazy event, couldn't relax. Their heads turned, and their eyes met simultaneously. They smiled, knowing this smile was about more than just what had happened. They could feel the warmth of each other's affection growing.

Tom was the first to get out of his bed. Daren sat up.

"Careful. Don't wake the others," she whispered, watching Tom step around the children in their sleeping bags.

Tom, with a smile turning up the corner of his lips, took a seat next to her on her mattress. "What are you still doing up?"

Daren had been up for a few hours, mulling over the event in the sanitarium and wondering whether she should share her gifts; whether she should reveal them to Tom.

The moment she looked into his innocent face and trusting eyes, he tilted the decision in his favor.

"You want to do something else crazy with me?"

Tom arched a sly brow. "You bet I do."

Daren and Tom made their way behind the building where she looked out into the run-down park. Daren knelt down on the dead, stale brown grass and closed her eyes.

Tom looked at the rusted swing set, the bent and broken-down basketball hoop, and the tacky graffiti. "What are we doing here?"

Daren's eyelashes began to glow. She placed her fingers into the dirt up to her knuckles. She heard a rumble, like a busy freeway in the night. Veins of light cracked in a web through the ground. She removed her hands.

"Whoa . . . ," Tom said, backing away.

Daren opened her eyes to watch the concrete disappear, and the metal and stone vanish. Sprites of light were budding from the ground, forming complex shapes. Flowers coalescing from light and pillars of luminescence forming trees and bushes along the exterior.

Tom sat down next to Daren to watch the show and placed his hand on top of hers. Huge heaves of flowers broke through soil, making the silent effort to open their buds. Like Roman candles, peacock-colored sprites burst from the center of the blossoms, pollinating the sky and ground with life.

◀▬▬▬▼▬▬▬

A few hours later....

The sun had defeated the clouds and brought morning to Southern California.

G.R. MORRIS

The dawn fractured crystalline sunbeams over rolling hills and through buildings like a Cubist painting. The bright blue sky sparkled like jeweled dust of crushed quartz. It was as if at any moment the warm light would part the city like a stage curtain, revealing the world beyond the one in which they lived.

The compound consisted of a small complementary house in the front and the larger orphanage in the back. The space behind the five-story neo-Spanish building was now an acreage adorned with nearly every species of Rosa.

It was as if God himself had painted the land with flowers, creating a much larger picture of another beautiful rose. The shape consisted of mostly white roses in its center, different shades of red around the borders, and black throughout the rest.

Before, the acreage had been littered with trash and ugly weeds cluttering the grass. Now there was the Floribunda Diadem rose and an abundance of Frau Karl Druschki's, the Antoine Rivoire, the Rosa Awakening, and various other colorful hybrids, most of which were as big as saucers.

Beyond the center of the garden and surrounding the rose symbol bloomed other forms of nature's beauty. The entire garden burned with color, as did smaller roses no bigger than a dime that framed the artistic form. Beneath the flora was the contrasting bright green lawn displaying speckled blooms of every hue. Along the exterior of the garden, several types of fruit trees created a natural fence and provided the perfect amount of shade.

The first two orphans to witness the heavenly change had spoken for hours. They lost track of time.

"I'm glad you feel safe enough to share this with me. A little surprised, to be sure, but glad." Tom smiled.

Daren looked into his eyes and blushed. "There are hundreds of other kids in this place, and even though it's crowded, I feel alone. Except when you're around; you know, it's as if I've known you forever. I trust you."

"We better get back," Tom said, standing up. He pointed to the giant rust-covered clock in the middle of two gargoyles near the roof. "I'd really like to stay and enjoy the rest of this, but there's Conover, you know."

"Yeah, she's gonna be so pissed."

With a mischievous smile, Daren followed Tom back inside.

Even when Tom wasn't with her, Daren would never be alone in this special place.

On the first day, butterflies migrated there. Later, several different and very specific types of animals were drawn to it. Above, flocks of birds nestled among the trees and soared across the sky. Sparrows, robins, finches, and doves all called this place their home.

From below, playful furred creatures jumped and danced about; bunnies, squirrels, chipmunks, and an occasional fawn were drawn to its luster. It was the kind of place that other types of animals avoided; the cats and the pigeons that once held residence in the park were now miles away.

December 23, 1976

For the next couple of months, Daren spent mornings in her special garden and sat with the plants for hours, basking in their sweet smell. The place seemed to melt away any agitation.

The way the light reflected into prisms off the morning dew of each flower made the place seem magical.

To her, it was sacred.

She had been raised in a decaying building in one of San Diego's worst neighborhoods. The exterior stucco of the orphanage cracked like varicose veins. The weather-beaten building wore shingles like an old hat. The interior wasn't much better, as most of its walls were tattered and some were patched with black, moldy cardboard. The wallpaper itself was at some point in time white, but now it was mostly gray with splotches of brown.

Those were, of course, the walls that had paper, and even in those spots it was peeling. In the orphanage's tiny kitchen, the ancient gas range was always springing leaks and constantly being patched up with various taping. "Dammit! Can we get some more holes in these pipes?" counselors would often say.

When they brought it to Conover's attention, she chuckled under her breath at the bursting blue flames. "I'll get around to calling someone."

They skimped, they skimped on everything: rust-splotched vents ; faded, gray, once-white, frayed underwear dripping dry over soap-scummed sinks; bare light bulbs; wobble-legged chairs—everything was recycled.

To accommodate the counselors and nearly one hundred orphans, the place had three economy-size refrigerators, which clicked and whined with age. Their warm motors invited what the cooks jokingly referred to as "walking protein."

Although Conover made everyone keep the rooms spotlessly clean, they had never been able to get rid of the cockroaches. "The little monsters are always hiding and chewing through the walls!" the counselors said.

The counselors were more concerned with Daren than they were with fixing the dilapidated architecture. As time passed, they repeatedly placed her in the confinement room for the slightest infractions against the rules, whether justified or not. The initial loneliness she felt the first few times she was sent there faded and was replaced by relief when she had to "do her time."

The view from this room was a single window looking out on a graffiti-covered brick wall. Nothing more than a four-foot-wide passage ran between the buildings. The window would not open; it was painted shut. Only when she pressed her face against the glass and peered straight up the narrow shaft could she barely make out blue from a thin sliver of sky.

The world is beautiful. Someday I'll be out there, she thought. She saw her reflection in a broken mirror and saw the dirty smudge on her cheek.

Daren looked at the amount of rust and mildew on the walls. "Gross!" She quickly wiped her face.

The room had a sink broken in half that looked like it had been used as a urinal. Its brown pieces were still there on the floor and dripped green muck. There was a hole for a toilet, with plenty of swirling flies, and a dilapidated bed.

Clumping up the sheet, she sat around the yellow and crusty red stains.

She stared at the bowl of broccoli-pea soup at the base of the door. It was near the flap where they slid the tray in. *If they think I'm eating that, they're loony.*

As soon as she folded her arms, lowered her head, and closed her eyes, images of people screaming in pain from demons eating their flesh flashed in her mind.

Breathing heavily, she opened her eyes.

Daren missed her garden. It was a shield, a haven from the visions that tormented her. It allowed her the silent seclusion from the others, gave freedom to her mind.

G.R. MORRIS

Daren slapped her hand on the bed. "Come on, I can do this." Closing her eyes, she dove deep into the river of the world's pain. She felt the sting of suffering; she connected to the mind of every being on the planet. She infused with every thought, tasted their immorality, experienced the perversions.

Her nose wrinkled in distaste.

Tears rolled down her clenched face.

Their victims were her victims. Their evil delights were hers. "Stop!! Stop!!"

She hit the floor, arms trembling; she gripped her sheet, and her nails scraped the mattress.

She exhaled. "Get ahold of yourself, girl."

She let go and rubbed her eyes. "All right. Focus."

Lowering her head again, Daren took a deep breath. "Okay, I can do this." She used her power to "see" through the brick wall.

She set her mind adrift, looking past the neighborhood to rolling hills, the vast Pacific Ocean, and over great mountain ranges. She was enjoying the escapism and looking for *him*. "Where are you?" she whispered.

Her vision turned to the garden. Looking upon her flowers, she grinned. For a moment, she again heard the whisper of the name "Kevin Knight."

It was like a chant calling out to her in dreams since the day she was born.

The midnight sky brought a chilling cold over the orphanage as a gust of wind flossed its way through the magnificent garden. The ocean of petals fluttered and began to glow in the moonlight.

Darkness seemed to part along the foundation of the building. Barely audible moans and muffled screams from hell were silenced. The very essence of the garden had restrained the shadows. For now, evil was held at bay. But it did not account for the hellions that were already inside.

The toddlers nestled in deep slumber squirmed in their beds, as nightmares were commonplace. Minute sprites of light were pulled from the blossoms and spiraled in the air like chaotic fireflies. The wind seemed to push through the walls of the building.

Asleep in her room, a wary smile surfaced on Daren's lips.

The halls were filled with the radiant microscopic specks and the smell of potpourri, strawberries, and various fruits. It was fragrant perfection, pleasing every nose. Then it reached the children. When the heavenly air hit their skin and moved into their lungs, the squirming stopped. The unconscious rug rats dreamed in peace, and when the garden's essence reached Daren, she called out to him in her dreams.

"Kevin! Where are you?"

Her smile congealed, then melted into horror.

She heard a growl. It held the deep, rumbling tone of bones being broken with slabs of rotten flesh. She felt something behind her that had slaughtered lives without number.

She heard its footsteps get louder.

Daren ran.

Meanwhile, in the kitchen, Conover was preparing coffee for the next day.

December 24, 1976

"We've tried a bunch of electric weed whackers, mowing, covering it with newspaper, tarps, bleach, digging them up—nothing is working! What are we gonna do about the garden? It keeps coming back. It's been attracting way too much attention," one of the counselors said to her. Conover was pouring milk into several saucers for eight stray cats.

Another counselor walked by. "The orphan's milk? So, that explains all the missing milk."

Conover scooped some sugar into her cup and smiled. "She does what she's told, and so will you unless you want to lose your legs."

"I wasn't here." The counselor's voice cracked and she continued walking down the hall.

Conover took a sip of her brew. "It's of no consequence. Let the stupid press come. Our special girl won't be special for long. Don't worry; she's gonna be sorry. I'll make sure of that."

PART SIX

MESSIAHS FOR DUMMIES

"Even the most ignorant aliens in the universe agree on one thing: cause and effect, action and its reaction. The foundation of free will is cause; it is action. The opposite is the effect and its reaction. If at any time in your life you are not the cause, you are therefore not acting, you are the effect, and you are re-acting. If you are not the cause, you are not acting, you are not free..."

—Nullados

CHAPTER THIRTEEN

"Destiny is no matter of chance. It is a matter of choice. It is not a thing to be waited for, it is a thing to be achieved."

—William Jennings Bryan

A preternatural darkness consumed the night, dousing the San Diego jail and hospital in death, taking various souls of unfortunates to their demise. A maleficent violence bound in death had come to quell both Kevin and Daren, but the clinging shadows had long been broken by the morning sunrise. Soon they would learn that Daren just being born had created a stir; a ripple in reality. History has told humanity of great leaders, people like pharaohs and kings; individuals who would inspire monumental change. They were exceptional people like Gandhi, Isaac Newton, Buddha, and Jesus Christ.

History has told humanity of great leaders, people like Gandhi, Isaac Newton, Buddha, and Jesus Christ.

And then there was a sixteen-year-old boy named Kevin.

A part of him, much like Daren, wanted to help everyone.

Kevin had a love of humanity in his heart, and Robert—a peregrine creature from beyond earth, an alien—was trying to bring it out.

They didn't talk much at first. There comes a bit of silent shock when someone discovers the supernatural. Kevin lived twenty miles from the police station, and they were driving in the opposite direction. He noticed the bright sun, and as they passed a bank a neon sign flickered 11:56 a.m. and 97 degrees.

Robert drove away from the commercial part of town, playing with the radio as he steered along the curved roads, braking, downshifting, and stomping on the gas when it was needed.

A swarm of pulsating black goo coursed through Kevin and glazed over his white blood cells. The nuclei bubbled and popped, and from the sizzling pustules demonic eyes opened.

Kevin looked down and clutched his chest. "Look, are you going to get this thing out of me or what?" he complained.

"Why are you asking me? You're the hero."

Kevin displayed a lackluster smile.

Robert handed him a mother-of-pearl digital watch. It had an orb in its center filled with a white fluid.

"Don't just stare at it, put it on."

Complying, Kevin felt a numbing chill on his wrist and a little bubbling black ink bled into the white fluid. Numbers floated inside the orb and a countdown ticked down.

"That's the longest anyone has ever had. The Spectre hawk says about a year before that thing completely takes you over. So chill."

Kevin swallowed. "Right. Chill."

Robert tapped a claw on his cigar, dropping ash. "There's nothing I can do; sorry. No one has ever successfully purged a minister without killing the host. Where we have failed, you will succeed."

"We?" Kevin asked. "So there's more than one of you things?"

Robert didn't move.

Kevin gawked at Robert's reptilian hands gripping the steering wheel. "You do your shopping looking like that?"

Robert still didn't flinch and continued with eagle eyes fixed on the road ahead.

Kevin stared at the green and red scales on the alien's skin, which decreased farther up his face, although his arms and hands were covered in the layered platelets.

"That's right; aliens exist. I'm what they call a Demonian."

Kevin looked down at Robert's hand as his crimson claws shifted gears.

Robert smiled, displaying his numerous fangs. "Frightened?" He aimed his reptilian eyes at Kevin.

"N-no, I talk to monsters every day," Kevin said, leaning slightly away.

"You could call me that. One person's alien is another's monster." Robert flattened the gas pedal. "I'm the last survivor of Demonia. Much like you, I was chosen."

"Chosen? By who?"

Robert raised one of his red eyebrows. "That was faster than the others."

"Others?"

"You aren't the first being I've trained. But you are my first messiah. Do you believe that everything happens for a reason?"

"I don't believe in fate, but yeah."

Robert looked up at the roof of the car. "Looks like you win another one, Moses. This savior is an idiot."

"Thanks."

"I must apologize." Robert tapped Kevin on the leg. "Here I am, insulting my hero. For future reference, if you believe everything happens for a reason, that means you must believe in fate."

Kevin looked up and to the right, as if in deep thought.

"Like the saying goes, what if everything happens for a reason? There are no accidents. To answer your question, I chose myself, just as you chose me."

"Choose . . . right. It's too bad you were too late to save me from this thing inside me," Kevin said.

"I arrived precisely when I wanted to, when I was supposed to. You'll just have to trust me. For now." Robert winked. "Every action and reaction in life is an agreement made with everyone. I was—"

"This is bullshit."

"Coincidentally, the day after I was pulled from my world to protect you, it was destroyed by something."

Kevin rolled his eyes. "Let me guess; I'm going to stop whatever that is from destroying Earth. I'm going to save the world!" he said, throwing his hands in the air.

"You will do whatever it is you've chosen to do, just as I will," Robert replied.

Robert drove through back alleys, making several U-turns through parks, with no clear destination in sight.

Kevin had had enough. "What the hell are you doing?"

Robert glanced in the rearview mirror. "Here they come," Robert said. The strobes of a cop's light bar flared across the early afternoon's empty highway as the cruiser pulled out behind them. "Autopilot engage!" He removed both hands from the wheel and pressed his scaly thumb on the cigarette lighter.

As a thin, soft, lime-green glow surrounded his digit, the dashboard retracted, revealing an embedded flat-screen monitor. Below it, there was an oval panel projecting floating holographic alien hieroglyphs.

G.R. MORRIS

"Cool!" Kevin said. He watched Robert's left hand shift the projected trackball and his right hand wade through the hovering symbols. "What's that?" he asked. The car was driving itself.

Then came the gunfire. The bullets streamed from open windows, some cars that collected behind them, and even random pedestrians.

"Whoa! Why are grandmas packin' Uzis and shooting at us?" Kevin ducked down.

Robert gripped the trackball. "It's the Chronos paradigm, plotting course—okay, that should cover the red lights. The probability matrix, check. And there, done!" Robert's fingers sank into the orb as it submerged into its holding base. "The real world isn't wholly real," he said, twisting his hand.

After a loud click, he pulled his arm out of the base, and a holographic timer floated above the dash. It was counting down.

Fluttering light surrounded by luminous mist in various colors spread out in a web inside the car.

Kevin covered his head with his arms. The Hummer moved through the empty spots between the many cars. Robert turned on the radio and took a drag on a cigar.

The drumbeat of bullets bouncing off the car accompanied the background music. Dozens of citizens were rolling down their car windows and shooting at Kevin and Robert. Bullets were even bouncing off the glimmering, metallic-looking tires.

A BMW full of gangsters sped next to them and opened fire.

Robert blew a few smoke rings. "Five." Then he waved, "Four, three, two, one." He floored the gas and jerked the wheel.

The timing was perfect. The Hummer crushed the side of the BMW and cut through a horizontal stream of traffic.

Kevin peeked up and watched their front bumper graze the back bumper of a crossing car. Robert adjusted the rearview mirror.

The BMW's frame exploded into a mess of metal, and he smiled at the ten-car pileup that walled off some of their pursuers.

"And now comes the Gatling gun." Robert smiled and lightly tapped Kevin with the back of his hand. "Watch this."

Kevin clutched his armrest.

With the gas pedal welded to the floor, the tires emitted a guttural howl as all four wheels skated at 120 miles per hour, then launched into a corner at an acute angle. The light emanating from inside the car appeared to bend, leaving glowing trails behind them. Robert pressed a button connected to the steering wheel, and the headlights retracted.

Coming out from an adjacent road was a black semitrailer truck that pulled in front of them. The trailer door raised, and Robert pressed another button. Missiles burst from the spaces where the headlights should have been.

Just as a man was revealed to be standing in the back ready to fire his Gatling gun, the two missiles, nearly scraping the bottom of the door, collided with the mounted weapon.

A salvo of the semi's parts crashed into buildings, and the Hummer plowed through the flaming mass. A half dozen cars sped to their location and trailed behind them.

"What are you doing?!" Kevin's legs pressed against the floor as if he had a brake of his own.

The Hummer headed straight for a building.

Kevin squeezed his eyes shut.

They passed through the structure like a ghost; the cars behind them didn't. They smashed through the doors into pillars and stairwells, then the rest into each other.

The Hummer was submerged in light. The holographic timer ticked down to zero. The car was traveling at 140 miles per hour, yet suddenly launched itself out of an apex like a laser blasting out of a gun.

The Hummer moved through the streets and, in a blur, pushed through a surge of streaming lights, surrounded in a tunnel of phosphorescent beams. Surprise splashed over Kevin's face. A trip that required two hours was cut down to two seconds.

The illumination froze into an amalgamation of police light; time came to a precipitous stop.

A woman's voice with an English accent spoke from the dash: "Course completed, switching to manual operation." Robert's car pulled over and, killing its rumbling engine, coasted to a stop in front of a very large hotel.

The road was eerily tranquil. Dozens of police cars had clustered on the street, engaging in some kind of raid. But the sirens, the gunfire, and the noise of the crowd were hushed, frozen in time.

The unyielding sun stung Kevin's eyes as he squinted in the bright sunshine glinting off the field of metal. Smoke from cigarettes remained still, and birds hovered against the sky. Ghost snakes of heat, frozen into misty pillars, rose from the pavement. Children playing in the swimming pool at the townhouse across the street were like petrified dolls, motionless marionettes on a stage of water.

Robert put the car in park. "Looks like they're trying to take out my help."

"You're gonna have to let me borrow this car someday," Kevin said.

They stepped out of the Hummer onto the sidewalk and surveyed the stillness, a commotion that was hushed along the tree-shaded streets.

To Kevin, the air seemed leaden; he found it taxing to draw a deep breath. For what little saliva he had, it was almost impossible to push past it to what seemed like an immovable boulder in his throat.

The day was hotter than the devil's armpit. It was humid enough to see droplets of water forming on windows, which was rare for Los Angeles, where the air was nearly always dry. The bright, cloudless sky was clear, gas-flame blue, an oven baking in the unusual December heat.

Kevin rubbed his eyes. They were grainy and sore from lack of rest. His mouth felt fuzzy and tasted like cardboard, and there was an unpleasant film of tartar on his teeth.

A sharp, deep, crackling voice echoed in Kevin's head like a static signal tuning into clarity from inside a steel box. *"Don't be alarmed, this is your conscience, ooooo."*

Kevin's eyes widened as he recognized the voice of the big-toothed lawyer in his mind. "Get. Out," he mumbled under his breath.

"What? I'm your Jiminy Cricket. Look pal, your friend is hiding a lot of secrets. Don't let him know I'm talking to you."

Robert noticed Kevin staring at the road.

"I know you need to sleep," Robert said. "But what makes you think you can?"

"Yeah, I got a few questions," Kevin said sarcastically.

"What is wrong with hearing me out?"

"Shut up!"

"Excuse me?" Robert raised an eyebrow.

Kevin ran a hand through his hair. *Both of these guys are monsters, so how do I know to trust either one?* he thought.

"Sorry. I'm just tired," Kevin said.

The lie brought a little chill to his wrist under the watch. Another droplet of black appeared behind the digital display. Stabbing pressure pounded behind his eyes.

"You're going to be sleeping for a long, long time. But first," Robert placed a hand against Kevin's chest, moving him behind Robert, "stand back."

"Wait, what's that supposed to mean?" Kevin blurted out.

Robert reached into his long dark trench coat and flipped open what looked like a thin, black cell phone, then pressed a button. "Chronos paradigm deactivate in sixty seconds."

Robert pressed another button and put the device away. The Hummer sparkled in glistening colors of every hue. Snakes of energy flowed from every seam in the car's design, coiling themselves around the vehicle in all directions. Glowing spheres of incandescent light merged with its frame.

The car was in metamorphosis, a shriveling conglomerate of luminous color. A few seconds elapsed as an explosion of dazzling light consumed the entire length of the street.

After the light had passed, the Hummer was gone. In its place, a Volkswagen Beetle parked neatly at the curb.

"Freakin' sweet! What was that?" Kevin asked.

"One of my changeling toys. Follow me."

Robert visually inspected the city, probing at the clouds and even scrutinizing the sky, then he crossed the street with Kevin steps behind.

"Oh no," Kevin mumbled.

"What?" Robert turned around.

Kevin had sprinted off, heading for an apartment building next door. A weeping four-year-old blonde girl was sitting on the steps clutching her doll. Several stray bullets were heading her way after breaking through a large glass window.

"We don't have time for this!" Robert screamed.

"Make time!" Kevin yelled.

"Oh, for the love of—" Robert said, pressing buttons on the control.

"Additional time allocated," the mechanical voice replied.

"We've got ten seconds to get her to safety," Robert said. He launched his body through the shattered glass. Kevin rolled under the floating bullets and threw the girl frozen in time over his shoulder.

On the way back, Robert waved his finger. "You can't keep it."

Robert carefully led Kevin around the inert swarms of bullets and through the double doors of the Hyatt Regency. He took his first steps into the hotel and pointed at the clerk behind a desk, who was unaffected by the frozen time. "Take care of this girl. She lives next door," Robert said.

"But—" Kevin protested.

"She'll be safe with him. I promise."

Some of the sludge in the watch thinned and vanished. No time was added to the countdown.

"Being a goody two-shoes won't rid you of me. Besides, how do you know I'm the bad guy? Perhaps I'm a Jungian shadow." The voice said.

The man, who seemed to know Robert, was leaning back on a chair, legs crossed with his shoes up on the counter. He had short dirty-blond hair with five-day stubble, a black T-shirt, and camouflage jeans.

It was Jason.

"How is . . . ," Kevin said as he noticed Jason was moving.

Jason raised an arm and showed a bracelet coated in flickering symbols. Robert's glare provoked the man to reach under the desk and pull out a cube covered in glowing buttons surrounding a small screen in its center.

"Put her in Commons Twelve in Defiance," he said as the clerk typed on the device. A wooden door materialized on a bare wall.

Robert opened it. Behind it was a brick wall. "Remember. Follow me to the truth, but if you do you will no longer be normal."

They heard the soft buzz of an engine. Stopping inches in front of the doorframe, Robert looked back for the cue to pass through.

Jason nodded, and the tip of Robert's black boot disintegrated as he started through the doorway. The rest of his body followed suit. The deeper he went into the room, the more he vanished.

Jason picked up the girl from Kevin's arms. "She will not be harmed," he said.

Kevin looked at the clerk.

"It's okay. Go on in," Jason said, waving Kevin toward the door. "He's waiting."

Robert's voice echoed. "You want normalcy and the truth. You can't have both. Choose."

"What if there's a pool of acid on the other side?" the voice said.

Kevin shrugged. He stepped into the opening and felt his body tingle and vibrate and then galvanize into a burst of light that was quickly followed by disorienting darkness. A second before he disappeared, he saw bullets fly. Outside, time had returned to normal.

It was like walking into the sun without the heat. But before he could voice his discomfort, the room's brightness dimmed.

"What is this?" He looked down at his feet. He was standing on shimmering energy that was nearly transparent and smooth as glass. As he raised his head, the energy split off into two white, flaring paths.

Like carpets of light, they led to two white doors. Streams of luminous color swirled through every wall around him; there was no other way out.

The black doorknobs on each white door displayed a single word. They were blurred. He could not read either one.

Black words began to coalesce on the wall above them. ONE LEADS TO HAPPINESS, THE OTHER TO SORROW AND DEATH.

Kevin put his hands on his hips. "How is this fair? They both look the same!"

"Very good," Robert said. "Look again."

Kevin could now see the white inscriptions on the black doorknobs.

The door to his right read SAVIOR, and the other read GO BACK.

He reached for the door marked Savior and paused. "Wait, isn't this a little vague?" He pulled his hand away.

He heard another man's voice echoing in the room.

"And you called him dumb. Perhaps he is the savior."

"Quiet," Robert said.

"Who was that?" Kevin asked.

"This room reacts to your desires; it provides you all you want or need to make your choice. I will not force you. The decision to continue must be yours. You have already noticed that the only fair choice is an informed one."

"Well, duh," Kevin said.

"Choose carefully. Every single choice is a domino that influences the next. Once you walk through that door, you can't change your mind; you are not free to go back."

Kevin smugly nodded. "We'll see about that."

"The door to your left is safety." As Robert spoke, a screen appeared, hovering at the room's center, showing Kevin walking into his old house, then being surrounded by police and being placed in handcuffs once again. "It leads back home and back to the police. You could choose that and spend the rest of your life in prison."

G.R. MORRIS

Robert breathed. "You will be forever safe there, be taken care of, and surely live a long life with no risk and no freedom. But you will live a relatively normal life."

"The door to your right is risk. But it's also the truth." Another screen appeared. This one showed Kevin sitting in a cab, being chased by supermodels in bikinis.

Wow, those girls are hot. Like this is a choice, Kevin thought. He turned the knob on the door marked Savior.

As he stepped through, Robert yelled, "Wait! You didn't finish watching the video!"

Kevin heard his words as he let go of the knob, but the door slammed shut. It was too late.

"Impulsive," Robert mumbled.

Nothing. Pitch black.

Keep it together, have to keep it together. Kevin closed his eyes. "No. No, no . . ." He dropped to one knee, and his breathing became shallow. "I'm not scared of the dark," he mumbled.

"Liar. This is what following him brings you," the voice said.

Kevin swallowed and pressed against the sides of his head.

Get out of my head! Kevin thought.

"Open your eyes, hero," Robert said.

It was still completely dark except for a spotlight, which was illuminating a rotten corpse in a pillar of light that came from above. The mangled mess that sat feet from him, deformed by necrosis and barely recognizable as human, was sprawled against a corner, covered in maggots and some kind of green alien goo.

Kevin saw something familiar about the dead body. "Wait a second, I uh . . ."

"He is mocking you. Don't listen." The voice was muffled.

Kevin stepped closer.

Robert hissed a snakelike chuckle. "I wouldn't do that if I were you."

It was him.

Kevin was staring at his own corpse. Startled, he flinched.

The body was gone.

"You saw what your fear manifested. Your mind was the spotlight. But remember, you are not your mind; your thoughts can be observed—even by you."

Kevin scanned the room for his doppelganger.

"You are not your body," Robert said. "The body sheds itself and is ever growing, ever changing. Existence is malleable; your focus determines your reality. If you think negative, you will be negative. If you think about why terrible things happen to you, the mind will come up with reasons to justify those things."

Kevin looked up at the dark ceiling. "So, if I hope really, really hard, I can will myself a million dollars and a hot babe?"

At the far end of the room, a door opened, seemingly by itself.

Robert's voice now came from the next room. "It's not that simple. Doubt is consumptive."

Kevin was now in a white padded room of an insane asylum. Kevin fixed his eyes on a glowing exit sign above a black door. He stood behind a geriatric white man in a straitjacket, who sat cross-legged in the center of the room.

"Sir?" Kevin took a step forward.

The man leaped to his feet, his back still to Kevin.

Jason's voice echoed. "Aren't you worried that he'll fail?"

"Failure can be a gift, a message that tells you how to grow," Robert said.

Kevin took another step.

G.R. MORRIS

The grizzled man turned around and stared at him with his milky white eyes.

His raspy voice was soft and weak. "You're going to have to knock me out or kill me to get by."

Kevin smiled. "I've been trained in every hand-to-hand fighting system. You want me to beat up this . . . this blind peasant?"

The man shook his head. A few dandruff-coated cockroaches tumbled out of his beard. "I don't need arms or sight to beat you, kid. Take one more step and I'll drop you."

Kevin, now in a fighting stance, took another step.

In a white blur, the old man's callused feet smacked across Kevin's face.

Kevin stumbled back and three more shots hit him in the chest and stomach.

His head whacked on the padded floor.

The old man coughed out a laugh. "Too easy."

A crusty, sour-smelling heel slammed against Kevin's temple, nearly fracturing his skull.

It rattled his mind and the lawyer's voice broke through. *"Why are you choosing to fail?"*

The old man danced. He hopped side to side and clicked his heels together.

Kevin barely breathed out his words. "I didn't choose this life."

"Oh, but you did! the voice said. *"Let me help you. I will relieve you of your burdens."*

Ears ringing, arms wobbling, Kevin tried pushing himself off the ground.

A foot slammed against his back, and Kevin was down again.

"Nothing bad will happen, no one will know. Come on, you have a whole year! Besides, you want to become the savior, right? Let me help you!"

Kevin winced. "I want the hell out of this. I want to be normal."

"Fate won't let you."

"Screw fate."

"Then let me help you leave Robert. Let me give you the power."

The instant Kevin uttered the word "Deal," a gushing of dark goo flooded into the ring. The time clock changed. Months were removed.

A chilling cold flushed through his body, and Kevin leaped to his feet.

"I'm not finished yet."

"Eeh?" The old man cocked his head. "Did you say you wanted me to knock you down again?"

"Bring it, geezer."

The crunch of popcorn being eaten pushed into the room. "Oops, mic is still on," Jason said.

Standing on one leg, the elderly man brought a knee to his face.

Displaying his inhuman flexibility and balance, he cracked his raised leg in all directions.

Kevin charged and delivered a series of punches and kicks, which were swatted away by the old man's crusty foot. The same leg struck Kevin's stomach, his chest, then spun into a roundhouse kick to Kevin's jaw.

The elderly man's target bounced off the padded wall.

Kevin gritted his teeth as black veins pulsed in his eyes. "We had a deal," he mumbled.

The teenage hero's vengeful strikes splintered the air in an inky prismatic onyx.

His speed caused the man in the straitjacket to hop and block with both legs.

But Kevin's power pummeled through the old man's bones.

The assault pushed the fight three feet from the exit door.

The savior felt the rage, the bloodless chill on his wrist, the soulless sting down his spine.

Kevin lowered his arms. "No. This is wrong."

The old man dropped to one knee.

"No! Repress your shadow at your peril," the voice whined.

A flurry of kicks stormed at Kevin from all directions, with every strike hitting its mark.

Kevin still stood.

Barely.

The crazy old man leaped and speared, heels first, like a missile.

Kevin's body launched off the ground and jettisoned through the back wall. He fell on a black floor in a hail of plaster and cotton.

The ceiling, like the floor, was inscribed with red letters.

They said, FAILED.

"Don't feel bad, kid, nobody beats him their first time." Jason laughed.

"Come on, Rumplesnakeskin, your boy lost. He ain't our guy. Just admit you were wrong for once. For once!"

Kevin gripped his aching chest. "I can hear you."

"Hmm . . . Robert breathed. "No. His fragility is a precondition of his heroism. It's evidence of his courage when he chose this life."

"I can't believe this. Our savior lost and he took the deal. He took the deal!"

"He became conscious of his shadow."

The lawyer's voice boomed in Kevin's head. *"You can't win. I am the right hand of Kain. Send me to hell and I shall come back stronger. The door is open."*

"The hero failed the test," Jason said.

"Did he?"

The pressure was building behind Kevin's eyes. The sludge moved in his skull. "I knew it. I told my mother, now I'm telling you. I'm not the savior."

"I failed hundreds of tests before I was allowed to be your guide," Robert said. "The armless man won. Can you win against something with more arms than you?"

Kevin rubbed his head. "This is stupid."

"If you don't evolve beyond the physical, you will never know the truth. You will die and forever be a puppet of darkness."

"Your species has always been monkey puppets. You are Robert's puppet," the voice said.

"You're evil. Shut. Up." Kevin covered his ears.

"The minister is taking over your mind. Force it out."

The voice laughed. *"I will cocoon you in darkness forever."*

Kevin got to his feet. His eyes glimmered. "Shut. Up!"

The dull sting coming from the demon in his mind evaporated. The countdown on his watch remained the same.

"Force it out. Right. It would be helpful if you told me how." A door made of light materialized in front of him.

Kevin walked to it. His path was blocked by a curtain of light too bright to see past into the room. He dipped in four fingers of his right hand, then yanked them back. Glancing down, he wiggled his fingers. "Okay. Still all there." He shrugged his shoulders and walked through.

He stood in the middle of what looked like the lobby of an old hotel. Behind him, he saw no sign of the door made of light. Instead, antique brown oak doors had been boarded up, along with its windows. Streams of light pierced through the cracks to display dusty, metallic boxes piled several feet high in the corners.

Kevin shook his head. "Great," he said, looking around the room.

Robert pointed to a thick stained-glass window. "Welcome to Africa."

Kevin's eyes narrowed at the light shining through. "A desert."

"The Sahara. This hotel is invisible to most organic eyes, and to most technologies. I trust that the portal wasn't too awkward for you."

Kevin eyeballed the sand dunes for any other threats on their way. "I've been possessed by a monster, witnessed a ton of people getting murdered, and I can't go outside without someone trying to shoot at me. Other than that, I'm great."

"As a child," Robert said, "I read about you in books; mostly religious texts and some folklore. It's surreal being here with you now."

The corpse on the floor wore a uniform. The police badge lying next to him reminded Kevin that he was with a monster. He glanced at Robert, then down at the corpse on the floor.

Robert smiled at the fear in Kevin's eyes and lit a thick brown cigar.

"I'm the last creature you should be scared of. Besides, again, I don't think I could kill you even if I tried."

"Yeah, yeah, because I'm some sort of savior of the human race."

Robert smirked and pointed up the stairs to the second floor.

Magazines and newspapers from all different historical periods plastered every step, and even some of the walls. The décor screamed of history, from black-and-white photos of John Wilkes Booth and Pol Pot to color photos of Adolf Hitler.

Kevin's walk was calculated as he moved toward the dark oaken staircase and looked around at every wall. The walls carried maps of various cities in numerous countries. Pegged to them were several markings for specific locations. "We've been looking after you, protecting you," Robert said. "We even saved your mother on a few occasions while she was carrying you."

"Some people believe you're a myth made to give the changelings hope."

Kevin smiled. "I know the feeling."

"For a long time, I was beginning to lose faith that you'd show up. I don't know how many times I've seen things that never happened, like ghost images of things that could have been."

Kevin rolled his head back and closed his eyes.

"So . . . ," he said, slapping a palm over his face, "you're a time-traveling alien from the future." He took his hand away and opened his eyes, half expecting he'd be back home in his bed.

Robert was looking at his cigar. "You'd be surprised how close one timeline came to calculating leprechauns' existence. But anyway, here you are."

Kevin paused, his eyes stopping at one group of photos of him in his house and a floor plan of the jail in which he had been held.

Robert walked in front of him. "You have no idea how much planning has gone into all of this." He trotted carelessly over the media and led Kevin up a staircase and into a hallway.

"Come on, hero. Your life was planned out long before any of this." Robert waved a hand at photos of concentration camps on the wall of the staircase. "How much different would you be if you were born a Jew during the Holocaust? Would your choices be any different?"

They reached the top.

"I can tell you. You would not be the savior."

They moved down a shallow hall. Kevin smiled. "Yeah, that would be a shame." The hall was lined with gun racks holding a plethora of guns from different times and worlds, all labeled alphabetically.

"Cool." Kevin began to reach for a six-foot-long chrome Gatling gun.

Robert swatted his hand. "Not yet."

Robert escorted Kevin into a small office that reeked of burned flesh despite the smell of pine-scented disinfectant. The walls resembled the rest of the building, except the maps in this place were blotched with bloodstains and extensive writing.

Four black granite gargoyles were legs for a large polished oak desk, which reflected the overhead fluorescent lighting. It stood prominently in the center of the room. A forty-inch screen was embedded in its center and, on either side, a substantial bank of buttons.

A plain white mattress lay adjacent to the corner, and on the opposite side, also lying on the floor, was a body. It looked as if a large animal had taken bites out of it.

"Are you just going to leave this here?" Kevin pointed at the carcass.

"Oh, you bet. They taste better after they've petrified. Crunchier," Robert grinned. "From where I'm from, I'm vegetarian. That reminds me," Robert said, opening a drawer and handing a book to Kevin.

Robert slid out the heavy Victorian oak and leather chair from behind the desk and sat quickly, folding his hands on the table before him.

"Adventures of Kevin!" he said dramatically.

Kevin raised an eyebrow and put the book down on the desk, and Robert smiled. "It loses a lot in translation, but trust me, it's pretty impressive in my language."

"Sure," Kevin said.

"I'm helping you, not because you were my hero as a child, and not because I used to have action figures of you in my room. It's not because of my hundreds of years of training for it. It's my purpose."

Robert opened his desk drawer again to put the book away, and Kevin noticed something else in there.

An old black leather-bound book with the title smudged. Tomorrow's E—

And there was something else written under that title, but it was too worn to make out. This book was in English. Kevin picked it up.

CHAPTER ONE
Devils Due

"Give a hundred pounds to a body builder, and he's easily going to lift it. But give that same hundred-pound weight to a starving child, and he's bound to fail. Everyone's challenges are customized to the individual, because we chose them to improve ourselves much like the body builder who can choose heavier weight."

Ellodion: Time observer. Interview, page 2.

Robert abruptly pulled the book from Kevin's hands.

CHAPTER FOURTEEN

*"It would be illogical to adopt consequentialism unless you
had absolute foreknowledge of events. I pray to God we do."*

—Ellodion

December 25th, 1975

What else is in that book?

"You don't want to look at that," Robert said, pushing
the drawer closed. "No one should know his future. Besides,
it's book two of a series. You should really start at the first one."
Robert smiled. "Which is hundreds of miles under the Earth's crust
at my old job."

"Let's go get it!"

"That would be a very, very bad idea."

"Fine. But anyway, what the hell is this?" Kevin asked, pointing
at the dead man.

"Breakfast." Robert smiled. "It was delivered here from the station
by my servant."

"Yeah, who was that guy?"

"That's Jason. Don't worry. He will protect that girl you saved. I've worked with him on over six hundred jobs for the HPA. I trust him implicitly."

"HPA?" Kevin asked.

"Human Protection Agency. Think of them as millions of aliens controlling everyone, including the Changelings."

"What do they want?"

"What do all species want?" Robert blew smoke. "Survival, but at any cost, including removing humanity's free will."

Those words reminded him of the demon crawling in his mind. He felt the goo swimming beneath his skin.

"Everyone has a right to live," Kevin said, scratching his arms.

Robert raised an eyebrow. "Do they? Even at the cost of everyone else? I'm not talking just humans, but every species on every world in every universe."

"And you work for them?"

Robert lightly shook his head, "I used to work with the CID: Changeling Investigation Department. Think of it like Internal Affairs for the police. Mainly the changelings' political leaders—them and eighty percent of all other alien life in the multiverse want you dead. The changelings generally view you as their messiah."

"Let's hope I live up to your expectations."

"Every prophecy has a doomsday scenario where all life is either in danger of being destroyed or will be destroyed. You are either the savior of all life or the ender of all life."

Kevin stared at his palm and at the tiny dark bubbles swelling in his flesh. "And you're sure I'm not going to kill everyone?"

Robert leaned back. "I know everything."

Kevin grinned wryly. "That clerk looks pretty strong; make him your savior and you can count me out."

Robert, brandishing a toothy smile, chewed on his cigar. "No one is going to be as strong as you will be."

Kevin stared at the blood on Robert's teeth. "How's taking the life of an innocent and eating him a good thing?"

"The plant life on my planet is similar to your bodies. Here, I'm a monster for eating your people, but on my world, I'm a vege-

"Well, this carrot isn't going to let you eat it," Kevin interrupted.

Robert popped a human thumb in his mouth.

Kevin shrugged his shoulders. "Morals are subjective—so what?"

Robert waved his finger. "Now, I did not say that. There are two paths for every being: good, which is the light, and evil, which is the dark."

Kevin stared at the blood on Robert's teeth. "How's taking the life of an innocent and eating him a good thing?"

Robert finished chewing, then sucked deep on his cigar and blew smoke into the air. "Many things I do are dark because they are on the path that I chose. Sometimes, however, the people I eat have chosen the dark. Eliminating the dark is the same as bringing in the light. Consider, for example, killing in the act of self-defense."

Kevin waved his hand in front of Robert's face. "This is all fantastic, but please do something about the smell."

"It stays. Get used to it; you're going to have to eventually. It's the smell of the future. You'll travel there soon enough. Have a seat on the bed. You've got some explaining to do."

"Sure, but I thought you knew everything," Kevin said while taking his seat.

Robert smiled. "Do you believe in destiny?"

Kevin lowered his head and ran a hand through his stringy black hair, gripping his scalp. "Oh brother . Of course I don't. I hate the idea that I'm not in control of my own life. But I guess I should believe. I mean, I haven't done anything in my life without being forced."

"You won't get rid of me that easily." Kevin barely noticed the demon's voice.

"You are not just the being currently manifest. Don't sacrifice the being of who you could be to the being you think you are now. Everyone knows the evils they could burn away to improve."

Robert put down his cigar and pointed at him. "In spite of the suffering I have witnessed, I agree with you. The reason we all exist is that we chose to. You've been living in a fishbowl, Kevin. And like a fish, you're completely surrounded by something and yet unaware of its existence."

Kevin looked up, elbows still on his knees and palms on his cheeks. Robert had his attention.

"You see, Kevin, there is an entire world around us that only a select few ever get to see," Robert said, pressing a button on his console. The walls fluttered, flickering and fading away, revealing a much larger room.

Sand in the desert twirled, dancing around the small, broken-down hotel as iridescent colors transformed into hundreds of serpents of energy.

Like a flower in spring, the hotel bloomed out into an encompassing sphere of incandescent light; spots of brown turned gray as wood became steel.

The entire building had shape-shifted. Kevin was in what now looked like a domed football stadium, minus the bleachers and the lines on the grass.

G.R. MORRIS

Billions of small screens painted the slowly rotating walls in a voyeur's dream; the enclosure depicted a vignette full of people from different countries going about their daily lives. Each screen was dedicated to the life of a human. The desk, the body, and the bed remained in the center while Kevin stood transfixed, gazing up at the large floating screen above him. "Wow, got any popcorn?"

Dozens of screens depicting smiling people in hospital beds enlarged. "I always like watching people who survive a life-threating illness, then explain it that it was the best thing that ever happened to them. The suffering took them away from normalcy, they were brought to an awakening of each moment. This gave their life meaning and perspective it once lacked."

Kevin rolled his eyes. "I didn't come here to watch a Hallmark movie."

The screens shifted to dark demons and brilliant glowing angels fighting.

"The darkness and light have been at war for eons, always hidden from the human world. I was brought in by the dark, changed by its seductive power, but it gave me needed strength against the ministers. They are the bastardized, undead corpses of what humans call angels. The angel and demon war ended in a stalemate long ago. Humanity was saved, but at the cost of all angel life. Demons were forced back to hell, but they've reemerged on Earth because aliens and humans are choosing the darkness.

"Then I found you: my childhood hero," Robert paused, pressing a button on his console. The hundred-foot screen diminished, and another took its place.

The new screen displayed events of Kevin's past.

"Tell me, what kind of incredible insight are you getting from recording me brushing my teeth? Oh good. You know that I snore. Zooming in on my drool? What the hell."

Robert tapped his screen. "The first changeling to observe the futures, the creator of the Timeweb, wrote a prophecy about you, and from that spawned religions."

Kevin folded his arms and looked disgusted. "Nice to know I'm the cause of wars based on religion, again."

Robert blew a stream of smoke. "Each religion believes in its own possible future. I believe that you will save us fr—"

"Wait, how do you know yours is the right one?"

"I've seen it." Robert's palms opened over his console. "You save us," Robert said. "Every religion has some light, some truth. The more truth a religion has, the greater the light and the less the darkness."

The smoke danced in the air; it spun and dove into Robert's hand. "The degree of truth in a religion is equal to the degree of light of people within it." The smoke burned bright white. "When one seeks truth, they'll find it to the degree to which they are ready. Only if they are free to do so."

Charcoal smoke crawled from his scaly lips.

"Eighty percent of all alien species are being forced"—the dark smoke formed a cage that dropped over the light smoke—"into a religion that says you are going to destroy everything."

"The other twenty percent?"

"Controlled by the HPA, which now controls CID, which also wants you dead."

"Sounds awesome."

Robert pressed a button. "Fortunately, we can make the outcome we want."

The center display retracted into the surrounding rotating wall and was replaced again by another screen; images of a large-scale underground war came into view.

"Everything is going according to the changelings' plan. They're making sure of it. Each passing second means more control, sacrificing billions of human and alien lives in the process. Please understand: the changelings believe that their survival is dependent on humanity's survival."

"Let me guess," Kevin breathed. "Even if that means killing almost everyone and making the rest mindless slaves."

"You got it. The aliens working with the Changeling Council embraced the power of the darkness and formed the Coven to stop the council," Robert said. "These aliens believe if humanity survives and you live, all life will end; all existence will cease. They've already slaughtered thousands of changelings."

"They couldn't have been surprised by that," Kevin said.

"That's not the only problem. The changelings I worked under for more than eight centuries now want me dead, and most of them are after you, too."

The screens shuffled again, and new screens hovered and expanded to accommodate one another. "But you are not alone," Robert continued. There were now two large displays showing a hospital in a deluge of rain. The images changed to a portrayal of people dying floor by floor in liquid darkness.

"It was agreed that there would be balance. If the light wished to intervene, there would first be darkness. Once there was a deluge of darkness, the light could respond in kind. The birth of a light child is a response to the changelings' actions and the imbalance of light and dark.

"The darkness you see is nothing more than a coalescence of negative decisions fused with violence. It's an agent of dark, not darkness itself. Think of it as a fraction of a speck of sand on a desert."

Kevin placed a hand on his chest.

"That's a minister. They're the assassins of the Coven," Robert said. Kevin's face grew white.

Robert blew smoke in Kevin's face. "Shake it off. That's your lack of faith in yourself as the savior."

"Are they just here to kill people?" Kevin coughed.

"To kill you, bring darkness unto the world, and destroy the light. The Coven is ruled by Kain, a dark entity completely devoid of light who, as you've read in the Bible, received dominion over Satan."

Kevin shook his head and waved his hands back and forth. "Whoa, whoa, whoa. What? You mean to tell me this Bible thing isn't fiction? Next you'll be telling me about unicorns."

Robert smiled and ambled away. "Some stories are embellishments of truth. Some are parables, examples of what one should do, providing they desire the path of light. The writers of each book of the Bible had their own agendas. The bad stuff is there to balance out the good. If there were evidence to the degree that it would convince everyone, it would remove the option of choosing the light or the darkness.

"But none of that is important; whether or not the Bible is true or false is irrelevant. Walking the path you have chosen is what matters," he said, continuing to push buttons on his desk.

"I don't understand. You keep talking in past tense. Chose and chosen; not choose," Kevin said.

"Precisely. There's a war going on, sort of a test to see which side— light or dark—will have dominion over existence. Rather than explain this further, let me show you." Robert pointed to the center screen.

Kevin looked at Robert with bewilderment as the screen now displayed what seemed to be an average man going about his day.

"This is Ron," Robert said, pressing a button and displaying a series of ascending numbers.

Kevin watched him get up out of bed and brush his teeth.

Ron's phone rang.

"Hello?"

"Hey, buddy! Great news! I got you a big part in a movie. Some poor fella died in a car accident, and, by chance, Warner Brothers wants you to replace him! Turns out you look almost exactly like the guy. Pretty lucky, huh?"

"Lucky. I guess so," Ron replied.

"Look, I need ya to get down here and sign papers ASAP! They want to start filming immediately! Can you be here in like twenty minutes for a screen test?"

"I'm on my way!" Ron said.

The camera sped forward through him eating a quick breakfast and getting into his car.

"Am I being brainwashed with religious dogma?" Kevin asked.

"Your mind could use a bit of washing," Jason's voice bounced off the walls. "It's full of crap."

Kevin looked around the room for speakers.

Jason's voice reverberated again. "Stop being a victim."

"Keep watching," Robert said.

When Ron's car came to a stoplight, the camera resumed normal speed. The light turned green, and he stepped on the gas.

The camera switched to a trucker asleep at the wheel, the semi crashing into the driver's side of Ron's Subaru.

The roads were wet; the cars began to pile up.

The camera switched back to Ron's car. A large part of the windshield was lodged in his throat, nearly decapitating him.

The monitor went dark.

"What follows is the result of this man's death ," Robert said.

The camera then zoomed in on a stop sign partially blocked by a tree. "The perfect metaphor," Robert said. "What if someone decides to stop believing in stop signs? Does it just go away?"

Kevin raised an eyebrow. "What?"

"If we abolished all traffic cops, would that change anything about the stop sign?"

Kevin laughed. "It would make the stop sign pointless."

"If there is a law, there must be someone there to enforce it. Otherwise, running the stop sign is perfectly fine as long as you don't get caught."

"You are talking about morality, aren't you?"

Robert smiled.

"But why wouldn't God just show himself?"

"See that bush? Right there in front of the sign?"

"Your point?"

"Judges usually give people leniency, even in traffic courts, if they can prove that they didn't know the sign was there."

The monitor turned back on, and it was an image of the United States flag burning. A nuclear explosion in the distance was turning buildings and people into ash.

"Without Ron, the communists expand into other countries, the United States loses the Cold War, and things escalate into World War III."

Robert switched off the monitor, and it floated away, back into the rotating wall of screens.

"Adjustments were made. Changing the memories of everyone who encountered Ron and manipulating his appearance to closely match the actor's was no small feat. Thank God they were all diamond walkers. All it took was a few keystrokes and a lot of time and planning."

"What are diamond walkers?" Robert was staring at him. "What?" Kevin said.

"Just wondering what you are going to look like with blond hair."

"What's that supposed to mean?" Kevin sat down on the mattress.

"All these people dying made me hungry," Robert said, stepping over to the corpse.

His scaly hand quickly grew and wrapped around the top of the head. With one twist and a tug, he ripped it off and its spine snapped and skin tore.

Kevin furrowed his brow and his mouth opened.

Leaning back, Robert started typing on the console with one hand, and with the other, he thrust his reptilian tongue into the decapitated head's eye socket.

Another video began playing. This time the video started with Ron waking up from his bed, stepping barefoot on a glass bottle, and cutting his foot.

But Kevin was distracted by Robert guzzling an eyeball and slurping down brains. His face went green.

"Mmm, like spongy steak," Robert said, with a mouth full of bloody pink. "Oh, sorry, where are my manners? You want some?" He laughed, pointing to the corpse.

Kevin shook his head and tried to focus on the video screen.

"Ron decided to have some late-night fun and get drunk. As you can see, the cut isn't very deep. So, here he is washing it up, but now he's going to be leaving his house at 7:35 a.m. rather than 7:25 a.m." Kevin could hear Robert's fangs crunching through bone.

The images began to speed up, appearing to fast-forward in time.

"On his way to work, Ron drives around the twelve-car pileup. This accident happened five minutes ago. If Ron leaves on time—if he doesn't cut his foot—he hits this accident and dies."

The depiction of Ron's life sped through several years, showing him becoming the president of the United States.

"If not for the mistake of leaving that empty bottle next to his bed, none of that would have happened." The story of Ronald's life retracted into the walls and was replaced by Kevin's.

"Whoa, whoa, whoa! I'm taking a shit! Seriously, man?" Kevin yelled.

Robert grinned. "There's nothing the Timeweb does not see and record. Unless, of course, someone blocks it. Don't worry; I made sure no one could use it to locate us."

"Timeweb?"

"We're watching it now. It's a machine housing the Skyviewer program. It also views every branch of time and every hypothetical reality. Every life is connected; every choice affects another. I've seen something as simple as someone picking his nose cause changes in someone's life. In this, the most probable future, you will save us from extinction."

Kevin rolled his eyes. "Sure I will."

"You've already made the choice," Robert said.

"I thought you didn't believe in destiny."

"Destiny implies that you are not in control of your life. Existence itself is determined by choice. Every event consists of the choices people make. This makes life fair and differentiates existence from destiny."

Kevin furrowed his brow. "This can't be true."

Robert lightly shook his cigar at him. "Is it really so hard to believe? I think of it like comic books and movies."

"Now you've lost me."

"Comic books—you read them every day, and you dream of being this Superman character, yes?"

Kevin shrugged his shoulders.

Robert pulled up images of young Kevin jumping on his bed with a blanket as a cape. "You know part of you has always wanted to be like Superman. I know you. You want to be the savior."

Kevin was reminded of the Superman emblem in his back pocket. "Maybe I just want the choice."

The voice spoke again. *"You adore freedom. I can feel what you truly desire. Let me free you. Follow me and be free to live your normal life."*

"Normalcy is the desire birthed from the fear of losing control."

Can Robert hear the demon in my head, too? Kevin wondered.

"You have no idea the kind of impact those books will have on your life. Your desire to be like this person will change your life and the entire world."

"Now, consider certain movies, ones where fanatics devote almost their entire paychecks to a particular series."

The images changed to Kevin sitting in front of a TV, then jumping up and shooting a toy ray gun from the same show he was watching.

"I ask you, was it random that those fans were born during this time, and if so, would they be disappointed if they died prior to this movie's creation?"

Kevin tossed up his hands. "Like I said, life's not fair. We play with the cards we're dealt."

"What if it was fair?" Robert slid himself away from his desk, took a deep drag on his cigar, and blew out several rings of smoke. "I noticed you chose the door with the pretty ladies. I ask you, do you believe in soul mates?"

Kevin paused. "Yes."

"One person meant for another." Robert pressed another button. "If people don't choose that soul mate, then the universe is one big arranged marriage."

Kevin watched his father slip on an icy sidewalk and fall against his mother. It was how they met.

"I have seen the wonders of attraction, how people go through their lives with a specific preference in their partner, from how they act to even the color of their hair."

The video changed to his parents holding hands in a restaurant.

"These, of course, are influenced and constructed by previous interactions. Each experience with a previous person determines the choice they will make with the next. Even if you were a regular guy, it matters what you do. You will interact with over a thousand people in your life, and each one of them will interact with over a thousand. Your choices are dropping stones in a pond with the ripples affecting reality in ways you cannot comprehend. What that means is, what you do and do not do matters more than you think. Every action or no action or even hesitation matters."

Robert stared at Kevin and rolled the cigar between his red claws.

"I'll try to dumb this down for you. In order to be with this soul mate, nearly every single star in the universe has to align to get them together. They have to be born to specific parents during a specific time, at a specific place. They have to have certain personality characteristics developed by their experiences."

Kevin was staring at his desk. "I have no idea what you just said. I'm sure it was great, but I wasn't listening."

Robert sighed and changed the video again.

"The past molds a person into who they are and how they act; without it, those soulmates do not remain attracted."

The multiple screens showed dozens of couples going on dates.

"Eventually, they have to meet, and other people must not break them apart. They obviously must stay alive, at least long enough to get together."

Kevin watched the couples' lives fast-forward into marriage.

"Some soul mates even have children or give birth to lives that they thought were accidents. Those new lives would also not be there if not for them—and all of the things that needed to go right in order for them to get together."

Kevin's eyes widened. "Wow. I never thought of it that way."

Robert sighed. "Believe me; it's been a pain in my scaly ass getting you together with yours."

Kevin's head perked up. "What?"

"All I'm going to tell you about her is, I'm keeping her safe."

Kevin's mind came to the consistent dream of a blurry woman in a brown cloak.

"Saw her already, have you?" Robert smiled.

"You reminded me of some stupid dream I've been having since I was in diapers."

Robert shook his head. "You just blow it off, just like that?"

"It's just a stupid dream. Anyway . . . who was that woman I found on the street?" Kevin asked.

Robert tapped ash off his cigar. "Elspeth."

"There was something unreal about her. My heart started beating really fast every time we touched. I felt strangely connected, like our meeting was," Kevin made air quotes with his fingers, "'written in the stars' or something. She never spoke a word to me. I tried to feed her, but her tongue was gone.

"So I gave her something to write with. She wanted to know what year it was and said she wasn't supposed to be here."

"Then she passed out. That's all I know. She had this whole Mother Teresa feeling about her, like someone super important to the world. I could just feel that, you know? Just who was she?"

Kevin saw another screen come up toward them and enlarge. It showed imagery of a bleak future, a decimated earth covered in ash and bones.

"Elspeth was a code name given to her by mercenaries," Robert said. "They fought against the slavers, the most organized, most technologically advanced alien race in existence. They steal technology and enslave entire worlds. The mercenaries accused her of revealing their location and cut out her tongue."

Kevin looked up at the screen that now showed his mother making breakfast in the kitchen. "Did she love me?"

"Very much. Put the past behind you. You're going to have to change. But you have to want to change. Let wounds heal."

Kevin's eyes followed Robert as he took an apple out of his desk and extended it to him. "I apologize for all the things I'm about to do. You will soon see that it was all necessary for you to see truth. What do you think this is?"

"An apple."

Robert cocked his head, "Is it?"

Kevin looked at the apple in Robert's hand. "What?"

"It's an apple because that's what you've been told."

Robert paused. "What would it be to someone not of this earth?"

Kevin raised his shoulders and pursed his lips. "I don't know . . . an apple?"

Robert tossed the apple to Kevin. "Catch," he smirked. "Are you sure?"

Kevin looked at his hand. He was holding an orange. His jaw dropped. "How'd you do that?"

Robert grinned, adding smoke to the air. "It was always an orange. I simply told your mind it was an apple. It wasn't until your other senses told you that it really was an orange that you could truly see it. You need to realize that your senses are there simply as aids; not as guidelines. Man relies on them to a fault."

Kevin gripped the orange, feeling its softness and smelling its tangy, crisp juices.

"Before you caught the orange, I deceived your mind into believing it was an apple. Where this power is an illusion, yours will be real. Take a seat on that bed."

Kevin stepped over to the mattress and sat down.

"So how is becoming Mr. Chiquita Banana going to save the world?"

Robert pointed at the orange. "How do you know that tomorrow gravity will still hold you to the ground . . . that the sun will still shine? How do you know I'm not still tricking your senses to believe it's an orange, but it's actually a pear?"

Kevin flinched. He was holding a pear.

Robert continued pacing and sucking on his cigar. "The truth is that everything is energy and light or the absence of that light and that energy."

"So this is magic?"

"There are four forms of power : the power from technology, the power from your race, and the power from your mind, but all power stems from the powers that drive existence: the light or the darkness. They are magnifiers based on the choices you make in your life."

"So, doing something good gains more light?"

"And causing evil gains darkness; you emanate the shadow."

"So why doesn't everyone just choose to be good?"

Robert smiled. "There is great power in the darkness. It's much easier to attain; it's faster. It's the quick fix that most people crave. Think of the darkness like eating nothing but chocolate or junk food; it tastes good in the moment. It's satisfying and addictive. Now think of the light as taking a vitamin pill and eating a balanced meal. Eating poorly will eventually make you sick and die. But, in the moment, it's a lot less work and more pleasurable; you're satisfied right away."

"But once they realize that the darkness is bad for them, why don't they just stop and turn good?"

"If you eat a lot of fatty foods, it's going to make you fat, and it's going to take you a lot more work to get back to where you started. In other words, you don't just start gaining the power of the light once you decide to stop choosing to do evil. You lose power. You have to give up all those abilities that made you strong."

"So back to level zero?"

Robert looked down. "Being mortal, yes. Only then can you start on the path of righteousness. It's the path of atonement." Robert pressed another button on his console. "Alice, would you step in here for a moment?"

"I'm on my way." A woman's voice came from a speaker on his desk.

"What makes something wrong or immoral?" Robert asked.

A tall woman in a white business suit and glasses, with long chestnut hair rolled up in a bun, walked into the large room right through the immense rotating walls of monitors. It was then that Kevin realized the screens were just transparent holograms. "Wow, they look so real."

As she got closer to the desk, Robert put down what was left of the corpse's skull and held up his hand.

"Stop right there. Just hold very still."

"Yes, sir," she said.

Robert reached into his desk drawer. "Why do you suppose not a single civilization, nor any country or planet, has deemed the random murdering of innocent people within their own borders as legal and moral?"

Kevin shrugged his shoulders. "Coincidence?"

Robert was holding a .45.

"What are you gonna do with—" Kevin watched as the woman's right kneecap was blown off.

She fell to the ground, holding the bloody mess. She was screaming. "Why!" she cried. Her mascara was running down her face.

Robert was laughing.

"I won't be a part of this," Kevin said, standing up.

Robert pulled the trigger again. The bullet splashed out the back of her skull. "Oh, you're no fun."

Kevin took a deep breath. "You're an asshole."

"Am I?" Robert's fang-toothed grin was wide.

As Kevin was walking away, he heard the click of another button. He saw the woman's body vanish. In the pool of blood left behind was a brightly spinning diamond that eventually tinkled to a stop on the floor.

Kevin turned around and looked at the face of a smug reptilian alien.

"Alice, would you step in here for a moment?" Robert said again.

"I'm on my way." Kevin heard the same voice.

An identical woman walked through the displays and stepped around the blood and the diamond on the floor.

"Do me a favor and clean up that mess and put that diamond in with the others I have in that chest," Robert said to her.

"Yes, sir, I'll go get my cleaning supplies and be right back." She walked away and back through the video screen walls.

Kevin walked back to the bed and sat down.

"Those are diamond walkers. Not the first time you have met one, I assure you. In fact, only a few million humans are real. The rest are artificial constructions; most of your buildings, your roads, your food, and even the animals on this planet are fakes. Some people call them replacements."

Kevin's eyes grew wide.

"What is living? How do you define alive?" Robert asked.

The woman came walking back with a bucket and a mop. Robert picked up his gun and quickly pointed it at her.

"No, don't!" Kevin yelled.

Robert put the gun down and stuck out his tongue.

"What makes something evil is the objective negative outcome it creates in the universe. Justice and acts of good—such as killing in self-defense—gain you power of light. The intruder who breaks into someone's house in an attempt to murder will have lost so much light that the person who defends himself will be brighter, thus making it justified to kill in self-defense. Humanity's abundance of light is what gives them dominion over the plants, animals, and insects. Thus, it's not an act of evil to kill them; so it's certainly not evil to delete a program pretending to be human."

"That was messed up, man."

Robert slammed his hand on the desk. "Don't let kindness be your highest value. It's the excuse that evil people make in order to control others. Truth is the greatest value. Kindness is not always appropriate. Discipline of children is painful in the short term but results in proper behavior in the long term. Even in this instance suffering results in a good outcome."

G.R. MORRIS

"I still don't feel good about killing them," Kevin said.

"Because your mind can't let go. It's convinced they are real. In many aspects, they are just as real as any human being. They can die like humans, have babies like humans, and feel emotions like humans. The only real difference is they don't have a soul. Instead of being powered and guided by a spiritual essence, they are projected, created by that diamond you saw on the ground."

Kevin was staring at the woman soaking up the blood with the mop. "How can you tell the difference?"

"Other than with certain tech and special abilities, you can't. Well, I shouldn't say that," Robert said, looking back at the corpse. "I can definitely taste the difference."

"You mean that's a—"

"A walker. I'm not a monster, you know," he said, showing his fangs.

Another woman, identical to Alice, passed through the stacked moving video walls. She stopped in the middle of the stadium. She was holding a glimmering box constructed of diamonds cupped in front of her.

Robert stepped away from his console and walked up to Kevin. "Do you think life is fair?"

Kevin looked up at the tall alien standing right in front of him. "You know I don't."

"Come. Follow me." Robert held out his scaly hand.

Kevin shrugged his shoulders and got up. They both began walking toward the woman presenting the mysterious box.

"I am about to prove to you that not only is life fair, but also how the universe truly began and just how important you are—to everything."

CHAPTER FIFTEEN

"Light is meaningful only in relation to darkness, and truth
presupposes error. It is these mingled opposites which people
our life, which make it pungent, intoxicating. We only exist in
terms of this conflict, in the zone where black and white clash."

—Louis Aragon

December 25th, 1975

All right, smart guy," Kevin said. "So how did everything start then?"

Robert stopped in the center of the stadium, a foot away from the woman and the box. He pulled out another cigar from the pocket of his black leather trench coat. "You can't create a cigar without the right ingredients. Even before it was made, it existed as a concept and a thought. The ingredients have always existed, but it's not until someone puts them all together that people call it a cigar. Mankind didn't evolve from apes; they were created with many of the same genes. All that is and will ever be has always been and will always be."

Kevin looked at Robert, perplexed. "Everything has always existed?

Robert reached into his jeans pocket. "The evidence is all around you." Robert pulled out a silver rectangle. He flipped it open, and a small blue flame burned at its top. "If I hold this lighter here long enough , this cigar will always burn at 451 degrees Fahrenheit." He lit his cigar. "Have you ever heard of a time where two plus two did not equal four?" Robert took the mysterious box from Alice's hands. "It would be hard to conceive of a world where it would be otherwise."

He pressed his thumb on the front of the box, and light bent around the scaly green digit. The top of the box popped open.

"Diamonds refract, reflect, and absorb light," Robert said, pulling out a key made from the precious gem.

Alice nodded and walked away.

Robert knelt down and pressed the key into the floor, and the black canvas beneath their feet began to bubble. Kevin saw no keyhole but heard a click. Light burst across the floor. A ten-foot circular prism of color spread out from where Robert turned the lock.

Great, this can't be good, Kevin thought.

"You'll be fine," Robert said.

Iridescent tentacles erupted at their feet, and before Kevin could say another word, they snaked around them.

Mummified up to his waist by the blinding tubes of light, Kevin looked down at his arms. They were breaking apart, quickly dissolving and turning into particles. His body was disintegrating and being drawn into the colorful, coiling masses. His sight blurred; his voice was gone. But there was no pain, just a pleasant warm tingle and surging curiosity and fear.

It took only two seconds for them to be gone.

The floor dimmed.

G.R. MORRIS

Alice returned, pulling the key from the ground. "Have fun, you two," she said, and placed the key back in the box.

Kevin felt a gust of air burst across his body. He could see nothing. Blackness. *He took a deep breath. Focus. There's nothing out there.*

Then Robert's deep crackling voice boomed. "Beyond space and time, there were two fundamental forces. Infinitely dense and infinitely powerful, these forces govern physics, nature, and the laws of the cosmos. One of them was the darkness, an emptiness, a nothing—but all that is negative."

Kevin could see a small light hovering far away. Although bright, it did not illuminate any of its surroundings. Kevin hurried toward it, but it did not get any bigger. He stopped.

Robert's voice seemed to fill up the room. He could feel its vibrations. "There was a light inside that darkness, a something inside the nothing. It was knowledge, choice, and all that is positive. There came a moment outside of time, where the collective something could choose to be something rather than nothing."

The light began to get brighter, and a thick, colorful fog began pouring out of it. The room became like a painter's canvas as colorful gems dancing in harmony swirled into the sea of darkness from the expanding luminance.

"This is where you come in; where you chose to exist in the form of light. Before you were the flesh-and-blood Kevin, before you even had an identity, you were a form of energy, a being of light and thought. You were, just like everyone and everything else, a part of an infinite collective of all that is, massed with a grouping of proto-galactic clouds, everything and nothing and what will be and what may be.

"Think of it as the ingredients of all existence floating in nothingness. Much of that something began as just thoughts and concepts. Thought and information transfer always precede action.

So what came first: the chicken or the egg? The answer is neither. It was conception."

Kevin watched the black of the room pulsate. Clumps of smoky gelatinous tar attached themselves to each of the expanding multicolored clouds of light. They were being pushed back to where they came, but the center of the room grew brighter, spreading its glory.

"A battle against the darkness was being waged. The convergence of choice and existence became one."

The room divided in two. Kevin was up to his waist in darkness, while the rest of the room was bright and full of life. A conglomeration of mists and clouds was taking shape, forming a large sphere. Sprites of multicolored energy darted around the room, bouncing off the dividing line of the darkness.

At the center of the room, there was something as bright as the sun, resting on the pool of blackness. Directly below it was a cloudy mass, a throbbing sludge that repelled the light.

"For that brief moment, choosing to exist was victorious. In that moment, the first communication was made."

The blinding center of the room vibrated when it spoke. "Let us take the form of what we will create, and let us also beget multiple opposing minds so that we may justly and unbiasedly determine existence."

Kevin heard Robert's voice again. "Who alone, not possessing a fullness of the light, cannot live with it. Only one dimmer than shadow can witness the seed of ultimate darkness.

"This required them to transfix themselves. Man could not see the representatives, and the representatives could not see the unapproachable light or dark. Determining the existence of their children was like baking a cake. All the ingredients have always and will always be there, but it was for them to decide how to put them together. It was for their children, with the aid of their creators, to decide together. It would be an ultimate collaboration determining the direction of their future."

A throng of light billowed in a cloud and began forming human shapes, and as it grew near, Kevin saw a face. It was his own visage looking back at him.

"What the hell is this?"

"This is you."

"What?"

"The process works like this," Robert said. "Once the human soul is pulled from a bank by the human representative, it chooses identity: its appearance, name, and where it'll exist. If the soul chooses to be downgraded into, say, a pig or a rock, it would be under that which did not downgrade.

"Choosing life grants a higher collection of light essence than inanimate objects. Humans and aliens have the most. A rock has great security but lacks freedom to grow from choices, like computer programs responding to commands."

"Whoa, whoa, whoa . . . hold on!" Kevin said, sitting down. "Aren't humans just choosing based on things that happen to us, like they do? How's that free will?"

"Everything chose to exist."

Kevin rolled his eyes. "You have to exist before you can choose something."

Robert smiled. "What does it mean to exist? Existence is not binary, it's a hierarchical progression that begins with a premetaphysical construct called order. Order was the seed that grew into the metaphysical spirit. That spirit moved up the hierarchy of existence when it merged with your physical body."

"Don't those things exist?"

"Do they? Do concepts exist?"

"No, I guess not. Since they aren't physical."

Robert smiled. "Right there. You just used logic, which comes from math. Certainly, you behave as if concepts are real—not just subjective. The idea that only scientific or empirical evidence is true is self-refuting. Both scientific and empirical evidence require a priori evidence, or logical laws, for example, which are independent of observation or experience. Science and empirical evidence are contingent upon certain conditions. A priori evidence is necessary and must be the case at all times. A blind man in a straitjacket chained to a chair in a dark basement can still do math without observation. That same man could not pursue scientific disciplines like biology, because those require observation."

"But they wouldn't exist unless there were minds to think them, right?"

"Two apples put together with another two apples will always be four apples. There are no minds required for that to be accurate. Conceptual effects can be measured unbiasedly."

Kevin heard Jason laugh. "Even infants problem-solve."

Robert nodded. "They make generalizations without having to experience the world directly with transitive inference. Concepts exist, but they don't exist like other things do. They exist at the lowest level. That is not to say they are less important. In a very real way, they are more real than anything else, since concepts are used in evaluation."

Kevin took a deep breath. "Okay, get on with it."

"The first choice was free of time and free of influence; an isolated conscious action that all choices thereafter are founded upon. Each choice influences the next, but you chose all of that. We all did.

"After choosing its life experiences, its mind is wiped so that it cannot see the future it has chosen, enabling free will."

A conglomerate of nebulas collided just above the central luminance of the room.

"Before planets, before any Big Bang, there formed a sphere," Robert said, "within it, a space so vast the Milky Way galaxy itself would take up only a small corner."

The brume condensed into a crystalline globe. Light surged along one side and began to create patterns of light, emerging with almost endless convex symbols against its celestial whiteness. Darkness, moving like an obtuse cloud, poured along the other half. An equal number of symbols crumbled away, unveiling concave symbols of opposition.

"Infinite representatives were formed to lay the groundwork of their own realms during the coalescing of the forum. Certain prerequisites were determined to have basic shapes; some apples would be red and others would not. The oval shape of the room had also been agreed to and, later, the uniform circular pattern of the universe."

The sphere was large but empty, except for one basketball-size diamond orb in its center, its exterior coated with innumerable symbols. The diamond orb began to spin. Shafts of light shot out in all directions in a myriad of colors, each one striking a symbol and causing some to glow and others to darken.

"The doors had been opened, and by the billions, beings of unquantified power emerged from convulsing liquefied darkness and flashing light."

The orb hovered within the globe, as did the countless representatives. Some were monsters of living shadow, others humanoid figures, made completely out of space.

They sat on a glowing halo of light, or a cloud of spinning darkness, proudly displaying their insignias. Each of them looked ominously powerful, infinitely vast in their wisdom, and alien to one another in appearance.

"Every representative of every form of life was there to pay homage to the first epoch and to contribute their own ideas of how reality should be formed."

The last multicolored design faded silently away, exposing the last rift of energy, and as the one remaining entity entered, no symbol or portal remained.

"These symbols would be both the insignia for each realm and signify the doorway into it."

The moment the last being entered the forum, they all folded their arms in unison.

"Are these gods?" Kevin asked, drumming his fingers on his leg.

"You could call them that, and some people do," Robert said. "There is nothing evil in acknowledging that other gods exist. The evil comes when you put other gods before the most righteous. Worshipping a flawed idol will put you on its flawed path. It would not be accurate to say that these idols don't exist simply because they are concepts. Concepts are, in one sense, real.

"As I said, these beings wanted to remain unbiased and fair; they all agreed to not look at the debate's end."

"Debate?"

"Stop interrupting!" Robert yelled. "I have a whole speech going on here."

"Sorry, I'm beginning to get bored." Kevin laughed. As the nexus was sealed, three-dimensional globes appeared in front of each personification of an unfinished, desolate, unpopulated blue planet. A humanoid of shadow dressed in all black descended toward the luminous orb.

A celestial voice reverberated in the walls and into every being in the room. "Great is this war of words and its repercussions. Speak, my children."

Robert's voice sounded more enigmatic than usual. "The ultimate debate would now begin: to decide whether to use evil and force or to use good and free will."

The booming, perfect godlike voice spoke again. "Very well . . . Levi, let us start with you. Please make your case against free will."

In a near blinding flash, the scenery changed. The walls, the floor, and the ceiling were vast and appeared to be made of white diamonds. Robert was reclining in another black leather chair in the center of the room, his decapitated meal lying next to him.

"Cool place. So that's how everything began?"

Robert was smoking another cigar and took a deep drag. "There was no absolute beginning, for there was no origin, but there is, and always will be, change.

"After the war of words, and over a span of countless eons, the cloud of existence churned forth endless substances, concepts, and creatures with perceived randomness."

Kevin was admiring the shimmering colors dancing along the diamond dome. "Where are we?"

Robert was holding a six-inch diamond and ran his thumb around its edges.

"This is a changeling training node." Robert stood up.

There was another bright flash.

Kevin felt something sprout beneath him, knocking him off his feet. Something very soft pushed him in the air. The scent of his favorite fast-food restaurant was pleasantly overwhelming. When his eyes adjusted, he was sitting on a giant hamburger, and the floor was covered in French fries the size of baseball bats. The ceiling and the walls remained as flattened smooth diamonds.

Robert stood, at least a hundred feet away, on the rim of a giant milkshake looking down. "Eat. I assure you it's safe."

Kevin tore off a piece of bun. "This stuff is real?" He put the clump of bread in his mouth.

"Real in the sense that it has the same nutrients and the same taste, but not in the sense that it was created naturally."

Robert was right. Kevin could taste the texture and crunched the sesame seeds. When he swallowed, it was just as satisfying as any burger he had ever had.

Robert reached down and scooped up some ice cream into his mouth. "This is unit forty-seven out of eight billion buried far beneath the surface. We can use them to replicate any point in time and mimic the behaviors of people by using the Timeweb. In this way, the changelings can ensure a success rate at 98.2 percent.

"They're also power sources for walkers, and they can use them to create other things on the surface."

"Like what?" Kevin said, grabbing a handful of meat.

"Food, weapons, trees, grass—just whatever you could possibly want."

"What if humans dig down deep and find one of these things?"

Robert chuckled. "This is shape-shifting technology. Just what do you think they are going to see?"

"Good point."

"All of mine are," Robert said.

"Why not make a paradise, a utopia for humanity?" Kevin asked.

"There is just no way we would do that," Robert said. "It would interfere with the needed suffering, pain, and the so-called accidents that people must experience to grow and evolve. None of it would fit with any of the prophecies. All life, all existence is like a delicate puzzle balancing on a single needle. If you remove one piece, the whole thing falls. Even your stepfather was your choice."

Kevin placed his hands on his head. "What? You mean I chose to have an asshole stepfather?"

"You would not be here, or be who you are, without him. There is an obvious plan to these choices."

Kevin spit out a chunk of meat. "Plan?"

"The purpose of existing is to evolve to something greater, to bond spiritual reality with its physical reality. Existence is meant to change, to grow, and then to become one with the light—unless, of course, the force of darkness defeats the force of light."

"What makes me special? Why me?"

"You are Ron's beer bottle. We believe that before all physical life was created, we all saw what was going to happen and that the darkness would potentially win. Someone stood up and volunteered to save existence from annihilation. We believe that guy was you."

"Okay, if everyone chooses everything before all of this, why doesn't everyone just choose to be a rock star? Why doesn't everyone just choose a life free of pain?"

"Not everyone wants to be a rock star; not everyone wants to be rich. With every benefit, there is a specific challenge. Not everyone needs or wants these same challenges. Growth requires adversity; the events in your life are selected by you to become the person you wanted to be. The cliché 'everything happens for a reason' is true. It happens because that's what you wanted.

"The greater the challenge, the more you grow and evolve. Sort of like the saying 'what doesn't kill you makes you stronger.' When born into a rich family, someone is bound by the gifts he or she has chosen. No one deserves a free ride; all forms of riches must be earned. The person who chose to be born with money has the kinds of problems that arise with having that money. Show me a person who does not have problems, and I'll show you a liar."

"Remember, those problems are chosen, so even people born into money can learn from those problems. Even the representatives have problems."

"Wait, aren't they omnipotent?" Kevin interrupted.

"There is human perception of logic and objective logic. Can a representative who is wholly good commit an evil act or violate the laws of logic? Yes. A representative constantly grows, and his identity is always in flux, as is yours. It can exist as something else at the same time and in the same respect, because it exists outside of time."

"But wouldn't committing an evil act go against who that good person is?" Kevin asked.

"Wouldn't murdering puppies go against who you are?" Robert said.

Kevin shrugged his shoulders. "So?"

"So you and I both know you won't ever do that, but how do you know you have free will?" Robert smiled. "What would be the point of doing something illogical? Knowing it's illogical? To prove you can?"

"Yes," Kevin said.

"Okay, then next time we see a puppy, and you don't kill it, it proves you can't."

"Good point."

"Just because something is never going to happen doesn't mean it can't. Remember: when you decide something, you cut away all other options. Choices exist in a hierarchical structure because some things are worth doing more than others, or actions are impossible. One cannot even walk in a direction without preference of direction. Of course the category of choice excludes, and some bells cannot be un-rung. You do not have the freedom to go back.

"The representatives chose to limit their laughter, as some humor is dependent on not knowing the punch line."

Each choice has its pros and cons. It's ultimately which positives and which negatives each soul has selected."

A wooden door appeared and opened.

"Here comes your secretary," Kevin smirked.

"Get off that burger. You're a fraud." Jason slammed the door behind him.

The door vanished.

Kevin hopped down to the ground.

The buff blond man in cargo pants launched a haymaker that connected with Kevin's jaw. Jason's roundhouse bounced the hero's body off the giant bleached bread.

Kevin fell to his knees.

Jason stepped back and pointed to Robert. "Pathetic. He's not our savior."

Kevin's head pounded and the demonic voice boomed in his ears once again. *"Do what you will. Your moral system is your own creation. The only person who can hold you accountable is yourself."*

"You're obviously evil," Kevin mumbled.

"Evil is such a harsh word. I'm the enemy of light, to be sure. But if you follow me, it will be liberating."

"Shut. Up," Kevin yelled.

"Great, our boy is losing his mind again," Jason said.

"Take my power. Be free from responsibility. You are a prisoner in a jail of destiny."

"Choose between freedom and the truth," Robert said.

"Truth," Kevin said. And that word warmed his body.

"I can feel you smiling. Don't. I'm using you."

Robert whispered, "Your fate is not your own, it's the fate of everyone connected to you."

Somehow Kevin heard his words, he felt them.

Kevin closed his eyes. "I'm not listening to you anymore."

The demon began saying something. *"You will lose to my master Kain and I . . ."* But the rest was too faint to understand.

Kevin clenched his fists. "GET. OUT. OF. ME!"

His mind focused on the dark streams of goo snaking through his veins. He imagined them collecting at the back of his throat.

His body tingled and his eyes blurred for a moment. His fingernails glossed over with black and the color faded to normal.

Nothing.

He still felt the hellion crawling just beneath his skin.

Kevin stood up and cracked his neck. "I'm not done with you."

Jason nodded, then darted toward the hero with his first attack.

Kevin ducked under the fist and slammed Jason's gut with four punches.

When Jason barreled over the hero flipped, one leg kicking him in the chest and the other in the face.

Kevin landed. Jason was dazed.

Enraged, he charged the hero again.

Thirty-one strikes, all blocked.

Jason was winded.

He took a step back and smirked at Kevin. "Nice job, kid."

Robert raised an eyebrow.

Kevin picked up a French fry and brought it to his lips. A flash of light, and the large potato stick in his hand was gone. Kevin bit down on a white boxing glove that was covering his hand.

CHAPTER SIXTEEN

"A system of morality which is based on relative emotional
values is a mere illusion, a thoroughly vulgar conception
which has nothing sound in it and nothing true."

—Socrates

December 25th, 1975

evin could smell cigarette smoke in the air and hear the near deafening roar of a crowd. He pulled the leather from his mouth and spat.

"Not funny."

He was sitting on a chair in a boxing ring designed with a yin and yang symbol on the mat. Hanging from metal rafters were dozens of fluorescent lights on chains that swayed from the stomping and roaring of the crowd. Standing in front of him was a short, balding, fat man with scraggly gray hair and broken yellow teeth, handing him a mouth guard. "You've been training your whole life for this moment. Now get out there and make me proud, boy," he said.

Looking down, Kevin saw he was wearing white boxing shorts, white socks, white boots, and white boxing gloves.

"Stand up! Stand up!" the fat man screamed.

In the middle of the ring, a man with a large black mustache and black top hat was reading a card and speaking into a dangling microphone. "In the black corner wearing all black, weighing 366 pounds, the Heavyweight Champion of the Universe, the Reptilian Roundhouse, the Stinging Snake, Robert!"

Robert was dancing. He was jumping up and down, raising his gloves in the air. The crowd cheered.

"And in the white corner, weighing in at 175 pounds, hero of all life, the savior, the one the only, Kevin Knight!"

The crowd quickly turned to booing.

"My place, my rules. Deal with it," Robert said.

The two fighters walked to the center of the ring for instructions from the referee. The man with the large mustache put the card away, and the microphone rose into the ceiling. "You guys know the rules. No low blows, nothing lethal, no weapons. Just a clean fight." The man stepped back.

Robert towered above Kevin and smiled. "All of this is much like actual reality. It is malleable; you have to have faith that you can change it. All of existence is nothing more than energy composed of light and intelligence. You can change everything. You can be as powerful as you want—as you believe—you can be."

"What are you guys waiting for? Let's get going!" a person in the crowd yelled.

Kevin backed up, shook his head, and raised his arms. "This is bullshit. You're gonna kick my ass."

Robert moaned. "With that lack of faith, yes, I will."

The crowd chanted "Ro-bert! Ro-bert! Ro-bert!"

G.R. MORRIS

Robert tapped his glove to his chin. "Come on, hero, give me your best."

The memories of William's beatings and his years of training were coming back to him. Kevin shuffled his feet and bobbed and weaved his head.

Jason sat in the audience wearing a T-shirt that said SAVIOR IS NUMBER 1. He gave Kevin a thumbs-up while drinking from a giant silly straw.

Robert had his arms down at his side. "Come on!"

Kevin landed a left jab to Robert's chin. Then another and another. And another.

Nothing. It was like hitting a stone statue. Robert's head did not even budge.

Robert showed his fang-filled smile. "No."

"Stick and move, boy! Stick and move!" the old bald man screamed.

He's not going to hit back, Kevin thought. He went at him with a succession of hooks to the face and to the stomach. Robert just pushed against his head with an open glove. Kevin stumbled back.

"All right. My turn," Robert said.

Kevin thrust up his gloves, shielding his face and stomach with his arms.

A blur of black and green moved across the ring. Robert's arms were too fast. A storm of pain came at the savior. Kevin's head whipped to the right and then strained to the left. He felt the crushing pain in his ribs and abs, all of which came almost simultaneously.

Kevin dropped to his knees. The room was spinning. There was blood on his lips. His eyes were already swollen.

"Let go of the natural world!" Robert yelled.

The room was a total blur. Then he heard the countdown.

"TWO!"

His ears were ringing.

"FOUR!"

"Asshole," Kevin mumbled.

Stumbling, he grabbed the ropes and pulled himself to his feet.

The man in the top hat looked into his eyes. "You okay?"

Kevin nodded and put up his gloves. Robert walked back up to him.

Kevin threw a series of punches. They were pushed away. More jabs and then hooks; all blocked.

A bomb went off in his stomach. He leaned over and puked blood. Robert didn't stop. He struck again, crashing into Kevin's chin and rocketing him from his feet.

Kevin slammed against the ropes and flopped face down on the ring.

The room went dark.

"THREE!"

"FOUR!"

He could hear Robert's voice over the cheering crowd. "Come on, Kevin, get up!"

"SEVEN!"

Robert yelled again, "Get up!"

"EIGHT!"

Time crawled, and Kevin's heart pounded. A warm glow pushed through his veins. *What's happening?*

Kevin was on his feet. Blood trickling down his nose vanished, but he still squinted through his swollen eyes. How the hell?

The chants turned pro-Kevin. "KE-VIN! KE-VIN! KE-VIN!"

Kevin raised his gloves. "Let's go."

"That's my boy," Robert said.

How could Robert do this to him? Kevin's body burned in rage. A feral snarl clawed its way up his throat. "I'll kill you." He lunged, swinging and missing. Robert slung Kevin, bouncing against the ropes.

He couldn't bring his gloves up in time. Robert's haymaker hit his face like a train. Kevin's head snapped back.

Where is the pain? The sting of Robert's punches was gone. A faint warm white glow swelled from Kevin's pores and raised the hairs on his body. Kevin's eyes were savage in a halo of white.

Robert's next punch hit the air, then Kevin's fist bashed into Robert's kidney.

Robert flinched. Stumbling back, he put up his gloves to block.

I hurt him! Kevin stepped forward and took off swinging. Robert blocked, but each one of Kevin's blows was a little stronger. A straight right crashed against Robert's guard, skidding him several feet across the ring.

Kevin ran forward and slammed up a fist so powerful it broke through Robert's block and into his chin. The uppercut lifted him off his feet.

The Stinging Snake's body stopped midair, inches before it hit the mat. His body spun and flipped. He landed on his feet and Kevin charged. Before the savior could even throw a punch, Robert's arms moved in a blur.

Kevin felt the barrage of boxing gloves thrash into his midsection. Twenty shots in a single second.

Dazed, the savior tried to bring up his guard. Too late. The Stinging Snake delivered a crushing blow.

Kevin's nose gushed blood.

The hero hit the mat once more, face first. The ref began the countdown.

One..

Two. *I can't move.*

Four..

Six. Kevin's arms flopped.

Seven. He tried bringing his wobbling legs up to his chest. His face still stuck to the mat.

Eight. *I can't lose this. I can't.*

Nine. Kevin raised his head.

TEN!

The ref waved his arms. "It's over! It's over. The Stinging Snake wins another one!

Robert raised his arms and looked down at the hero. "You are still the caterpillar. You are not ready."

Robert vanished. The bell rang, and there was another explosion of light.

Kevin was sitting in a large spa. In the reflection of the water, his bruises and cuts were gone. The sky was clear blue, and as far as he could see, there were rolling hills of green in every direction. The sun beamed crisply.

Robert was sitting across from him, chewing on an unlit cigar. "Nice fight."

"What the hell was that?"

"A demonstration and a test."

"So, great—I'm not human?"

Robert spit out his cigar. "Look at me. You are more human than anyone who has ever lived. It was a genetic necessity for your father to turn human to give life to you."

Kevin's eyes narrowed. "My mom used to tell me that 'last angel' fairy tale all the time. You want to tell me who killed him?"

"You will meet him very soon."

Kevin splashed Robert in the face. "Cryptic asshole."

"See? A human reaction," Robert said, wiping his face. "Because you were born from a fallen-angel-turned-human who mated with another human, you are the purest form of human who ever lived."

Kevin rolled his eyes. "Awesome. So?"

Robert paused and looked down at his reflection. "The changelings have imprisoned all of mankind. You have no idea the things I have done. What they have done."

"What made them such assholes?" Kevin asked.

"Make no mistake, the changelings are not evil. No race is wholly evil. They are controlled; brainwashed by their leaders. Evil is an action, but it is always either about a person or by a person, which presupposes individual intrinsic value. What a tornado does is not evil."

Kevin glanced down at his Superman swim trunks.

"Where the hell are my clothes?"

Robert held up a crystal and rolled a claw over its edges. The sky filled with images of the fields of human brains connected to the Timeweb machine. "This is what happens when you believe the ends justify the means."

"Wow. The changelings did that?"

Robert tapped on his cigar, letting ashes fall into the water. "Where better for evil to hide than within a nebulous and encompassing ideology brimming with moral relativism? Murdering billions to prevent the extinction of the human race is good because their society has said so."

"Why not just conform to the idea of a pragmatic naturalistic moral system and guide humans accordingly?"

Robert stepped out of the spa, revealing his black swim trunks and his scale-covered body. "I suppose you'd objectively ground that on subjective empathy? *Feelings?* For something to be objectively moral it would be so, regardless of how anyone *feels.*

Robert laughed. "Something is not true just because you *feel* it is."

He pointed up, and thousands of screens depicted animals eating each other and people killing one another. "There is nothing illogical with always doing whatever is in your best interest. What happens when oxytocin rewards people for murder? What do you do when people decide the world would be a better place without you in it?"

"Different people disagree about what is moral; doesn't that mean it's relative?"

Robert pointed his cigar at him. "Do not mistake subjective perception for objective reality."

"What?"

"Some thought the earth was flat; others thought it was round. It was always round."

Kevin stared at Robert. "How am I supposed to stop them? Do we kill them?"

"If we have to; remember, killing is not wrong. Murder is."

Kevin watched his clothes coalesce on the grass. "What's the difference?"

"Context versus subjectivity. Murder is killing the innocent. We don't live in a world without moral absolutes. It's why doors have locks and societies have laws. If a kid wants to be popular on the playground, he has to play by the rules."

"Whoa." Kevin also stepped out of the spa. "How are the changelings wrong, I mean, objectively?"

"The changelings want the freedom to create their own values, yet they take this away from humanity," Robert said, throwing Kevin his clothes. "Take this away from a changeling, and he'll protest in the name of justice or in an alternative invented value system. Of course, this means their protesting has no objective value either."

"Your point?"

"Typically," Robert said, walking away, "every claim has someone who disagrees with it, but nobody wants their personal value systems circumvented. They intrinsically desire this freedom. Since freedom is really good, it must be freedom from something really bad, thus assuming some objective good and bad.

"Everyone desires moral freedom, the freedom to choose their own moral system and the freedom to exercise it." He stopped. A wooden door popped from the soil and grew at Robert's feet. "Moral relativism is a contradiction; it undermines itself because the mere idea of it is unlivable. The universe naturally seeks to balance out justice and sometimes that only comes from death. No one is without sin and sometimes the suffering in death and the pain in life brings about that equilibrium. That cleanse from sin only comes to those who chose that suffering prior, otherwise the justice comes from a redeemer, from lacking in afterlife placement and lacking in rewards."

"Okay, I get it. What they are doing is wrong, but we still need to stop them somehow." Kevin pulled on his white shirt. "What else do I have to do as this savior?"

Robert opened the door. "The path of the savior involves defeating the darkness from within; overcoming fear. It involves defeating the Coven, but most importantly, it involves growth, from nonbeliever to believer."

Kevin laughed. "Good start. But we'll see."

"Don't forget," Robert said, turning around, "the changelings are not your ultimate enemy. The darkness that drives them is."

"Great, so I'm supposed to fight evil, is that it?"

"Evil is one element of negativity that is the darkness. Ironically, the darkness is being used as a tool to try to stop them."

"Well, that sounds dumb." Kevin pulled up his black jeans.

Robert scratched a fang and raised a black eyebrow.

"There's a lot of power in the darkness—as you'll soon see. Speaking of which, that's where your nemesis comes in."

"Oooh , my nemesis, you say." Kevin yawned and followed his teacher.

The room glowed a soft white: white walls, white ceiling, and white floor. There were hundreds of shelves lined with large crystals. There must be millions of these things in here, Kevin thought.

Robert put his crystal in an empty spot on a shelf. "Eventually, after you grow, defeat your inner demons, stop the Coven, and free humanity by stopping the changelings, you will have to face the Dragon," he said as he walked down the long room. "The Dragon is the darkness's response to your existence. Ninety percent of all alien life—including some changelings, I might add—worships the beast as their savior from you."

"Let me guess, the Coven worships him."

"Of course. Most changelings see you as their savior, but they worship Raksasha."

"So, am I going to have to fight this Raksasha, too?"

Robert dragged out a slow smile. "I hope not. Many prophecies about you are inspired from her words. The prophecies that you are going to save all life, I mean."

"Wow, what a pain in my ass. When do I get started?"

Robert stopped. "Nobody believes you'll ever defeat the Dragon, but I have faith."

"So what's the future look like without me to save it?"

"The changelings limit technology," Robert said, picking up another crystal. "They hinder humanity, first striking at their brains and next creating multiple languages to divide them. During the 1930s, neurologists claimed the term 'silent cortex' to be false, but they were wrong."

Kevin sighed. "Story time for me, I guess."

Robert poked him in the shoulder with the crystal. "Hey, you asked. Anyway, the constant wars and man's inhumanity against man begin to take its toll on mankind.

"Guns are outlawed. Automobiles are abolished in favor of mass transit systems. The police freely enter whenever and wherever they want. Dictatorships are rampant. But humans inherently desire to be free—free from control, free from the changelings. Humanity fights back one last time, and with so much death, so much hate, the darkness floods the earth, with hell itself washing over the globe.

"Civilization falls. Earth is an easy target.

"Eventually, aliens try to take over. The survivors are hunted down and slaughtered. Then, there is the possibility that your opposite will come and negate all that is. Either way, the species becomes extinct. But this is, of course, if you decide to opt out."

Kevin was scratching his head. "How can I opt out if all my choices are already made?"

"You're here to learn and grow from your choices. People make decisions all the time. The key to free will is that you don't know what choice you made prior to your life on earth. If you ultimately knew, it would eliminate your free will. None of us knows for sure how any of this will turn out."

"So I could have chosen not to be the savior?"

"And the pope chose to become a serial killer. I don't think so." Robert rolled a claw around the six-inch diamond. "This was fun, but these things have a limited energy supply. Back to the real world."

Kevin's flesh vibrated and rippled. He watched as the top of his skin began to break apart. Pockets of flesh bent into floating bubbly images. He shattered like glass; the bubbles burst into streams of light and shot into the sky.

Kevin, back in the stadium, stared at the rotating walls of monitors. Robert was next to him, and Alice was presenting him with a golden box etched with a symbol of a leaf.

Robert began walking back to his desk. "Thought always precedes action, and ignorance is a gift. Without it, we would not have free will."

Kevin followed. "I don't get it."

"Even though you knew you were going to fight back as I stood there, and you knew you were going to hit me, did that prevent your free will to do so?"

"No."

"Would you have acted differently if you knew how the fight was going to end?"

"I would have fought a little better," Kevin said.

Robert pointed to the bed, stepped over the headless corpse, and sat back down at his desk.

Kevin sat down. The smell of death had fermented the air. "What happened to me back there?"

"At mankind's creation, they were flawless. Blood healed all wounds, and the brain had supernatural abilities. About six hundred and eighty million years ago, a single human appeared, pulled from the bank of souls upon a paradise encompassing the entire globe. Reality's blueprint had already been established through an ultimate, omnipotent democracy and eventually constructed by humanity's representative. Adam named the planet Eden and was the first human to be created by a higher power."

"You mean God?" Kevin queried, looking down at the rotting corpse.

Robert nodded. "Adam was alone, and even though his advanced brain allowed him to communicate with the animals, he longed for a companion. But Adam's power was limited to change and not creation.

Creation of life meant pulling an essence from existence to mold into a physical form. Everyone agreed that this kind of power was to be relegated only to the representatives, or through the biological choice of each living creature. You know, giving birth.

"Each blade of grass and each rock had already decided to be molded, and humanity was given dominion over them. Therefore, Adam could change a rock into a bird or a blade of grass into a tree.

"It was chosen to be a law of the universe that no one, not even the representatives, would create things out of nothing. Creation requires elements already in existence, like baking a cake. The laws of the universe, such as logic and math, were decided upon to restrict chaos.

"So the representative gave Eve to Adam. Adam and Eve were stuck in a limbo of no progression. A side effect of this was that they could not produce offspring. Without their offspring, of course, there's no human race."

"You mean to tell me that God placing the tree right where they could get it was all part of everyone's plan?"

"Even with the tree right in front of them, they weren't going to eat it. I mean, they were told not to. But that's where the changelings come in. The HPA gave me my first job—to offer an apple to Eve. It was designed to dampen their powers by limiting the human brain's abilities. Free will benefits those who need to grow through trial and error. In essence, the gift of the apple made them mortal." Robert fake-coughed. "Where's my thank you?"

"What?"

"Without me, there's no human race. You're welcome."

"Let me get this straight. You're the serpent the Bible talks about; that stupid book?"

"I guess the tongue gave me away," Robert licked his eyebrows.

"Wasn't it supposed to be the devil? You care to explain why there are so many inconsistencies? "

"The Bible was never meant to be inerrant. It was meant as evidence, so that you could choose. Let me ask you something: do you choose to believe two plus two equals four?"

"So what?" Kevin said.

"You are compelled to believe it. You don't really have a choice.

"Many people who require proof would no longer believe—they would be compelled, which would eliminate the choice. That is why there is no objective proof for either side."

Kevin raised an eyebrow. "According to that book, being the serpent would make you evil, wouldn't it?"

"You think so? The creator of the Timeweb theorized that there must be a balance of good and evil. Because both Adam and Eve were born of light, evil was required to balance. But this was a means to an end."

"Okay, so your point?"

"Do you believe people are born good?"

"I don't know what to think right now."

Robert chuckled. "Your greatest battle won't be with some monster or alien. It won't be some arbitrary concept like the weather or society. It will be with your own nature.

"A pattern with species is to tell each other that they're perfect and the fault lies with everything except themselves. It's crushing to humanity's growth to always play the victim."

"I guess all of this eliminates natural evil."

"There is nothing natural about evil. You may as well praise water for being wet and a stone for being hard. Only perfect knowledge of the future would put someone in the position to correctly judge the effect any action will eventually have."

"From what I have seen, some choices and some natural disasters are actually beneficial in the end. Humans making the mistake of rarely getting in disasters way, does not outbalance the vast number of benefits they provide to nature and in relation, man. When evil came upon the Earth, man was given dominon over animals and nature. This dominion comes with responsibility of controlling evil that spreads like a cancer over nature."

Kevin nodded. "You mean human sins actually *cause* animals suffering and bad weather?"

Robert smiled. "Influence to a great degree. Yes. Negative and positive energies. The Darkness and the Light. Combine that with the thought that we chose everything as part of our growth; correct, natural evil becomes a joke."

Robert pointed at Kevin. "You can choose nothing you do has meaning, or choose everything has meaning. With no meaning comes no responsibility. You don't have to do anything. You might view the suffering coming from meaninglessness a small price to pay for being able to be utterly useless. Or . . . choose everything you do matters. Your mistakes are real mistakes. Every bad choice you make tilts the scales of existence toward evil and less good. If you choose a meaningful existence, then there's no fooling around. This means real responsibility and every decision is important. This means ultimate accountability for everything you do. All choices matter. Question is, what do you want?"

Kevin stared blankly.

Smirking, Robert opened the golden box on his desk and pulled out a shimmering red apple. It had two bites missing. Otherwise, it looked perfectly fine; better than fine, even. Kevin could actually see his reflection.

"Don't tell me that's the apple?"

Robert closed his eyes and nodded.

Slack-mouthed, Kevin waved his hands. "Hell. No. I'm not eating some six hundred million year old apple."

"Oh, it is far from ordinary. It's an ageless changeling fruit genetically engineered to look like an apple."

Kevin paused for a moment and thought about everything that had just been revealed to him. "All of this is hard to swallow. So everything that happens, good or bad, is a result of predetermined free will."

Kevin took a deep breath. "So . . . I guess I'll summarize. Everything has always existed, and the makeup of all existence is light and darkness. The light wants continuance, and the darkness wants oblivion. Before things exist physically, they exist spiritually, and at that time everyone agreed—including myself—that I would be the savior and make sure that the darkness doesn't win. We all watched how everything will happen. So to have free will, the memories where we made all these choices from this spiritual existence, was wiped from my mind. That about right?"

"Yes. And sometimes that process repeats itself."

"What?"

Robert winked. "You'll see."

"Why didn't you make it less complicated?"

"Because you would have asked follow-up questions. Someone as intelligent as you can look at something convoluted and view its simplicity. Some people need an explanation for everything; some people have a thirst for knowledge. Essentially, you've been dehydrated."

Kevin stepped over the corpse, walked to the desk, and picked up the apple. He held it up to his face, examining every inch.

"This apple once reduced the human brain's abilities," Robert said. "Now it's been altered to do the opposite. One bite and you'll have full control of your brain. Because the brain is a physical thing, it is limited, but the mind is not. This will free the prison of the mind from the brain."

Kevin stopped for a moment, looked at the apple again, and began pondering all the things that Robert was telling him. *Did I choose to eat this?*

"Changeling food is grown underground in a green room, near the earth's core. You won't find anything like this in any supermarket."

The smell of the fruit alone caused Kevin's eyes to water. The once-cardboard taste in his mouth was now moist and pleasant; his eyes sparkled in delight like they were seeing for the first time. Like waking from a long nap, Kevin was no longer fatigued; he was wide awake.

He filled his lungs with air. "Amazing! Well, every single alien race thinks I'm the antichrist and wants me to die. Except one, and now even that one, for some reason, is trying to kill me. What do I have to lose?"

Robert folded his arms. "Factions of each race believe as I do, but, yes, every single one thinks you're going to kill everyone—other than the majority of the changelings."

"Well, fantastic. It's not like I'm not used to people trying to put me in the grave," Kevin said. "So I'm going to be some supergenius now?"

"Not exactly."

"Well, whatever, I'd better not wake up in the hospital . . . I must be crazy." Kevin consumed almost half of the apple in one bite.

His mouth watered at its pure taste. The fruit's juice coated his tongue in shifting sweets. He could recognize half of them: watermelon, cherry, strawberry, then blueberry.

They were all potent yet perfectly wonderful. The pieces seemed to sizzle on his tongue. "Wow, man! This is good! But I don't feel any different."

"It hasn't reached your system yet. Finish the apple."

Kevin devoured the rest as if it were his last meal. He savored every morsel as the perfect juicy flavor overloaded his taste buds.

"I think you'd better sit down and rest," Robert said with urgency.

"What? I've never felt better in my life!" Kevin replied, breathing in deeply. The smell of death no longer bothered him. He smiled, but then his body began to tremble. The shakes vibrated through him, chattering his teeth. "Whaa . . . what's happening?" He clenched his fists.

"Don't worry. Your body is going into shock. It's trying to catch up."

What appeared to be varicose veins began sprouting all over Kevin's skin. White foam oozed from his mouth and sprayed in all directions. "Help me!" he cried.

Falling to the floor, he landed on the corpse, his convulsions spreading its maggots throughout the room.

Robert sat smiling in his chair. "God, this is hilarious."

Small streams of light escaped Kevin's every pore. Blood trickled from every fingertip. Kevin's body shuddered, suspended in the air, hovering several feet above the corpse. Maggots danced in the air that flowed around his body.

He crashed to the ground. The foam stopped. The veins subsided, and the blood clotted. Kevin's eyes closed.

After moving Kevin to the bed, Robert pulled an arm off the officer and began chewing. His loud crunching of the bones should have been enough to wake Kevin, but he was gone. Robert sat at his desk, finished his meal, and kept a watchful eye on his sleeping friend.

PART SEVEN

WILL THE REAL SAVIOR PLEASE STAND UP?

"And God said, Let us make man in our image, after our likeness: and let them have dominion over the fish of the sea, and over the fowl of the air, and over the cattle, and over all the earth, and over every creeping thing that creepeth upon the earth."

—Genesis 1:26

CHAPTER SEVENTEEN

"Growth is never by mere chance; it is the
result of forces working together."

December 24th, 1976 —James Cash Penney

Daren sprinted down the shattered street of a broken city. "Kevin!
Save me!" she screamed.

She was several decades past living in the orphanage. Times
Square was in shambles, the buildings ablaze and spattered with the
remnants of its populace.

Daren looked behind her and stumbled over a rock. A deep,
deafening roar boomed, vibrating everything to its core. The ground
quaked beneath its power.

"Ahhhh!" Daren dropped to her knees. Covering her ears, she
looked up as a shower of glass filled the sky. She crawled under metal
debris. It was the remains of a tank; one of many scattered throughout
the city.

She saw the flags of China, Iran, Russia, and the United States side by side, marked on everything. She knew this was not country against country.

This was the world against a monster.

"Wake up, Daren! Wake up!" she screamed, darting into an alley.

She could smell burning skin from the piles of bodies just around the corner. She could hear screams suddenly hushed. What disturbed her most was feeling her name spoken on the wind in a demonic growl. It was getting closer, teeth crunching through bone becoming louder. Her breathing became shallow, and her heart thundered against her chest.

Daren emerged from the alley and ran through the streets. Hundreds of soldiers stood grouped together, their guns dropped on the ground in front of them. She saw their faces bone white, their limbs shivering.

Running by, she heard terror-filled mumbling. "D . . . d . . . don't turn around."

As she picked up speed, she heard the soldiers' bodies pop and felt their blood splash on her back.

Just a dream, just a dream!

A tidal wave of blinding fire exploded hundreds of feet in front of her and instantly towered over the tallest skyscraper. She looked to her left and saw another firewall. She looked to her right, and there was another. All of New York City was being devoured in a ball of flame.

With nowhere to run, Daren pleaded his name. "Kevin! Save me!"

An explosion of pure white light encased her body and splashed over the city block. A calming voice came back at her, echoing in her mind. A blurry white image of a man approached.

"The girl from my dreams. Who . . . who are you?" he asked, reaching out his hand to help her up.

"I'm Daren."

G.R. MORRIS

The dream abruptly ended.

The night's darkness was in hasty retreat, and sunrise was barely peeking over the hills of Ramona. Light splintered through the trees of the San Diego suburb, washing across a shallow valley until it reached a field of dead grass. It splashed against withered, leafless black trees and the squalid building beyond.

Dawn fractured through windows smeared with dozens of greasy fingerprints. Dust swirled in the slant of lights and lined the rotting creases of the black, charred floor, salting the knotted wood. Gradually, the sun's warming illumination crawled over a room full of kids who were oblivious to the extraterrestrial slumbering among them. The orphanage had the icy feel of a penitentiary; bars across the windows complemented dreary stone walls. The children's sleeping area was the largest room in the building, expansive enough to hold seventy bunk beds with adequate room for a half-dozen mattresses.

The first golden rays of a new day touched Daren and her clandestine future. As spacious as the room was, she routinely found herself bedding down near the windows, always at least ten feet from anyone else.

Daren felt the glow of the sun move over her tenth pair of frayed, gray, permanently stained replacement rags. Staring at the ceiling, she watched a cockroach push itself through dusty cobwebs.

Her eyes had opened two hours earlier, the sting of bruises pulling her from rest. She ran her fingers through the tattered brown bed sheet. *When will my torment end?*

Tom, the one orphan Daren felt she could socialize with, took a seat at the foot of her bed as he regularly did before the 6:00 a.m. alarm. He sat with all the self-possession of an African lion. Arms wrapped around his chest, flat-footed, peering around the room—her protector.

"Good. You're awake. I heard about you and Conover again. How are you doing?"

Daren continued staring at the ceiling, motionless.

"So what, you've grown really fast. I'm so sick of hearing the same diversity speeches about how boys and girls are different. It's not like you're doing it on purpose. At least Conover's starting to go easy on ya." Her sole companion grimaced, pointing out the glistening shiner on her face. "If I had bruises like yours, I'd be hitting myself all day."

Daren glanced at him and sighed.

He turned away from her as Daren remained silent. "I'm gonna knock those glasses right off her giant warty nose! I can't just keep letting her get away with this." He grunted. "I have to do something!"

"Please don't. This will pass," she whispered. She could see in his eyes that nothing she could say was going to stop him. Not this time.

"I don't get it; why don't you do something?"

"I hate it here," Daren said, sitting up. "Conover is always glaring at me. It's uncomfortable. It's weird! I wish you could have seen this: after you went to sleep—after she made me clean the bathroom and kicked my head in—ten minutes later, there she was. She was standing right there!"

Daren pointed at a paint stain on the floor, a foot away from her mattress. "It was awful. I had to leave the room just to get away from her gawking e—"

"Stop it," Tom said.

Daren looked at him, confused. Then she saw his concern for her on his face.

"You'll get through this. I'm here for you. Okay, what happened next?"

She shook her head. "I told her that I had to use the bathroom again. I've been in confinement every other day this week."

Tom placed his hand on her shoulder. "Good thing you never actually have to use the bathroom."

"You know," Daren said, "honestly, if I had known you'd keep asking me about that every day, I would've kept my mouth shut."

He shrugged his shoulders. "What'd you expect? It's crazy someone never has to go. I mean, never? No pee or poop?"

Daren scrunched her nose. "Gross. I don't know how you guys can do that stuff."

"I've seen you throw back some bowls; where does all that stuff go?"

She shrugged. "I'm almost never hungry. It used to freak me out, but you know what? After all that icky stuff I've been cleaning since I got here, I'm glad."

Tom smiled. "You're so cute and perfectly clean. I'll bet you never fart, either."

Daren's hands went to her waist as she made a fake pouty face. "You're gross. And I keep telling you I don't. Do you think I'd ever lie?"

"You're fun," Tom said, patting her leg. "Sometimes I wonder why you picked me to trust with everything."

Daren lightly pushed Tom's chest. "Aw, come on. You know why. After the sanitarium, you seemed to accept my . . . differences. Better than I have."

Tom's hand made its way to her shoulder. "Hey, you're like a little superhero. I mean, I get it, you can't control what you do or how you're doing it, but so far no one's died because of your abilities, right?"

Daren sighed. "I just can't bear thinking of hurting anyone—even the witch."

Tom laughed, as he did whenever she preached about not doing anything to retaliate against Mrs. Conover. "Okay, Mother Teresa. Man, if that were me, if she'd done some of the things to me she's done to you, I'd . . . I don't know, I'd do something. That reminds me, did you eat the food on that dirty tray they slid under the door?"

"Of course. You know how I am."

"I do." Tom smiled.

"There's something creepy about a lady that just stares at ya nonstop. She doesn't look at anyone else like that, and she doesn't look at me like that," Tom said. "I'm just glad I'm not you. What do you keep doing that makes her so mad at you all the time?"

"Last time she blamed me for the shoe polish that she found in her coffee."

"Daren, someone told me"—they leaned in together, both looking at the door because Conover would be walking through it any minute—"someone told me it was Eddie. And I saw him run screaming from a baby mouse I saw the other day. I guess he hates her."

"Who doesn't?" Daren said.

Playful smiles washed over their faces, and the two loners bent forward on the bed.

"I hear she stomped down on your head in one of the toilets because it was too clean?"

Daren lowered her head and nodded. "She's done that to me more than once. I think she gets a kick out of seeing me in pain."

"I need to get you outta here," Tom said. "I look at her sometimes when she thinks no one is looking. Something happens in her eyes; they change. I don't know, though, it's like she's not human or something.

Word is, when she's taking some of us off to meet parents, she kills 'em. She's walking around looking like the Wicked Witch. You know, like in that book she read us that one time, The Wizard of Oz . I almost died. I bet I wasn't the only one picturing Conover riding a broomstick. God, for a moment there, I almost thought I'd end up like Billy. What kind of psycho locks kids away and beats them just for laughing?"

Daren pulled her golden blonde hair back and snapped on a rubber band. The sunlight breaking through the glass in the windows appeared to make it glow.

"Wow, you are just . . . just amazing."

Daren blushed, but her beauty always reminded her of her evident differences. She bit her lip and glanced away. She flashed back to the time she had changed into Mrs. Conover. "Amazing, maybe," she said, "but not always in control."

Then her skin began fluttering as if water was running underneath it.

"Daren! Your nose!" Tom said, as he watched it begin to grow.

Bug-eyed, she put a hand over her face, and as quickly as the nose had grown, it shrank. In that instant, she also felt something ominous, a dark sadness coming for her. She slammed her eyes shut and tried pinpointing the source. It proved fruitless, because it was everywhere. She realized it could be anyone or anything.

"Whoa," Tom said. "You weren't kidding."

"Yeah, I'd love to entertain you with my weirdness, but like I said, I don't know if I'll be able to control it. I'm not going to get stuck looking like her."

"What's with all the stolen duct tape in your mattress?" Tom asked.

Daren's cheeks reddened even further. Her breasts had started to develop.

She was getting taller; her waist was getting smaller and her hips a little wider. Her original form began to look less and less like a little girl and more like a woman. The fallout of her maturation soon became evident in the other children. Especially Tom; Daren caught him staring at her from time to time. She noticed everyone would stare at her, but he was the only one who she didn't mind.

The drastic growth and extreme attention were almost too much for her. Some of it was manageable, however. She knew she had to prevent the other boys from staring at her C-cup breasts. This required flexing her mental muscles until she could strap her breasts down with duct tape.

"You're one to talk," she said, deflecting the question. She lightly pushed him. "You're hiding bars of soap in your mattress holes."

Tom grinned. "I was saving that for you." He dragged his finger down her nose. "I've heard the girls hog the soap. That reminds me, why haven't you asked me for some more?"

The old wives' tale that women do not sweat was true for Daren. A microscopic liquid coated her skin, eliminating all forms of dirt and bacteria. The purifying cleansing solution made showering unnecessary. She was perfectly clean at all times.

"I don't want to get you," she touched his arm, "in trouble. You should probably get rid of them."

While Tom was talking, Daren could see out of the corner of her eye Joey whispering with a few other boys and staring at her.

A rotten tomato slammed into Tom's closing hand an inch in front of Daren's face.

Tom stood up and chucked the tomato back at Joey, smacking the bully on the side of his head. Mold and seeds ran down his face. Squishing the goop out of his eye socket, he screamed, "You're dead meat!"

"Come and get it, asshole." Tom spread his arms wide.

Daren's heart raced. Her eyes glazed over. *Oh my god, I'm falling in love with him!*

Conover's piercing shriek forced itself through steel and stone.

"Dareeen! Dareeen!" Her high-pitched voice almost mocked Daren's name.

All the kids froze. Tom reached into his pocket and flung a napkin at Joey. He caught it, they both looked at each other and nodded. He quickly cleaned up the evidence.

Everyone rushed to their beds.

Bang! The metal door flew open and clanked against the wall.

Conover stood with her arms folded, black hair sprouting from beneath the sleeves of the white nurse's uniform.

"Off the beds, right now! Clean, clean!" These kinds of entrances always lit a fire under every one of them.

"Twenty seconds!" she shouted. The green gaze of her fury instantly brought the children to their feet, turning the deepest sleepers into the spryest workers.

She slapped her ruler in her palm. "Twenty lashes to the last person ready!" Her voice was like a rake scraping a chalkboard.

Conover stomped over to Daren, placed her fists on her waist, and leaned down. She was screaming an inch from the top of her head.

"Ten!" All the children had their beds made.

Daren remained seated, her head bowed.

"Nine . . . eight!" All the children gathered up their personal towels.

"Seven, six, five!" Everyone was in a straight line at the door waiting for head count.

"Four, three, two!" Conover grasped a fistful of Daren's hair, yanked her off the bed, and dropped her to her knees.

"One!"

Tom charged at the Counselor. "Ahhhh!! Don't touch her!"

She let go, but gave a backhanded slap across his face. Tom fell.

The fluorescent lighting flickered as Daren gritted her teeth, looking at Tom on the floor.

Conover's scream sprayed spit. "Stupid brat! You will fall in line like the rest!"

"Ahhhh!" Daren's legs started to glow. Light bulbs shattered, and sparks fell like rain. Luminescence surged from her body as she shot like a bullet through the air.

She drove her head into Conover's stomach. The strike launched the counselor from her feet. They shot like a bullet across the wooden floor.

Daren let go. Like a rag doll, Conover kept going, the great momentum propelling the counselor's body against the stone. Her head whacked against the wall, leaving a small blood splatter.

"Noooooo! I—I killed her!"

Tom stared with cow eyes. "Wow. You're a superhero."

Four counselors within earshot sprinted into the room to witness the havoc and also saw Daren's new change. She clenched her teeth and clasped her head. *How could I want something to die! I took a life!?* Auburn color streamed from her scalp, painting over her angelic blonde locks.

Four other nurses rushed to Conover's aid. "Beth? Are you okay?"

Even with her face down on the ground, Conover's cackling was maniacal. "Heh, heh, heh. Your time will come, little one." She pushed herself to her knees and stood up. "Take her to confinement."

A few moments later, the nurses dragged her by her arms and tossed her into her cell. Her body bounced on her bed.

"This is where you belong. Maybe when you learn how to behave, this will stop," one of them said, sliding the steel door closed.

Again, Daren found herself locked away in her cell. After wiping her tears, she watched a few drops on the floor dissolve away the bacteria and dirt. She rolled her newly darkened hair between her fingers. *What's happening to me? I hope she's okay. Wait. She deserved it, didn't she?*

Confused, all she could do was focus her mind somewhere; anywhere but the home. She went to the window again, looked out through the bars to the courtyard, and closed her eyes.

Daren was not alone in tasting Conover's wrath. She felt Tom's voice reaching out to her, bringing her mind back into the cell across from hers. She could hear every word in his mind and feel his every emotion. But she could not respond.

"Looks like I'm also skipping breakfast this time. Come on, Daren, I know you can hear me. Still haven't figured out how to use it to talk back, huh? That's okay."

While Tom rambled on with a story about the time he hid cups of water to help Daren fake going to the bathroom, Daren dropped to her knees.

She focused on her breathing and, clenching her eyes, she lightly hummed. She sensed her voice link to the air itself, moving through the cracks in the walls.

"Thomas Alfred Bane! Is that all you think about?"

Her voice reached his ears, echoing through his room. She could picture him sensing the vibrations of her voice.

"You sound like an angel." He stood straighter with a sly smile. "I hoped that'd get your attention. You should've seen her face when they dragged you out. I don't think I've ever seen her so mad. It was awesome."

"I don't want to hurt anyone. Who knows what my powers could have done?"

"She's fine."

"Yeah, I . . ." She swallowed. "I don't know how to feel about that."

"I do have some good news. I overheard her saying we're getting out for lunch," he said.

She focused on the cell across from her, and now in her third eye she could see Tom lying on his back, staring at the ceiling.

"What's with your hair?" he said.

"Don't know. I just really wanted to not be me."

"You know, after lunch, she's having everyone play in your garden. I heard something's going down. Are you ready?"

Daren's eyes prickled. "How can she do this to me?"

"I'm sorry I brought it up, but I figured you should know. I'm sure those animals are in a better place."

Frustration crinkled her face. "She butchered them, right in front of me."

"You know, ever since you made that garden, I've been sleeping like a baby. My dreams are fantastic, and they're always about something happy."

Daren took a deep breath, and the tightness in her face was subsiding. "I knew you'd like it, but it didn't work out as great as I hoped."

"So, um. The garden didn't make it so you could talk to him?" He rolled his eyes.

Daren looked down and shook her head.

Tom sighed. "You're really hung up on this mystery guy, Kevin, huh?"

"Jealous?" She grinned.

He blushed. "No, I uh . . ."

And there he was, giving her that look again—the one that always got him an extra stick of bread at dinner.

She felt the corners of her mouth turn up.

"When everyone else was asleep, she woke me up and shoved a clump of dirt in my mouth. She whispered to me that if I did anything like that again, she would kill you."

Tom paused and took a deep breath. "I can remember the last time you said no to her. I still have blisters from all the scrubbing we did on the floors."

There was a brief moment of silence.

"Come on, princess . . . you still with me?"

With her eyes still closed, sitting on the bed with her legs crossed, she leaned over and put a palm over her eyes. "I'll think of something."

"So, this is pretty groovy, isn't it?" Tom said, putting his hand against the wall, feeling it vibrate. "Oh, man, think about what we could do with this. We could spook the socks off that jerk."

"Boooooo!" Her voice echoed through his room and Daren giggled. "It's a little late for Halloween, I think. Besides, something tells me that if I start showing off, the people in charge might do something worse."

"So," Tom said, looking around his room. "We're going to be in here awhile, so—what's it like to have your powers?"

"Weird."

"I mean your visions."

"Really weird."

"You don't want to talk about them?"

"What should I tell you? My visions are"—she sighed—"very, um, different. A lot of stuff is very private. Very scary.

"When I'm feeling good or happy, I see puppies and stuff like that.

Lately, with what Conover and the others have been doing to us, it's been like constant horror movies running in my head."

Tom's eyes widened. "What kinds of stuff do you see?"

Since the garden, her visions had changed. As the night came, she drifted into sleep, but she was still conscious of the room around her. The edge of everything was fluid and soft. All the figures were dark and misty, like demonic ghosts, and their words came to her from very far away.

The voices that she could hear throughout the world carried with them all the loneliness and ruined hopes of billions of lives. Daren would peer closer. The darkened, fleshy pillars were people twisted together somehow, contorted into humans meshed with monstrous red-scaled devils.

"Trust me, T. It's better you don't know. If I told you what was out there, you'd never be able to sleep. Ever."

"What about the other kids here?" Tom asked. "Can you see anything about them?"

Daren opened her eyes and walked over to the one-foot-square, barred window. "It's often better not to know what people think," she said, running a finger across the sill, "because then it's easier not to care."

Her feminine, almost godlike voice was like music. It echoed in Tom's cell, but in hers, her mouth was not even moving; her lips were closed. "Besides, nine times out of ten, I can't get most of my abilities to work, at least, not on command. My visions when I sleep are random, but they both seem to be linked to how I feel."

The negative emotions would spark visions of homicide, one group of images after the next. All things were seen: no act too atrocious, no depravity taboo.

Daren felt a presence coming for her, viler and darker than the demonic shadows she faced during her birth.

"Daren?"

"Yes, Tom?"

"You know just about everything, don't you?" She smiled. "Sometimes I think about how we all got here because life seems so random. Some parents just drop off their kids here like they aren't wanted. Then, some other people come in and pick them up, and they become part of their family.

"And then some kids have been here forever, and I hear the older you get, the less likely you are to ever get folks. It just doesn't seem fair, you know? I mean, what chance do I have? I was abandoned at birth like you, and I still haven't been picked. I hope you don't have to be here as long as me. Shoot, as adorable as you are, you'll probably be picked up tomorrow."

Daren blushed. She felt like a prisoner of circumstance, a cruel mistress of the fate that had dealt her cards. However, another part of her felt like a painter rendering her destiny on a blank canvas. "We'll get out of this. I really think so."

"You think so?" Tom asked, getting up from his mattress. "Not enough sleep to have a vision of us getting out?"

"I don't choose what I want to see. I wish I did, or I might not have done what I did this morning."

Tom lifted up the food slot at the bottom of the door and peeked out, looking for the guards. "How do you know which dreams or visions are real?"

Daren paused. "Like I said, they're all real."

Tom dropped the metal flap. "Whoa, scary. How do you know?"

"I just know." She breathed.

"Most of my visions are things that already happened, like when my hair changed color. Sometimes I see the present, sometimes the past, and sometimes the future. I hate it. I always see things I'd rather not see: children bald from chemo, moms stuffing children into dumpsters . . . I just can't."

"What am I thinking right now?" Tom said, putting both of his hands to his head.

Daren said nothing.

"No, really, what am I thinking? Your third eye stuff is neat. I mean, you can see what I'm doing in here and talk to me and even read my mind. So what am I thinking?"

"I don't feel comfortable—"

"Aw, come on."

"I don't want to see your darkness," she said.

"Fine. Let's play."

They spent their remaining time using the dusty walls to play tic-tac-toe and bantering about Conover. At lunchtime, the counselors escorted them down the hall toward the cafeteria.

Walking down the dank gray hall with the two counselors right behind them, they held hands. "Joey might try something today; are you okay?" he asked.

Daren shook her head, sighing audibly. "Joey is . . . well, yeah, I think I'll be okay. As long as you're here." Tom locked his eyes on hers and felt himself unable to look away.

She ran a hand through her beautiful, silky, shimmering auburn hair. She was pulling it back into a ponytail. She noticed him struggling for words and smiled.

Finally, he spoke. "You're so kind, and hardly anyone knows how amazing you are, even though they should." He glanced away.

He was trying to control his staring.

You keep to yourself, but you're easy to talk to, and I know you'll be honest with me no matter what I ask."

Tom paused and took a deep breath. Daren peered into his eyes and smiled.

He continued. "You're the only person I look forward to seeing every day, and I sometimes feel selfish because I would hate to see you get adopted. I don't ever want to see you go."

At the end of the soliloquy, his face had gone red, and Daren noticed that he was looking away from her—almost as if she were making him nervous.

Daren grabbed his hand again. "Let's just enjoy the time we have."

They arrived at the cafeteria.

December 24th, 1976

CHAPTER EIGHTEEN

"Better to reign in hell than serve in heaven."

—John Milton

"Daren must die." It was the voice of Darkness. "Unless…"

Evil's tentacles had spread far, even piercing the walls of the White House. The dark stains of impurity brought ominous clouds collecting in the capital's sky, shading the pale moon's luster. The night took possession of the streets. Bleak shadows chilled anyone who dared to challenge it. The families of Washington, DC, retreated into their homes to await the warmth of sunrise. The monthly Coven meeting had begun, and after shuffling papers, the president mopped sweat out of his eyes. He pushed himself away from the Resolute desk and made his way toward a painting.

"I know you don't care, but being the president of the United States means I've got my own problems."

A loud, deep, apparitional voice trembled in the walls around him. "You will not speak to me in this manner! Shall I remind you of the minister's appetite? Watching those beautiful creatures feed on the living is quite exquisite."

The president bowed his head. "Yes, Lord Blackthorne. I'll obey." He removed the canvas.

Blackthorne's notoriously terrifying voice always jarred his movements. Capturing a lungful of air, the president flattened his quivering right hand against the empty wall. A console appeared to grow from plaster. To the right of his palm, an array of buttons etched with strange symbols sprouted from the wall. Just beneath his hand was an obsidian panel covered in smudges of other alien fingerprints.

Light emerged from the console, moving over his fingers and down his body. In that brief second, a flash of his true changeling form was uncovered. Cells of reflective diamonds covered his body in layers, scales of beautiful mirrors that bent light, reflecting kaleidoscopic prisms into the room. His long hair resembled truffles of light, ever-shifting into a myriad of colors.

As fast as he had changed, he returned to human form.

"Welcome, Agent 187," a computer said.

The president removed his hand, and the etched buttons shifted from English lettering into changeling symbols.

"Please move away from the walls. Commencing initial containment and stage two security."

Within the boundary of the ceiling medallion, sizzling, inky black slime began moving down the walls into the room. The curtains closed.

A veil of darkness slid over every window, and all glass across the room became opaque. It took only seconds for the spectral goo to coat the Oval Office in a black shell.

Ooze on the wall in front of the president retracted, unveiling a massive orifice striped in teeth. Immersed within its enlarging throat, a stone path pierced a churning stream of blood. Waves of fangs undulated around the perimeter of the mouth.

"I hate demons." The president carefully stepped through and onto the pathway. Brimstone gathered in the misty air, the noxious fumes adding to the already grisly atmosphere. Blood, like inverted rain, dribbled upward into the sky, collecting in coagulating crimson clouds.

His feet sloshed through entrails down its carmine path, pausing at a door made of scarred human tissue. Giant eyelids parted at the center of the flesh and fixed their gaze on his face.

"Yes. Yes, it's me. Let me in."

The door opened. Thick, oily shadows moved as liquid, descending in a waterfall at the doorway.

All right, Gerald, just once a month. You can get through this.

Moving through its murk, he could just make out billions of tiny demonic eyes watching his every step. He could feel the goo slide over his flesh. The blinking orbs were unholy observers, fluid as falling rain in the dark cascade.

He emerged through the liquid shadow and continued down the nightmarish path. Hurrying his pace, he pressed on through the training observation area. Now surrounded by walls of jagged black rock, he recognized he was deep below the earth's crust.

Distant muttering accompanied flashes of ghostly, fiendish faces. The shuffling of thousands of footsteps and the pungent smell of unwashed bodies, excrement, and burned flesh invaded his nose. Hairless, horned demonic monks were on display like a zoo behind dim transparent energy.

Every part of their bodies displayed scars as symbols, and every inch of flesh held a variety of piercing.

The monks sat floating in meditation in front of various animals wailing in cages and howling in pain. The wildlife exploded. The monks clenched their eyes, and the bones and flesh meshed back together.

He heard the animals' cries, the sounds of their bodies popping as he passed by each window. This gruesome process repeated as he advanced down the pathway.

The trail ended in dark fire, the collection of black flames amassing several feet over his head. It was antiradiance, drawing in heat and pushing away light.

Tightly shutting his eyes, he jumped through.

Only one who is dark shall pass through dark fire. Then why is this always so freezing? He felt its life-giving oxygen passing over his body and the pain of bitter cold tasting his skin.

He landed on a red carpet covering a narrow path in a room with a vaulted ceiling. Coming to his feet, he saw that he was in a temple, and on either side of him were levels of seating where reapers cloaked in gray were sitting in reverence. Their robes concealed mummified bodies wrapped in gauze, and then there were the eyes. Thousands of tiny demonic eyes blinking in tar peeked through serrated bandages, watching for any would-be evil impersonator. In robotic unison, their heads turned, tracking his progress.

Creepy little bastards. The president saw the place he was looking for—the open obsidian door with steps going down.

The lower temple meeting was always in a place devoid of light. Stepping into the thickening darkness, his eyes began shifting in color, morphing into diamond-encrusted orbs.

With that replacement, now it was as if he stood under the bright sun on a cloudless day.

Upon entering the temple, he discovered a reeling chaotic mess.

G.R. MORRIS

The surrounding stone walls billowed in a sea of human bodies stretching like plastic wrap. He watched the thousands of rippling fingers and teeth scraping to get free.

<hr />

I hate this place. The twelve rulers of the Coven, immersed in their Mephisthophelean aspects, sat in silence while eating skin. The pink membranes of the newborn babies they devoured symbolized their lives: carnivorous, preying on the flesh of those weaker and slower. The creatures, sitting at the table constructed of layered, dark, demon skin, raised their heads in unison. Blood staining their teeth, they beamed smiles that were 90 percent leer and 10 percent hunger .

A man immersed in white was not partaking in the feast. He was sitting at the head of the table in a chair made of death, piles of severed heads stuck together with matted, cooked flesh. Each one of them still held eyes that moved around, staring blankly into the room.

All of them had a distinct expression of pain and horror, like they would scream if they still had voice boxes.

With his black goblet of blood held aloft, the man spoke, the words coming from an unseen mouth concealed by mystical shadow beneath the white robe.

"Before we officially begin, I must tell all of you that I'm disappointed in the treatment of Daren. I realize you want a war with the changelings, and I'll bring you that war." He leaned over the table and pointed at the others.

"But if you kill the changeling god, you'll have a war with me, and I promise that's not a war you want. If you think I'm going—"

"Out of my seat!"

A voice came from behind him, from an erupting dark cloud. The edges of his robe began to turn a shade of black, then flickered back to white. The man in the white cloak stood up.

"I said, get out of my seat!"

The man in the white cloak moved away from the head chair and bowed his head. As he raised his hands, the wide sleeves of his robe slid back, revealing arms in a blurred shadow. It was the head of the HPA.

"So wonderful of you to grace us with your presence, Master Blackthorne. To what do we owe this prestigious honor?"

Blackthorne gazed into the shadow of the white cloak; his withering, cracked lips compressed a little, indicating his irritation. He took his seat. "The incompetence of your men."

"Ooooo, gee, I'm soooo sorry," the man in the white hood said sarcastically, turning his back to Blackthorne. "If you're so competent, then why don't you go find Kevin yourself?"

An alien with skin layered in black scales stood up. "Why are we just sitting around and letting the bitch Daren live? I'm telling my faction to kill both on sight."

Blackthorne chuckled. "Do not worry; neither this light child nor this miserable savior puke will ever touch our lord. The Dragon is all-powerful. Your fear is misplaced. He comes soon, and when he does, he will win the fight against our oppressors." Blackthorne took a deep breath and pushed back his eyeball that was falling out. "Don't forget why we are all here, gentlemen."

The HPA leader nodded. "We all know why you're here, you zombie."

Blackthorne raised his fist and clenched it. "I should rip your throat out where you stand!" Dust fell between his cracking fingers.

"You won't get the chance," the HPA leader muttered.

"We are all here for the same purpose. Our motives may differ slightly, but we are all here to save our species."

President Gerald Ford raised his hand. "I know I might be a bit new here, but why do we have to do it in such deplorable conditions?"

Blackthorne pointed around to the suffering of the people moving in the walls. "A few people suffering; so what? A few babies die. So what? You joined our little group because you felt guilty about how your people were treating humans. Let me tell you, it goes far beyond my people and their imprisonment. Their slaughter of humanity by the billions doesn't stop with them. They cause the end of all life."

Gerald Ford looked down at the bloody flesh parts on the table, the bodies of newborns being eaten in bowls carved from human bone.

Blackthorne nodded. "You know they don't care about humanity. You've seen it. I saw them create a man who was slaughtering the people I was supposed to protect—the Jews." Tears, half-filled with blood, welled up in Blackthorne's eyes. "And when I died, I had every reason to suspect that they had wiped out my friends, my family, my whole race."

The wetness of his sorrow rolled down the withered skin of his cheeks. He lowered his head. "So I sacrificed my soul to Kain, the ruler of hell, to make them pay for what they did." Raising his head, he locked eyes with Gerald Ford. "Is there a limit to what you would do to save all life from ending?"

The HPA leader golf-clapped. "Magnificent speech." He looked at Gerald Ford. "Given that you're a changeling, what do you suppose he's going to do with you, eventually?"

Gerald Ford looked at Blackthorne with fear in his eyes.

"Be happy that I haven't killed you already," Blackthorne said.

The alien with skin layered in black scales raised his hand again. "So far, all three prophecies have been correct. What if we're wrong?"

"I'm not wrong. I am never wrong. I already have Daren, and

Kevin cannot hide forever." His creased finger pointed at the alien's nose. "Your pathetic anxiety, your concern should be for following orders; I will ensure the Dragon rules the universe and prevents our extinction. He will save us all."

Gerald Ford whispered to the alien next to him, "I've heard about this Dragon. How does Kain feel about him?"

"He worships him, of course. Now shut it!" the alien said.

Blackthorne leaned back in his chair and folded his arms. "I am curious, however. Vicesia, what are your findings?"

A thin male figure with skin the texture of wood stood up. "Master, if I may be blunt? Daren is not the goddess."

Blackthorne turned his head, glinting a smile at the man in the white hood. Leaning against a stone pillar, that same shadowy figure in the white robe folded his arms.

"This is ridiculous."

The wooden man adjusted his bifocals. "The blood samples you've provided clearly show that she does not possess the kind of light required to perform the acts of prophecy. In fact, this proves she is fragile. Any one of us could kill her."

"He's right." Another alien with similar skin stood up. "Our group also tested the blood 666 times per your request. Each time, the results were conclusive. Our group believes in science as much as we do in the sacred texts, and I have to conclude that she's not the one we're after."

"How can you be so certain?" Blackthorne said, tearing off a piece of flesh dangling from his wrist.

"Well," Vicesia said, shuffling his papers, "there is a strange genetic anomaly. She does not register as a changeling, or as a human, or even a mixture of both, although each of those strands are there."

"I know exactly what he's referring to," the other man said, pulling out a flat-screen the size of his palm.

A holographic DNA image appeared in the middle of the table. "I want you to observe the common DNA helix," he said as the image expanded.

"Each of these balls represents different elements, such as hydrogen, oxygen, and nitrogen. Now I'll bring up Daren's DNA."

The helix vanished, and another grouping of three connecting strands appeared in its place.

"You'll see here that all three strands contain an anomalistic white element. It's also present in the ester bonds. In fact, as you can clearly see, for every identifiable atom, there are two of these anomalies separating it. In other words, more than half of her is made up of this element."

A large, muscled figure coated in red spikes voiced his opinion. "Nullados never mentioned anywhere in the scriptures that she'd have this stuff."

The white-hooded man sighed. "It also never says that your race would be such assholes."

"I'll kill you!" the spiked alien yelled, slamming its fists on the table.

Blackthorne barely raised his voice. "Quiet!" The argument stopped before it even began.

"Please continue," Blackthorne said.

An alien whose skin flowed around him like water raised its arm.

"Yes? What could the Flobians possibly have to add to this?"

"Master, I've read in Conover's reports that this Daren person created life. Could this be true?"

Blackthorne aimed his finger at Vicesia.

"Oh!" Vicesia coughed. "I guess I'll answer that. The garden can be explained scientifically. There was no evidence in the blood of the animals to prove creation at the time of the event. The animals at the incident had memories, not to mention the age of the thyroid samples."

The HPA leader pushed away from the pillar, his white cloak ruffled. "What about the Timeweb? It shows us that—"

"It shows us a possibility," Blackthorne snapped. "I'm beginning to believe Conover was right."

Vicesia sat down and picked up a paper. "It's like she says in her report from when you first brought her in. A god shouldn't bleed."

"What's with gods and gardens anyway?" one alien whispered.

The other wooden man pushed a button on his pad, and the hologram disappeared. "Technically, if she's the god of the prophecy, we shouldn't even be able to do these tests. Besides, from what we've seen, she's as easy to kill as the humans. And, some of us think, she will be easier."

Blackthorne waved his bony finger. "Okay, that's enough of her. She does not die today. If we find more evidence that she is truly the goddess, I shall deal with it then. The Great One will kill them both, even if all of us fail . . . or even if, somehow, Kain fails."

The man in the white hood nodded, his expression always hidden in shadow. "That's what the Dragon was created for; he was chosen to stop Kevin and wipe out the oppressors. But I'm not going to just sit on my hands."

Blackthorne stood up from the table. "Agreed." He pulled a snow globe full of swirling black smoke from his gray suit jacket pocket. He threw it on the table and it shattered, spreading its smoke and its holographic insides.

A miniaturized version of another room showed four men looking up at Blackthorne. "So these are your best Skyviewer technicians?"

The man in the white cloak looked down.

"Yes. Please don't—"

Two of the men convulsed. Their entire bodies spasmed and grew into masses of undulating balls of surging flesh covered in black veins. Before the white-cloaked man uttered another word, they exploded in flesh chips and black blood.

Blackthorne took his cracking, withering finger and pointed it at the two remaining men. "Let that inspire you to find him."

The man in the white hood shook his head. "Must you always do that? You think we have Skyviewer techs growing out of our butts? Great, another week to genetically smarten up replacements."

A huge, gelatinous man cradled in a transparent hovering bowl giggled. "Master, I love how you motivate the help."

"Kiss-ass," the man in the white hood mumbled.

"You could learn a lot from the Thorbans: a little respect and loyalty," Blackthorne said.

"I guess I could also learn how to never stop eating and how to run away from a fight," he replied.

The slimy green throat of the Thorban expanded like a frog's, hissing and screeching sounds saturating the air. The jelly in its container bubbled, nearly splashing out of its bowl.

"Silence!" Blackthorne ordered, quieting the room. "Contact me at the Havens. You have twenty-four hours," he said, pointing at the man in the white cloak, "or I'll kill the rest of your technical division—and maybe a few more of you for pleasure. Find him!"

In another charcoaled puff of smoke, Blackthorne was gone.

December 24th, 1976

PART EIGHT

ANGEL TEARS

"There has to be evil so that good can prove its purity above it."

—Buddha

CHAPTER NINETEEN

"Love is obsession. It's the greatest influence of choice.
It pulls you to the hills of ecstasy and drops you to
valleys of despair. It is not just an emotional intoxicant;
it's the most powerful force in the universe."
—Raksasha

T oday is the day I'm supposed to save everyone from hell, Daren
thought. *Wish I knew how.*

"Let's hope we can avoid being locked up again," she
said to Tom.

"I guess we'll see what happens." Tom pushed the metal bar and
stood to the side. "Ladies first." He smirked and bowed.

"Together," Daren held back a giggle and held out her hand.

They entered the crowded, murky cafeteria. Daren could feel all
the eyes and smell the sour, burned, potato-skin soup.

Tom's eyes narrowed to crinkled slits. "I might've known Joey
would be there once again, getting more soup than the rest of us."

Conover sat at the center of the long, dark-brown oak table, eating beef Wellington off expensive white china plates.

The rest of the children ate from small pine bowls with wooden spoons, self-whittled and self-cleaned. They sat at hand-me-down wood tables held together with bent, rusty nails and semidried glue, spread out across the room in rows. The cauldron at the center of the room held thirty gallons, so there should have been plenty of soup to go around for the eighty-six children. Today, they made just enough; however, two servings sat on the table under Conover's watchful eye.

She pushed her white cotton bib down her shirt. "You sit in the back of the room with your boyfriend and watch the rest of us eat."

Tom walked close to Daren, holding her hand and making eye contact with everyone. Most of the boys stared at the girl like the starving stare at a feast.

Daren was genetically flawless. Her body was in perfect proportion from head to toe. The girls would have none of it; their eyes flashed and raked her with freezing contempt.

Tom jerked Daren away from a swarm of moist crumpled toilet paper. "Stop it!" he yelled, and not even one landed on her.

"All right, all right, that's enough," Conover cackled. "Don't waste toilet paper, now."

"Come on, Daren, let's go over here." Pine logs shaped into stools were stacked against the back wall. Tom grabbed two for them to sit on.

"Just look at that jerk sitting next to his mommy," Tom said, kicking one of the logs.

You could count on one hand the times Daren looked at or even talked to the other children, but she noticed that her peers had begun regarding her as stuck up.

"She thinks she's soooo much better than all of us, Tom," they would tell him, and he would always defend her.

"You don't know her like I do. She's been through a lot, you guys.

I can't believe you guys pick on her."

She could hear the conversation between two boys at the table a few feet in front of them. "Do you think Conover will take her to the attic?"

"What are you talking about? They're just trying to scare us into doing what they want. I'll bet you still believe in flying reindeer."

Tom sighed and turned to Daren. "Have you used your powers to check that out?"

She was looking down, following the rings on an upright log with her finger. "There are things like dark clouds that stop me from seeing into it. When I try to push through them, it hurts." She looked up at him. "I don't know, like lifting really heavy weights."

"You think all the rumors about that place are true?"

"I've seen a lot of horrible things."

Daren and Tom were the last ones to stand up from their stools, and not a minute too soon. The final scoop of slimy potato skin mush was just about to be served to Joey. Tom Bane could not believe it; Joey was going to get three servings today.

Joey smiled at them, raising his empty bowl, knowing that he had just finished Tom's food and now was about to eat Daren's.

White burned in her eyes, and she crushed a piece of wood in her fist as she stood up. "Hey! This isn't fa—"

The rest of the orphans gawked at her, and she sank back to her seat.

Tom put a hand on her shoulder, then his arm curled around her waist, tugging her next to him. "It's okay. I'm here."

Shaking her out of her emotional state, he tapped a finger on the tip of her nose.

Daren nodded.

"You're cute when you're angry," he whispered. "Everything's going to be okay when you're with me. I promise." He smiled with wide eyes, watching the light play on her face as he contemplated the treasure in his arms.

Drinking in his glance, she felt a tingle flutter through her body as she stood up from the table. She slipped on a piece of wood.

Falling deeper into his arms, she brushed her nose against his chin. She could feel his heartbeat against hers as her chest grazed his.

Oh, to hell with it. Blushing, she threw her arms around him. The hug was very warm and kind, and she felt a deep glow burn inside her chest.

Conover chucked a stack of plates . "Stop! There will be none of that! Fraternization is not allowed!"

The hug didn't stop, and Tom squeezed back. Daren followed every movement of his eyes, as if he might escape if she did not hold him with her gaze. She felt his heart beat fast next to hers. "I—I—um," she mumbled.

This is it! My first kiss!

She could feel his breath on her face, their lips just inches apart.

Darn it! Go on and kiss me! Make a move!

Tom looked up at the sight of Conover stomping toward them. Grasping the sides of her head, he kissed Daren on the forehead.

A spark deep inside her—an electrical impulse fluttering through her body—erupted at the surface of her skin.

The emissions were smaller than the human visual spectrum; microscopic oils that carried a shifting scent.

The scent was perfect, altering itself to please anyone within a few feet.

Tom let go of Daren and cooed. "Do you smell that? It's like we're in a strawberry field. It's amazing!"

Conover's clomping feet came to an abrupt stop.

G.R. MORRIS

"Roses? Someone brought roses in here?" She had an affinity for that particular blossom.

Daren knew it would take something more than the mere smell of flowers to do that to her. She was right. Unfortunately, the smell was the perfect pheromone, an unyielding attractor, an airborne love potion—and the power was getting stronger. She radiated the allure of ultimate femininity, causing the primal urge to pair-bond with her from every man, and abject jealousy from every woman.

The kids waiting in line turned around, all gawking at her. Conover, gritting her teeth, fell to her knees, overwhelmed by anger. Holding her head, she screamed.

"Ahhhhhgggghhh!"

All the females in the room screamed. "Ahhhh!"

Tom stood back with eyes glazed, locked in a prison of infatuation. Her beauty, at its inception, was perfect, in the way that a human can look perfect. Now Daren's skin began to alter, changing into something even more amazing.

Flawless, she became godlike, an inhuman perfection too pleasing to the eye; the temptation to stare was now unbearable for any mortal man. Daren's beautiful visage ensnared all eyes in the room. A simple look trapped them in emotion; contentment and arousal devoured the males. Jealousy erupted into rage in the girls.

Conover, ensnared in fury, charged at her. As she did, everyone, including Tom, chased Daren out of the room.

"My skin! What's happening?" she said, racing down the hallway.

Daren sped out into her garden, grabbing handfuls of dirt and smearing it all over her body. "Stay away! Stay back!" she yelled.

By the time they caught up with her, she was clumping the filth into her hair. The dirt was sliding off her skin and dissolving.

The new perspiration of godlike pheromones would soon break

through.

Go away! Her eyes clenched closed as she felt her skin tingle. The dirt stopped moving. For a moment, she had managed to control her body.

Droplets of rain started to fall from the dense clouds that hung overhead. Everyone stopped the chase and looked at each other as if waking from a strange dream. Then they saw the girl coated in mud. Except for Tom, everyone laughed, and some even pointed.

Joey, the favorite of the counselors, began the chant: "Doody Daren, Doody Daren!"

The majority of the others joined in. "Doody Doody Daren! Doody Daren!"

Conover, smiling, picked up a hose and threw it at her feet. "Wash up! I better not see a single smudge of dirt on those clothes, or you're not coming in."

Daren picked up the hose. "But there's no soap!" she said, watching the crowd of people shuffle back inside.

"Princess Precious will figure it out!" Conover said, clacking the metal lock.

It didn't take long—a few minutes and the chemicals in her body removed the dirt, but cleaning the stains from her clothes took longer.

Tom, looking down from a second-story window, pressed his hands against the glass. Daren saw the silhouette of Conover's wild, curly hair behind him.

As he mouthed the words "I love you," Conover threw her arm around his throat and violently pulled him away.

"You . . . you monster!" She was breathing heavily. Her eyes burned bright with light.

Get ahold of yourself, Daren. She slowed her breathing, and her eyes returned to normal. *Where could she have taken him?*

The second she was alone, she sat down, crossed her legs, pressed her hands together, and lowered her head. *You can do this!*

It wasn't easy, but after a few minutes submerged in her mind, something happened. Her clothing elongated with multiple prisms of light, bending around her body, pushing inside the cotton fibers. Swirling light stirred across her head, crystallizing into a hood shape. She created clothing like a shield: an oversize white hooded sweatshirt, baggy jeans, a baseball cap, and tennis shoes. *There, that should cover me up. She's going to be super pissed, and everyone's going to hate me because of these nice clothes, but they hate me now anyway. So . . . whatever.*

She felt satisfied that the thick, baggy clothing would mask her chemical messengers.

A nearby counselor heard Daren's fists pounding on the doors. "I'm ready. Let me in!"

Hypnotized by her beauty, he complied.

They passed by the kitchen and the cafeteria and headed to the sleeping area. *Where is that evil woman, and where is Tom?* she thought.

"Sir?" she asked a custodian.

"Yes, my lovely creature?" he said.

I must do something about my face. He's a zombie!

"Tell me, where is Miss Conover and where is Tom Bane?"

The man bowed. "My perfect rosebud! Beth Conover is in a meeting with President Blackthorne. As for Thomas Bane, I do not know where he is. Please let me help you find him. I will do anything you wish; please allow me to bask in your presence."

My god, are all the men going to talk and act like this? Clearly, the effects are still wearing off.

"Who is Blackthorne?" she asked.

"Oh, my little turtledove! He's the man who pays the bills around here."

"You may go." She rolled her eyes, entering the room.

"I would prefer to stay!" he whimpered.

Wow. Creepy.

The children in the beds stared at her with awe. When Daren saw Tom wasn't among them, she took off running.

"My perfect flower, I will wait for you!" the custodian called after her.

She threw open the doors to the women's bathroom. Holding the sides of the sink, she stared at herself in the mirror. *Focus, Daren. Focus!*

She squinted. *I've done this once; I can do it again.* Peering deeply into the perfect blue pools of her eyes, her skin became as water moving.

She was now uglier, or at least as ugly as the hottest runway model that would ever live.

Large warts began to appear all over her face, along with scars.

Yikes! Not that much! I don't want to look like Conover. Maybe just back to where I was.

She opened the door.

Maybe Tom will be there when I get back.

When she entered the sleeping area, the kids turned away. Daren sighed.

It's finally worn off. Guess I should be happy with them ignoring me.

She wasn't hungry. Once again, she set off, gliding a mattress across the uncarpeted wooden floor to put space between her and the rest of the children.

Tom was missing on a night when the cold stood in your breath, your body quivered, and your teeth clacked.

Cheap jerks, trying to save money while we freeze here. Oh brother,

Joey thinks he's being cute hiding behind Tom's bed like that, she thought, walking over to it.

Where is he?

Daren grabbed Tom's wool blanket, but Joey was standing on the opposite side of the bed.

"Oh, I'm sorry, your majesty!" he said, yanking the cloth from her hands. "Back off! This is mine."

Daren clapped her hands on her hips; arms crooked like sugar bowl handles. *You know I could kill you so easy. Wait, what? Where did that come from?*

Rather than examining this sensation, she backed off, fearing for his safety, and lowered her head.

"Yeah, that's what I thought." He chuckled, jutting out his chin.

She watched Joey walk away with Tom's blanket and went back to her bed. *You're just being paranoid,* she thought. *He'll be there next to you when you wake up. I mean, won't he?*

———◆———

It was very late by the time Daren snuggled into bed, taking advantage of the warming heat from the air vent beside her. Soon she dreamed, hot, lurid fantasies of violence and fire, rape and bloodletting, and a cold black fury that carried all before it. She woke muffling her own screams.

Daren rolled out of bed, wincing at the cold seeping into her bare feet through the skin against the stone floor. There she was, the Wicked Witch, stomping her heels into the room. "Oh no, no, no, no, no! I don't know how you got back in, but—"

It had been a couple of hours, and Tom's bed was still empty. "You evil witch! What did you do with him?"

"Stealing from us? Those clothes belong to the children who

deserve parents," she said as Daren walked up to her.

They were inches from each other, locked in a stare.

What am I doing? What am I doing?

"If you must know, Tom has finally found some loving parents." She displayed her green-and-brown stained teeth.

She knew Conover was lying; she could feel it, but she didn't need any special abilities to know it wasn't the truth. He was still somewhere in the orphanage.

I will find you.

Conover grasped Daren's wrist. "Well, princess, for theft, you get to spend the next month in your cell."

Daren drooped her head. "Yes, Mrs. Conover."

CHAPTER TWENTY

"I willingly believe that the damned are, in one sense, successful,
rebels to the end; that the doors of hell are locked on the inside."

—C. S. Lewis

December 24th, 1976, 11:30 P.M.

Her skin was almost luminous in the murk of her prison, and it was silent enough to hear the sound of every breath. The metal cell door slammed shut. She could hear the clanging of the two-inch chains rattling against her door and the clicking of the lock.

"Don't think you get to keep those clothes. When I find where you hid your old ones, I'll be back," Conover said.

There Daren sat, secluded with her thoughts and seduced by her memories.

Where are you? Daren closed her eyes and sent her mind through the halls, looking past every door and into every corner.

Normally, Daren tried to ignore the oddities, like the cockroaches inside the walls, where they roamed unfettered and unchallenged. The pests preferred overall to stay upstairs, nested in the attic.

A variety of insects seemed to be gathering outside each day, slowly working their way up the walls toward the top floor.

She felt a sudden chill; a dark cloud of energy prevented her sight from penetrating the attic and a room in the office. Daren looked up at the ceiling.

I'll bet this is where you are. This must be why you can't hear me.

"Sorry, people, I don't mean to pry, but I've got to find him," she said. Just a topic. Okay, everyone, what do you know about the attic?"

There were plenty of rumors going around about the restricted evil room, but few ever dared to venture to the top floor. There were, of course, stories inspired by imagination, and that's all it ever was. The counselors made sure of that. Children that went in never came out.

Daren saw it everywhere; the barriers that make the devils and angels invisible to mortal men were wearing thin. The dead were mingling with the living; every immoral choice of the living was slowly chipping away at the gate and spilling the horrors of hell into the world of men.

Daren sat in her cell, one flight of stairs down from the attic, listening to the clamor of noises from above with a sort of awe, scarcely daring to believe people were summoning demons.

She always felt nibbles of the damned and hints of voices from another world, but this was the first time she could not ignore it.

A voice cried out in a whisper. "You must see this." She raised her head, her eyes still closed, seeing Mrs. Conover sitting in an office on the first floor.

"She's leaving today?" Conover's groan was so loud Daren cast her eyes around the room to see whether any neighboring ears had heard.

No one was there to hear except Daren, watching Conover's every move from her cell.

Conover's hand jumped to the middle section of the printout she'd been going over. Someone had been manipulating foster dates again. She felt her anger rising. She ran her hairy-knuckled fingers down the page, checking the contact information and time.

"The parents are showing up in an hour?" she screamed. This meant trouble, big trouble. The Johnsons simply needed to sign the correct paperwork once they arrived, and Daren would be theirs.

Looks like I foiled your evil plans, didn't I? Daren smiled.

Conover decided she had better confront the administration while she was feeling the outrage. With files in hand, she stood up, took a deep breath, and stomped her way across the campus to the office building.

Daren watched the children's eyes widen in fear at the clomping of her hard black wooden oxfords echoing down the hall.

Before entering the office, she paused for a moment, staring at the plaque next to the door: PRESIDENT, and below that, DR. EDWARD BLACKTHORNE.

Behind the door, Daren saw the dark fog that had blocked her abilities before.

"Tom!"

Searing pain ruptured like fire through her skull. Pushing her abilities through the fog felt like running through boiling glue. Mental strain put the squeeze on her brain, and she felt as if it was in a vise, then set on fire. As she winced at the pressure, a droplet of blood trickled out her nose, and then she heard the voice.

The deep, rumbling crackle filled her head as the clouds began to part.

She felt the presence of the thing that created the shield protecting the room.

"Sweeeeeetieee!" The echoing voice carried the sounds of hell.

Daren felt a chill flutter up her spine. *What was that?*

Quickly reaching out with her third eye, she felt the lives in every room. The source was neither living nor dead and neither shadow nor solid.

The voice crackled deeply through her skull. The sound was coming from within the darkness, and it was calling out to her. Something beyond the physical scraped at her sensations.

Shake it off, Daren. Shake it off.

The office was normal.

Plain.

Empty.

"No. This isn't right."

The shadow around the office was clearing.

Daren grinned.

She could now see the office for what it truly was.

The office told a horror story of Blackthorne's Jewish heritage; from end to end, stars of David were carved into the ceiling, the back wall, and the floor. The other walls were decorated with images of the Holocaust. Paintings of dead Nazis stacked in burning piles , framed photos of Hitler with his eyes torn out, and emaciated Jews standing in lines waiting to die in concentration camps.

Many of them were violently cut with the words "justice" and "revenge."

Blackthorne had a collection of keepsakes, one of which was the skull of the first child he ever killed exhibited prominently on the center of his desk.

Daren briefly glanced at it and then quickly looked away.

She gasped and covered her mouth. *A newborn? That's sick.*

Also on the table, locked in an infinite spin, was a dreidel carved with satanic symbols and a large black demon-scale-covered menorah with branches made of serpents. The fanged mouths were filled with fresh blood.

Demonic items in glass display cases on the back wall were colorfully fashioned over the ages.

There was the infamous crown of thorns worn by a crudely sculpted head of Jesus with its eyes stapled shut. The entire collection of nails used for his crucifixion was stacked forcefully in its mouth. Even the exact copy of the original Hebrew Bible was there, but written backward.

Daren saw much more than antireligious items. There were vials of blood belonging to every one of the worst criminals the world had ever known, including Hitler and Pol Pot. One of the things that disturbed Daren most was the dozen blood-caked demon heads bookending each shelf. She covered her mouth.

She saw them being carved and sculpted by unwilling priests. When they finished their respective carvings, their throats were cut for one reason: to use the artist's blood as paint to color the sculptures.

Blackthorne's skin was as dry as cracked leaves; his body was that of a malnourished ninety-nine-year-old man. Shriveling, sallow flesh was barely holding on to bones. Sunken eyes, and his stringy hair—what little he had—was long and thin and fell over his charcoal gray suit. He smelled sour; the air filled with sickness and rotten meat.

He coughed up blood to splatter on his desk; a few maggots squirmed around in the puddle.

There was a kid crying in a small blood-caked cage.

"Billy! Nooo!" Daren yelled.

Blackthorne's bones cracked when he moved, and his arm quivered when he pointed at the child. "I'm sorry, my young one. You must die so others may live."

When he spoke, the flesh in his cheeks fluttered; it was thin enough to see his rotted teeth.

Blackthorne picked up a yellow skeleton key from a drawer in his desk along with a jagged bone dagger.

"Someone help!" Billy screamed, shaking his shackles.

Hunched over, Blackthorne shuffled toward the four-foot cage.

Daren breathed heavily. Her mind was already strained from breaking through the cloud that protected the room.

Blackthorne gripped his thigh as one of the bones in his leg snapped. "Damn you, Kain!"

Dust erupted from his knees, and flesh fell from his arms.

"I'm terribly sorry, my child." His quivering, ancient, rotting hand turned the key.

"I've got to think of something!" Daren cried.

The dagger slit the seven-year-old boy's throat.

Blood gushed out, and Blackthorne began lapping it up with his cracked tongue. The liquid spilled over his black gums and splashed over the ridges of his nearly transparent throat.

He bit down on the boy's face.

"I can't watch this anymore," Daren said, opening her eyes.

She paced around her cell for a minute, then sat back down and continued watching.

"Got to find Tom," she said.

Daren felt a horrid presence in Blackthorne's room. Her heart raced, and shivers pulsed over her body.

Blackthorne was sitting back in his chair; Billy's bones had been picked clean.

Blackthorne's skin on his face was thicker. He was no longer hunched over, but that was all that had changed.

"I don't understand. I've devoured the flesh of the innocent ten times this week but youth has not returned. We had a deal, Kain!" he yelled.

A demonic voice rumbled through the walls. "The deal was to keep you alive as long as you spread suffering. No one said anything about feeding your sin of vanity."

"But I look like—"

"No more on this matter! I will keep my end of the bargain as long as it's convenient. You will continue with these acts of atrocity and receive the gifts of darkness, or your soul burns with me in hell."

Where are you, Tom? Daren thought.

Conover tapped lightly on the door before opening it. Blackthorne threw the last of Billy's bones in a basement and closed the trapdoor.

"You may enter."

She entered his office and kept her eyes on the ground.

"I'm afraid I've found another mistake in our records," she said as he looked up. *Here it comes,* she thought as he squeezed his beady eyes into slits. It was a scowl showing both scorn and resentment.

"I'm assuming this is about Daren, am I right?"

"I've been going over these files, and the Johnsons are expected to be here in about an hour," she explained as she placed the reports on his desk.

"We have discussed this," he said, his cracked voice rising. "You said you could handle it!" With that, he grabbed the papers and threw them on the floor.

Mrs. Conover raised her head and watched his body clench with controlled fury, but she knew that she could not back off yet. "Mr. Blackthorne, I don't know what else I can do. They will be expecting her when they arrive."

He stepped up close to her face, green eyes blazing with fury. Before he could utter a word, she added, "We can't risk being accused of misleading our clients."

"Let me tell you something." His voice was thick with menace. "You will do whatever it takes to make sure she does not leave this place. Yes, you will!"

She stood for a moment, staring back down at her oxfords, before lifting her eyes to his desk and saying, "You're right. It would be sooo easy to slit that bitch's throat in her sleep." She raised her eyes. "Please let me kill her."

"I suppose torturing her isn't enough for you?" he said, drumming his cracked yellow fingernails on the desk.

"Her existence spits in the face of everything we stand for. Nullados prophesized that—"

"Shut your face! How dare you start lecturing me about the sacred text!" Blackthorne kicked his black leather chair, his hands curling into fists. "I warn you, Beth, any kind of insubordination means that not only will you be out of a job, but your life will be forfeit."

"I'll be sure to remember that, sir." Beth turned around slowly, body winding with a tight jumble of anger and fear.

She closed the door behind her, and his muffled, splintered voice pushed through the wood.

"I'm giving you two minutes to meet me in the attic."

She turned around to face the door. "Yes, master." She headed down the hallway toward the stairwell.

Blackthorne vanished in a cloud of smoke.

He was moving at the speed of darkness—in the blink of an eye, he was in the attic.

Conover wants me dead; not surprised. So this is who was stopping her from killing me. If he's not there, that means Tom is right above me!

The dark cloud protecting that room was also gone.

She thought of Tom's face; so innocent and vulnerable. She envisioned it through the connecting current image of Conover standing in the elevator. Beth would be up the stairs soon. Daren watched each step she took.

She saw Tom's pale face, damp with tears and clenched in fear. "Somebody, help me," he wailed.

On the top floor of the seven-story building, in a claustrophobic room, Blackthorne was summoning the dead. At the request of the president, bodies of children were sprawled in piles against the bone-colored walls.

Daren closed her eyes and, traveling with her telepathic mind, looked at a clock on the wall in the next room. It was 11:55 p.m. Slumped in the corner, she stared at the blood moon through her tiny window.

She took long glances through Tom's clear blue eyes, the way a detective might stare at a wall at a murder scene, desperate for clues. She saw through his eyes; he was peering through the slits of bars. Like Billy, he was in a small animal cage.

This is all my fault; if I weren't so careless with my abilities, he wouldn't be there.

The attic was in shambles—a few worthless paintings showing images of Christ's crucifixion, human bodies skinned and hanged by their intestines, and churches set ablaze.

Many years of blood had accrued on the floor, and the char of smoke stained the walls and ceilings. Their sources were sacrificed children, and the candles sat on every shelf and sill, stalagmites of crimson wax.

Everything was aged, withered, and so old they were fit only for the incinerator on the opposite side of the room.

I'll get you out of there. Hold on, Tom, hold on. I should tell him—no, they'll hear me coming.

Blackthorne smeared more blood into the pentagram on the floor. This pentagram was a pentagram within pentagrams—666 of them—all mixed with alien symbols drawn in several different types of blood. "Our god is greater," he mumbled.

He had been slaughtering children for years and had already walked the darkened path. He knew which types of animal, insect, human, and alien blood were required for the ritual.

"The blood of all can open the door to the damned," he said, after writing the last symbol in changeling letters.

The sins of man's depravity, the cruelty of man's inhumanity against man, through every maleficent act, had culminated in an infinite river of darkness. A rumbling growl mixed with the hiss of demons was slowly growing, like a timid whisper building to a scream.

The stone walls were boiling, raging with the echoes of the dead.

Below the building, dark veils gathered like smoke, bubbling up ghostly goop from the soil and through cracks in the pavement.

It throbbed beneath the trees, pulling them into its tarry wake. It was growing, emerging from the ground like a living flood. There were things inside it that came at Daren's senses like an alarm waking her from slumber.

12:00 a.m. Midnight.

She could hear them: the sound of swarming locusts blending with shrieks of pain. She felt them: the evil in the shadows and the souls stripped of all humanity and every ounce of dignity, wailing in agony.

All of this struck at her perception in waves, forcing her to block it.

Then there was the hint of sulfur; the air stained in brimstone flowed as a constant reminder.

It was then that she noticed the clouds in the sky were welcoming the evil and had taken the shape of the devil's insignia, casting its shadow over the grounds. *My garden isn't going to be enough for this.*

Just below that chaos, Tom's eyesight blurred, not only in liquid melancholy but also with extreme fear. "Daren . . . oh God . . . someone help me!"

Looking through Tom's eyes, Daren could see horrific silhouettes, devilish claws, and hellish faces pushing through the expanding walls. Daren was pacing. *I'll get you out of there somehow.*

Although she could not see it, she felt a denser collection of darkness in the form of a human figure. There was wickedness beyond evil; the one who ruled over the massing darkness, the king of shadows Daren instinctively knew as Kain.

His demonic snout was sniffing the back of Blackthorne's neck, studying him, waiting for the door to completely open before revealing himself.

Daren heard that disturbing dark voice rumble through her head once more. The sound slithered through her mind.

"Sweeeeeetie!"

Daren watched as Conover moved through the warren of darkened corridors leading to a door at the end of a hallway past her room. Walking up a single flight of stairs, Conover entered the licentious chamber. She raised the attic door. The stale heat moving over her face brought fresh beads of sweat to her brow.

Without room to stand, Tom was on his knees in his cage, watching preparations for his sacrifice.

Daren observed everything and sensed something else about to happen: the death of his captors.

"I have not been entirely up-front with you," Blackthorne said, opening a vial of blood.

Conover had her back to him, selecting candles from a shelf. She slowly turned around to see the sacrificial dagger covered in demonic symbols floating in the center of the room.

Blackthorne smiled. "Here. Hold this."

A glint of light sped through the air like a laser. The dagger stopped inside Conover's stomach.

"Wh—wh—what have I done?" she said, holding the sacrificial weapon's handle in both hands.

Dark, fang-tipped tentacles spread up like a web from the wound, punching through her chest and grinding into her wart-covered face. She screamed. Puss burst out her eye sockets.

Blackthorne stood up. "You weren't the first to replace Conover."

Gargling on her own blood, Conover dropped to her knees.

"There is one thing about changelings," he said, raising his arm. "They are easily replaced." The knife flew into his hand.

Life poured from her mouth as her body flopped face down. Her body had turned into a boiling puddle of dark flesh.

"Nothing personal. I needed your life energy to complete the ritual."

The black blood on the dagger was all that was left of Beth Conover.

The corners of Daren's lips raised in a gradual smile.

Wait, why do I feel good about this? This is awful!

"You're a monster!" Tom screamed through the bars.

"Patience, my young child; the monsters come later."

Stepping back and leaning against the wall, Blackthorne folded his arms, still wielding the dagger.

The front of the cage flew open.

Darting from his captivity, Tom rushed out into the room and stumbled toward the exit. Just before his hand grasped the doorknob, swirling clouds formed ghostly chains that coiled around his arms and legs. Tom's body jerked backward and skidded across the floor, the chains lifting him into the air.

"I love it when they run."

Fire erupted in the center of the room, directly in the middle of the pentagrams. Tom dangled like a sacrificial roast above the flames.

His flesh did not burn; instead, it froze. Icicles formed on his extremities. Every pore on his skin began to widen as small, circular wisps of dark energy drew blood into the circle.

Daren felt the light of his life force dim. She watched the encroaching dark while Thomas Bane was still locked in her mind's eye.

Daren screamed. Shimmering tears ran down her face.

Come on, Daren, think! You have all this power; think of a way out of here! Daren rushed to the window.

The nectar of the devils that bubbled out of the soil passed over the garden in a dark blanket and flowed around the first office building, smashing through the cross.

She felt her personal wilderness die. The luscious perfection of life cut out an icy grave in an instant. Her Eden was gone.

Daren winced. *My—my garden. Nooo.*

The large crucifix between the two buildings crumbled in crystalline fire, melting in an ooze of black liquid, leveling into a puddle of bubbling grime in seconds.

The river of darkness came as a tidal wave, roaring up the side of the main orphanage building.

The fluid evil splashed over her open window. It did not enter her room. But that did not quell Daren's fear. She stumbled, landed on her back.

She crawled away from the wall. Bordering on hysterics, her fists clenched and arms shaking, she was close to cowering in a corner.

Putting up a mental shield, she lost the connection to Tom.

She could not clearly see beyond the veil of evil, where changelings, humans, animals, aliens, and other monstrosities were ground together, still conscious and aware of the pain. Her mental barrier did not save her from witnessing their silhouettes, moving under the thin layer of churning evil as it flowed past the large window.

Daren's heart was pounding furiously. Hold it together. You can do this. You can save Tom.

"Don't you dare die on me, Tom. I'm coming!" she yelled.

After the rescue, she would somehow have to make it through the black shadows that encased the building. The quickening bleak was a tarry prison; a shell for the victims of evil.

First, she had to try to save everyone, not just Tom.

I can't let my feelings for him blind me to doing the right thing; I have to save everyone. If I try to escape and save them . . . no, I won't get there in time. Maybe I can do something from here.

All the children must live. I wonder if I can open a passage through my block. Daren closed her eyes and opened a mental tunnel through her barrier to the sleeping area. That was simple.

She saw the gore and felt the hate and future suffering.

She saw the moving shadows lurking above the children, the violent evil coming to devour their bodies.

I have to save them.

CHAPTER TWENTY-ONE

"And so it is, that both the Devil and the angelic Spirit present us with objects of desire to awaken our power of choice."

—Rumi

December 25th, 1976, 12:10 P.M.

orror had an audience; children's screams resonated through every hall. The once-boastful bullies had urinated on themselves. Even Joey had lost his bowels—and for good reason. The caretakers of the children had turned on him, picking him up by the arms.

Pressed against the window, Joey screamed like a baby.

The half dozen counselors stood still, like joyous and maleficent executioners, slyly grinning at one another as if they had just pulled the switch. Black sludge pressed against the cracking glass. A pulsing, demonic river was squeezing through the entire building.

The glass exploded.

"Mommy!" Joey screamed. Uncongealed sin burst through his gut and ripped through his chest. Frozen, crystalized by the cold, his bullying days were over. Those who slept near the window died where they stood, gurgling in a sea of bubbling, dark terror.

Melanoid murk erupted from the river of hell, projectiles hitting different sections of the room. Joey's body shattered.

From where they landed, insects of every variety swarmed into the children's sleeping area. Bugs sprouted from nowhere, discharged from the cover of every soiled mattress, and crawled along the walls.

The preppy girls' screams were the loudest. Large locusts scratching at the ceiling dropped into their hair, biting flesh and burrowing into their skulls. The makeup bubbled and drained off their faces. In a panic, the horrified females tried ripping their manes from their roots.

Daren empathically rolled her own hair through her fingers. "Bastards! You did this to them!" she screamed.

She could not believe the counselors would be in on it.

Let's try this. She lowered her head into her clenched fists.

Speckles of light like glowing dust manifested in the center of the sleeping area. Brilliant light burst and swirled around the room, the particles merging themselves into countless insects.

There's just too many of them! she thought as she watched hundreds of them flickering then popping into glittery flashes of light.

Kids were still dying. For every dozen insects that exploded, six more sprouted from the ooze.

Come on, Daren, do something. Think!

Whoa, that's disturbing. The counselors smiled and walked right to the swarm. They were the first to be completely submerged in the dark sea.

They opened their mouths; one by one, the large insects crawled inside. She watched as their throats engorged and tore apart. The obsidian-coated building became a feeding station for the monsters.

The vermin attempting to escape by piling through cracks in the walls were the first enveloped by the demonic river. The speckles of light moved into the waves of muck.

Nothing?

They were absorbed.

Opening her eyes, she clutched her tattered bedsheets , trying to catch her breath. Got to be another way.

Bulbs burst throughout the building, and though it was early morning in the city, the building was in the black of midnight. Sunlight reflected off the building cocooned by bubbling, liquid darkness. The remaining bulbs flickered, seconds away from shattering, so Daren began to reach.

Raising her head, she swallowed hard and pulled air into her lungs. Her eyelids closed on a sliver of tears.

She stretched out with her mind for a light source: a flashlight on a shelf in a supply closet. It fell to the ground and rolled down the hall, seemingly by itself.

The counselors did not want their prized child to leave, and had covered the door with hundreds of chains webbed together by a thick lock. Daren twisted her fists. The chains vanished, the steel door swung open, and the flashlight rolled to her toes.

Daren, picking up the flashlight, heard moans from the unbroken darkness crawling closer. She took off sprinting down the hall.

The flashlight went dead.

Blinking owlishly, Daren felt as if water was coating her eyes, and she could see again. She saw her own face smiling back at her. "More virgin flesh!" it whispered. The darkness was an inch from her nose.

She stumbled backward and her butt hit the floor. Terror was the size of a baseball lodged in her throat. She watched her own reflection gesture with her hand to come inside.

Just above the growing sludge, she could see the attic door.

"Tom!" she yelled, scooting away.

"Oh God! Daren! Help me!"

The same haunting voice, that demonic random chatter that was in her head, came to her ears, rumbling from the attic.

"Blackthorne . . . depart this place! Prepare the Coven for my arrival. The Defiance will fall!" Kain said.

Crimson crystalline fire exploded on the perimeter of the room, blocking the walls and preventing intrusion.

Blackthorne bowed his head in defeated reverence. "Yes, Lord Kain." In a spinning cyclonic cloud of gray smoke, he was gone.

Daren's attention to the attic was broken; the wall of darkness had quickened its pace. Crawling to her feet, she hurried her steps backward. She reached out her arm; the massing evil was just a foot away from her.

Then she saw her reflection. It smiled back at her. Its eyes rolled back in its head and exploded into maggots in their sockets tumbling down its face.

"That's nice. I've seen worse," Daren shrugged.

Let's see how tough you are. Summoning the courage to fight, born from the will to save Tom, she dipped her hand into the encroaching darkness. She felt icy-cold, bony fingers grip her wrist. She felt her fist beneath the black gauntlet vibrate. Beams of light erupted from her skin and pressed through the murk. Still moving backward, she tore her hand away.

With a few waves of her arm, the remnants of fluttering shadows on her hand vanished.

"I'm coming, Tom!" Closing her eyes and inhaling a sharp breath, she looked down through her mind's eye, staring at her feet. A vibrating blur of white light moved up her body.

She let it come to her, her eyes tightly shut while the fluid evil engulfed her. The light around her body instantly dimmed. *I better not have just killed myself.*

G.R. MORRIS

Focus, Daren. Focus!

A stew of animal and human flesh pressed against her skin in what felt like a mix of quicksand and boiling tar. The scalding sludge thickened at every passing second as she tried to swim through its mass.

The bleak grew so dense that she could not move. Her vibrant light was now but a timid glow, and all of Daren's senses were muted, except for the feeling of touch.

She heard the voices, like painful daggers ripping at her mind. Feeel Ussss. Evil had overtaken her body, forcing her to focus on her last remaining sense.

You won't beat me. That sensation was overcome by the claws and scraping teeth of hundreds of monsters pulling at her flesh. Light vented from the slits in her closed eyes, and she grinned in defiance.

Get—her arms glowed—*off*—her body was enveloped in a ball of blinding white light—*me!*

The darkness exploded, but the parallel forces of light and dark caused Daren's body to fly backward down the hall. She pressed her arms out, and glowing beams crashed against the walls, stabilizing her fall.

The path to the attic was clear.

She heard the thumping of Tom's heart slow.

Daren was stunned. She shook her head. She was numb, her vision was blurred, and her ears rang. Squinting through the water in her eyes, she watched the evil pour into the hallway.

The darkness rose like steam through the cracks at her feet. It wreathed around her legs with growing, ghostly skeletal fingers.

Tom's declining heartbeat was like a rising scream in her head.

The sludge had just reached the attic door.

She would save Tom; pain be damned.

Daren gritted her teeth. "TOM!!" Her shout bounced off the walls and vibrated away the dust. She collapsed to her knees, and the darkness around her exploded into nothing.

Flickering ghostly shapes the color of blood burst from the flowing darkness. They splattered against the tile and rolled toward her. Their naked misery attacked Daren's mind like they were her own emotions. She grabbed the sides of her head, trying to push out the noise.

The globules grew into humanlike figures.

"Help usss!" Bubbling inky bile spewed from their mouths. Four figures, one smaller that looked like a child, began coming into focus. Their eyes were missing, and their mouths were sewn shut. They were all on fire, their skin burned, and each one had scars that told their story of eternal torment. Some of them had their bellies torn out and were covered in bite marks.

She could hear the spatting of their blood-covered bare feet against the floor. The same sounds were coming from behind her. Daren pressed her hands together and closed her eyes as the demons approached.

A supernatural gust of wind rushed around her. Her hair began to float, and each strand became like bright flowing crystals. As she held her breath, her eyelids became coated in diamonds. Opening them, her eyes burned with white fire.

"LET TOM GO!" her voice boomed.

The demons stopped; they turned catatonic, and she felt their fear. They stepped back.

Sparkles of light rose from her body and began to spin. They transformed into a swarm of five-inch hot-white spikes of light.

The barrage exploded through the demons. Burning flesh splattered against the walls and disintegrated. The sparkling, untarnished projectiles splashed into the darkness like a horizontal storm.

The darkness receded and withdrew from the door leading to the attic.

Daren rushed to her feet and thrust open the trapdoor.

Empty. A room full of cobwebs and the echo of a demonic chuckle. "TOM!"

She closed her eyes, took a deep breath, then reopened them. He was here. Something moved him, she thought as she went back down the steps.

Her heart racing, she turned around and sprinted down the corridor in the opposite direction of the attic and the sludge. Echoes of pain and ghostly crimson baby handprints appeared like growing stains on the walls.

They moved with her, trailing at her heels. As she saw them, she heard a maniacal giggle, like a demon having its feet tickled. She could feel the lost souls in the room, the newly slaughtered young taunting her to join them.

"Play with us, Daren!" they giggled.

Daren lowered her eyes as she ran. "I'm so, so sorry. I couldn't save you," she mumbled.

Thank God I can still feel many people are still alive. Tom is still alive.

She was moving through what used to be a nursery. Her glowing eyes lit up the peripheral glass windows as she passed them.

She could see children's toys, chewed-up teddy bears, and plastic balls covered in blood rolling around by themselves. At the end of the hall was a stairwell.

Several flights below, she could see some of the other orphans caught in a demonic massacre.

Hands came from every side; long bony arms covered in gray hair and melting flesh tore at their faces as they dragged them, screaming, smashing skulls against steps.

Before she could take another step, the stairwell was blocked by thickening shadows. The path to her left was filling with the fluid of evil, and she couldn't go back. The hall to her right appeared to be safe.

So, I'm being led somewhere. Stay alive, Tom. Stay alive. I'll come up with something . . . I hope.

Daren reached the end of the corridor. The room's walls were made of smoldering flesh, blood dripped from the ceiling, and slithering tentacles moved through dark sludge coalescing into crackling bone.

Each tentacle had numerous suckers. At the edges of each mouth, a ring of teeth like fingers moved in a wave, beckoning its prey. She turned to look behind her, and the bleak misty death was still coming.

Taking a deep breath, she stepped inside. The place had a special quality of zero gravity for the toys and some of the hovering blood droplets, while Daren's feet remained planted on the floorboards.

The surroundings had a pulse, the rhythmic beating mirroring her own heart. Moans violated the air. Fleshy masses of faces bound together moved on the walls, mouths agape in torment.

Stalactites of red flesh hung loosely from the ceiling. The sight of hundreds of eyelids—apertures like small mouths—finally broke her will.

They were all around in the walls, the horrible glare of bloodshot pupils staring through her with hunger. Daren shivered in terror.

There was also something in the corner.

"Sweeeetie!" It was the familiar demonic voice.

Temptation pooled with curiosity caused Daren to push one of the floating baby dolls to the side and glance at the thing that was in the room with her.

It was a human figure; a shadow emerging into the room.

Tentacles sloshed in boiling blood burst from out its back, moving toward where the walls met.

Crackling bones and stretching skin coated in bubbling darkness protruded from the walls crease and began forming a solid horror.

Daren could only see it in silhouette, jet-black shadows, the arms spread out, touching the walls on either side. Vast dark obscurities, darker than the night, were like live fear—a form of evil itself.

"S—S—Satan?" she mumbled.

"Little girl, I am much worse than a fallen angel." Ghostly tendrils as fine as hair grew from the darkness, twining themselves around the bones in the walls, the strands growing thicker with every palpitation. Streams like coalescing veins pumped stygian mucoid against the walls. They threaded their way through and around the room, knitting trembling flesh onto the frame.

The faces were now gone, replaced by matted skin.

"The father of sin's only crime was loving humanity too much, and for that, he was banished."

Thicker strands surrounding the figure's blackening mass seemed to soak up light, throbbing as luminescence was pulled inside and destroyed.

Daren's empathic connection was now like a curse, an explosion of infinite lost souls crying out in pain. She could feel the creature's lies.

"A l—lie." Her lips trembled with her fear.

The horrific shadow was a deep hole in the fabric of reality, a tear among the unbalanced physics surrounding her.

She could not look at it, not with her actual eyes; she knew that visually diving into that abyss meant drowning in despair, being forever lost to it.

As the shadow stepped forward, the figure began putting strain on the attached tentacles.

"Very good, my child. It was his greed that placed him there; his own choice to rule hell. Now all his powers belong to me."

As the tendrils snapped from the wall, she heard a demon's squeal. Like bursting from a devil's womb, the monstrosity spun around in a gory explosion of bones, skin, and teeth.

Emotions, her own fear, and the pain of the souls around her engulfed Daren. Crouching down, she buried her face in her chest and covered her eyes with her hands. "Somebody . . . help us."

The creature existed in layers: its outer layer a walking pile of gore. Numerous pieces of body parts flowed like liquid skin. Coalescing tentacles covered in the lightless blob coiled around it, as if holding the mess together. Broken segments in the skin filled with reflective mist, displaying ghostly images of captured souls screaming out in torturous agony.

All of that was mixed in with a humanoid shadow with the face of a dark abyss.

"Look at usss! Look at ussss!" the captured souls screamed.

She understood that compliance meant death. Even to her. Daren closed her eyes, peeking at it through her mental peripheral vision. It was getting closer. Terror saturated Daren; it bathed in her fear, enjoying every moment.

At each step, space itself seemed to cry out in agony.

The air around the thing appeared to die. Particles of oxygen turned to vacuum, and vacuum turned to an absence, evolving finally into darkness.

Behind it was a trail of mirroring figures, echoes of itself fading and blending in a cluster of blackness.

"Mmmmmmmm—" a deep moaning reverberated in her flesh. Fear immobilized her, gripped her in a vocal vise. Daren's arms and legs began vibrating with light.

"That won't work on me," it said.

The light in her body dimmed, and the vibrations stopped.

It approached her and, with each step, left a steaming footprint, a permanent shadow on the ground. It was now a foot from her face. Instead of eyes, it had empty crevasses. The monster cocked its head and stared at her from its deep pools.

Not a part of Daren moved; she did not even breathe. Its head was a shadowy darkness, rising dark mist parted near its base. An oversize mouth displayed rows of fangs; they were daggers overpopulating a mouth of crimson gums. Its jaw elongated to the point where it could swallow her head and devour her entire body.

Smoke rose from the groups of shiny spikes spread from ear to ear. Rows of tusk-like spears pushed through shadowy flesh rose from below its mandible and wrapped around her face. "Tasty . . . ," it grumbled.

The sharp protrusions stuck into her cheeks and lifted her in the air, her feet flailing as she tried to wiggle from the iron grip. It pulled her into its open throat, so deep that she could feel the cold dampness of its stomach acid and see boiling blood down its gape. She smelled brimstone from the glistening tar moving on the jagged crowd of fangs. There wasn't a place inside the monster that wasn't coated in some kind of sharp edge.

She was lifted higher, above the thing's head, and thrown to the floor.

It could have killed me. Why did it stop?

She knew what the creature wanted; she felt its lust and then its purpose.

The deep voice from the abyss came at Daren from all directions. "You live because it is my will. I desire your willing compliance."

The creature paused, and the sounds around her stopped. All Daren heard were the screams of the foster kids. She felt them dying.

She felt the warmth of gallons of blood pool at her feet. Her pants stewed in the crimson river, and she watched as it swirled around her.

The fluid blurred, and Daren could see a human figure in a cave of fire; she could feel its pain.

It was Tom.

Daren stood on a bridge made of flesh-covered bones coiled in chains, suspended above a pit of human misery.

"Let him go!" Daren screamed. Below her, his body roasted above an inferno, coiled in barbed wire twisting through his bloody flesh.

Daren's eyes glowed for a second and then dimmed. She gripped the chains.

The creature spoke again. "Hmm, such delicious pain . . . the pleasures of the innocent. Now, your two choices: first, save the children from death and infinite despair and in return you pledge allegiance to us. Your utter devotion to the dark. I require no contract written in blood.

"Second, you can be cruel and let them die. Either way, we will leave. Choose: we leave with the lives of the children, or shall I spare them and just take you?

"Before you answer, think about Tom; can you live with that choice? All you need to do is speak. Do you give yourself to us? Yes . . . or no?"

Daren paused for a moment, thinking. She liked the idea of self-sacrifice; the noble act of giving her life for those who tormented her. Something told her that choosing the dark would be the right move.

She stared down at Tom's burning body and clenched her jaw at the sight. How can I just let you die?

She rubbed her arms, her own skin feeling his pain. Daren's eyes watered, which turned to steam.

Daren shook her head. Her heart thundered.

"His death will be on your hands," Kain said.

Something else said that she was too important, that the act of giving herself to darkness would make her powers and her body the puppet of evil. She foresaw that choice resulting in an even greater loss of life.

She saw the answer; she made her choice.

She stood straight and closed her eyes, forcing the word out through trembling lips.

"No," she breathed.

As she spoke the word, she could see the rest of the children, the counselors, and both buildings erupt in darkness, surrounded by icy flames and bubbling black.

She could see Tom's face, his skin coated in fire. His flesh boiled and burned. His death was painful to her ears, vibrating through her mind; she knew his screams would never leave her.

She fell to her knees, tears flooding her closed eyes and streaming down her face. Long, oily tentacles reached for her. The shadowy arms pulsed red with the blood it had already taken from the children. As it lurched forward, a black void thicker than quicksand and as slimy as mucus enveloped Daren's body.

Small tentacles grew from the muck, wrapping around her throat.

"Foolish little girl. You can feel it, can't you? You will join us soon. You know it to be true."

Daren's screaming started immediately. Her powers told her that Kain's words were true.

It dropped her to the ground, leaving black blood pulsing from her throat as the beast raged. It was as if hell was opening.

She felt billions of invisible eyes piercing her; the thing's form turned to solid black as its face opened in a scream, and the first wisps of smoke appeared at its feet. The mouth of the being spread open—it was as if it was swallowing itself.

It burned with a deep golden fire that consumed it entirely in less than three seconds; a fire that stretched toward her skin, one last desperate attack.

She appeared instantly outside in the moonlight, with the cold and madness echoing inside her head. Standing on the sidewalk, she saw a moth frozen in the air under a streetlamp. It was like she was in a time bubble; everything was under dark, pentagram-shaped clouds. Outside of that, nothing moved. She was far enough away to notice a border, something that made the entire event invisible to the outside world.

She watched as the black glutinous nightmare coating the building transformed into giant arms, its claws smashing through floors. Every strike was fast and precise, igniting everything around it in cold, crystalline fire.

All that was left of the orphanage was a pile of ash; both buildings were leveled in a matter of seconds. The arms burst into cinders and blew away in the wind.

Daren was breathing heavily when she finally got to her feet, but at least the carnage had stopped.

The moth bounced off her forehead as if she had just appeared in front of it. The bubble was gone. The clouds vanished.

Daren sniffled, and wiping tears from her eyes, she turned to walk away. *I failed. No matter what I chose, it was bad. How can life be fair if every choice ends in pain? What am I going to do now?*

Then there was a tap on her shoulder. "Excuse me. Isn't this where the Blissful Havens Orphanage is supposed to be?"

G.R. MORRIS

PART NINE

COMPOSITION OF THE REAL

"Physical concepts are free creations of the human mind, and are not, however it may seem, uniquely determined by the external world."

—Albert Einstein

CHAPTER TWENTY-TWO
"We are what we believe we are."

—Socrates

I s this how you imagined the afterlife?" His own voice called out
to him from a distance.

Kevin was sitting in a white chair in the middle of a plain, flat
circle that appeared to be hovering like a cloud of spiraling energy.
There was no breeze. The stale air was dry and nearly hot enough to
evaporate sweat.

Beyond the circle, the world was a bleached blur, a soupy mess
of incomprehensible shapes.

Kevin placed a hand on his chest and felt his heart almost beat.
"Robert!" he screamed, and the blurs sharpened into puffy white
clouds. The pain from the tips of his fingers digging into his palms
should have reminded him he was still alive.

The pressure should have drawn blood. Even his toes curled in
his shoes, as if his feet were showing their disdain when they pressed
hard against the flat ground.

Kevin heard what sounded like his own voice speak again. "He
didn't kill you."

Anger turned to fear. Breathing heavily and shaking, tapping the ground for stability with his feet, he stood up.

"Wha—wha—?" Kevin scrunched up his eyes, trying to focus on the large rectangle in front of him.

He paused and stared at a large, blurry frame that sat on the blurry street against the indistinct backdrop.

"It's a cab, you idiot. Get in!" A voice that sounded much like his own was speaking to him.

His vision began to clear. It was as if all his senses were waking for the first time. He turned around and looked down at the glowing white bench at a crowded bus stop. Hundreds of faceless people were going about their day in a wondrously colorful metropolitan city.

They were tall, featureless, skeletal beings, shrouded in a blurry fog. Creeping around in the distance, they moved sluggishly, as if underwater. Their arms were twice as long as their bodies. They dangled at their sides, dragging the tops of their hands over the glowing streets. Their heads ticked from side to side, like a strange metronome to every step. *Click . . . clack . . .*

Kevin heard a collection of noises just a few feet from where he sat. Pain struck his head. He cupped his ears. "Aghhhh!"

Closing his eyes, he felt as if an invisible field was quieting the acoustic bombardment and protecting him from the deafening attack. A multitude of smells and muffled sounds stormed his location. A barrage of information assaulted his senses.

"Wow." Looking up, Kevin saw cities floating thousands of feet in the air, obstructing his view of the sky. The ground, although transparent, was polished to a clean luster, appearing as deep as the sea.

"It's like I'm not even here . . . a thousand years of preparation, and this is the treatment I get," the cabbie mumbled. "Come on, I'm sittin' here!" His Brooklyn accent was almost practiced.

G.R. MORRIS

Kevin felt the warm ground vibrate beneath his feet and through his shoes. Looking down at his body, he saw he was still wearing a white T-shirt, blue jeans, and tennis shoes, all of which were just as transparent as the ghostly pavement he stood on.

I must be dead.

Considering his surroundings, the heat was the least of his concerns. "So ghosts sweat?" he said, pinching his soaked T-shirt.

Click . . . clack . . . click.

"Amateur. You still believe you are in your body? Come now, anointed one. I don't have all day."

Billions of pictures, some three-dimensional images, words, and symbols, all moved under a gray, glowing overlay that comprised the surface. Bright colors pulsated through the river of information beneath his feet. It flowed among the faces of his past; shimmering hues of iridescence and lustrous beams of light rolled, undefiled, beneath the transparent surface.

"Cool! What is all this?"

The things were drawing closer. *Click, clack, click.* But Kevin was still in a daze of wonderment and shock.

The cabbie rolled his eyes. "Yes, yes, it's very nice. Fantastic. You noticed the ground."

Kevin's head still numb, he squinted, trying to look through the fog. "Where are you?"

The sound was getting louder. *Click, clack, click, clack.*

"I'm not gonna keep holding your hand like this."

Kevin heard some fingers snap. The fog began to clear. His eyes grew large and his jaw dropped as he witnessed the fantastic landscape of lush greens mixed with a rainbow of color.

Even the air seemed to sparkle. Kevin swallowed, trying to push saliva past the lump in his throat. *This is too beautiful to be hell . . .*

I hope.

His entire body tingled. "Whoa," he said, looking through his palm at the open cab door. He was like a ghost; a bright glowing transparent silhouette of his former self.

"Hey, dummy. I said get in the car. Now!" Leaning down across the passenger seat was an older version of his face looking back at him through eyes magnified behind large, dirty, coke-bottle glasses. It was a mirror image, except for a beard sprinkled with potato chips and a torn brown leather jacket. His yellow-stained white T-shirt, torn blue jeans, and backward I LOVE NY baseball cap completed his stereotype.

"Whoa, what the—?" Kevin almost flinched seeing himself sitting there.

Click clack, click clack click, clack, clack clack clack.

Grabbing the side of the car door, Kevin paused. "Who? What are—?"

Something grabbed him. Long, pale fingers gripped both shoulders like a vise. Its hollow digits flattened and meshed into Kevin's upper torso. His transparent body was being filled like a glass with spatters of color containing images, pictures, and symbols.

"I wish you would stop imagining these things as monsters; you're giving them purpose. You're making them attack you. Pfft." The cabbie laughed.

Its hands did not move, yet its extensive arms flapped around almost as if in a seizure. Its head ticked at such a rate that it shook in a vibrating blur.

As the thing poured into him, he heard a bestial, high-pitched noise, like billions of warped words screaming all at once.

The cabbie leaned back in his seat. "Ha, ha, ha! Should've listened to me, son."

Spinning from its grip, Kevin beheld the faceless figure. It stumbled backward. The ticking of its head slowed.

The connection was broken, and the color was yanked from Kevin's body along with it. He could now clearly see the city's inhabitants: the knuckle-dragging demons that populated his mind.

Like incomplete mannequins, the creatures were almost entirely featureless: no hair, no mouth—except for a small inch-long cut where one would be. He felt the sound like a burst of wind exploding from the form's diminutive slit. A solid, genderless doll with no apparent joints or segments and no clothing.

"Spooky."

It bent and moved at will; it was rigid as steel in parts of its body in one moment, and in the next it was flexible as a wet noodle. As it moved, the arms sometimes flopped across the ground, and when it raised them, they were stiff and unyielding.

"Oh, come on, kid. Let's get out of here!"

Its arms and legs were aberrantly thin, like a collection of unearthly bones coated in ghostly white flesh.

"I can handle myself, thanks." Kevin stumbled backward, leaning against the cab. The creature's hollow fingers reached out like writhing, demonic snakes. He saw strands like hair swirling deep inside them, twining around, ready to strike. "Crap." Kevin turned his head side to side, looking for some kind of weapon.

"I'm done trusting people," Kevin said.

"What—what are these things?" Peering into the face of the lunging figure, he saw something nearly hidden behind the facade, deep inside the doll's head.

Almost hypnotized by its strange, chaotic beauty, Kevin stared.

Swirling like in a blender, symbols churned and circled around words just within the pale container that was its skin.

Kevin was yanked down by his shirt into the passenger seat. "Now you've done it!" a voice said from behind him.

The cab driver raised a shimmering diamond handgun encrusted in gems.

Kevin's eyes widened.

"Leeches."

A beam of light swirled around the barrel, igniting into a solid shaft of white luminance erupting into the creature's chest; the creature flailed its arms as it stumbled back. White symbols poured from its wound.

"Don't just sit there gawkin', kid! Close that door!" the cabbie yelled.

Kevin slammed the door. "Thanks for almost blowing my nose off."

The muffled background noise exploded into a roaring scream. Every being in the city was now targeting them with their cries. Thousands of the creatures, their arms raised, emerged from the blurry surroundings and came running toward the cab. The cabbie looked at Kevin and said, "Okay, Mr. Independent, what would have you done about all of them?"

"Be gone, foul villains!" Kevin smirked, snapping his fingers.

Nothing.

Kevin shrugged his shoulders.

The cabbie raised an eyebrow and hit the gas. In a blink, the metal of the car turned to light and shot through the strange streets.

"Independence comes to those who earn it and who are ready," the cabbie said.

———————◆———————

A few minutes later . . .

G.R. MORRIS

The car slowed to cruising speed, and the driver looked into the rearview mirror. "There's no white rabbit here, Alice," he said, chomping through a chaw of gum. "Hey, pal, what do you think of your savior's journey so far?"

"Suck it, that's what I think."

"This is what you signed up for, isn't it?"

Kevin folded his arms. "Just let me out."

"You chose this door both before you were born and in Robert's room. Don't you remember?"

"I've been fed this load of bull my whole life. Please stop."

"The truth comes to everyone eventually. It's their choice to deny it or accept it."

Kevin sighed, staring through his hands and arms. "I don't think I did anything to deserve going to hell."

"No one does anything they don't want to. I thought you would have figured that out by now."

"So are you taking me to meet Satan?"

"You're not dead." He smiled.

"What the hell do you—?"

"Welcome"—he let go of the steering wheel and panned both hands along the windshield—"to your mind." As the cabbie spoke the word, Kevin looked out the windows, and the landscape came into focus.

It was a world of beautiful chaos.

Of the place where they traveled, there were only two constants: the information street in which they drove, and a large palace far off in the distance made of multicolored crystals.

They had moved beyond the cities in the sky and into an open space.

The laws of physics were chaotic, as if warped from an M.C.

Escher painting; he saw other faceless creatures, upside down, walking on large, hovering orbs covered in stairs that led nowhere. The clouds were a kaleidoscope of constant changes with swirling color moving in prisms.

Countless crystalline butterflies soared high in the sky and exploded, pouring color into the clouds. Still high above the cab, mixed with the fluttering fragments, came wavy images of Robert's fang-toothed grin. *Ooo . . . that, ooo . . . I'm gonna . . .*

These were meshed with pictures of his mother and his comic book heroes.

"You live here?" Kevin asked.

On either side of the cab, separated by the transparent stream of information on which they traveled, was a multitude of foliage growing from an undulating foundation of white and black.

"I live in the minds of everyone, off and on. It's much too toxic to take up permanent residence."

Kevin's attention was still focused on the environment. "This place is crazy, so . . . great . . . I'm nuts."

Various sized plant life—some towering hundreds of feet into the sky and others the size of a one-story building—resembled living tree houses, crystalline yet palpitating and breathing with life. The branches spread into various structures, like veins on a heart, covering perfect squares, circles, and large rectangles.

"Everyone, and I do mean everyone, has a little bit of crazy," the cabbie replied. Half of the buildings were white, and the rest were black, but each of them had reflective surfaces and were the only opaque items in the city.

Hundreds of the faceless figures scraped their arms across the undulating surface, unaffected by the motion.

Many of the monsters were snatched up, wrapped in the plants' colorful veins, and pulled into the structures.

"Not more of those things again. Just what other kinds of crazy creatures are in this place?"

"Why are you asking me this question?"

Kevin shook his head. "Because I want to know?"

"We're inside your mind. You see all the monsters you want."

"What's that supposed to mean?"

The cabbie pointed at him. "It means if you think up a monster, you'll see one. You create your own problems. You can't separate the motor unit of the brain from the sensory. You aren't a passive collector of data since you can't look at something without focus. You can't focus without desire to look. Which means you choose your influences."

At the center of the city was a diamond palace surrounding an enormous tree, its trunk an endless tower of light. Filling the sky were its branches, like transparent tentacles covering a beating heart, shivering with countless faceless creatures swimming through rivers of words and forgotten images.

"I thought the default position was to not believe," Kevin said.

"No. You actively harvest information, which means you can't get rid of interpretation. Blank slates can't process information. You either believe in a proposition or you believe in an alternative proposition, like belief in a default null hypothesis."

If not for the monsters running through the streets, this place would be beautiful.

The cab traveled along one of the branches. Every road teemed with pictures and symbols.

"We're on the River of Information . . . the birthplace of thought. This entire reality is how your consciousness interprets your worldview." He pointed at the plants and buildings. "The architecture, the entire landscape, everything you perceive as solid is or includes but are not your beliefs; those leechy faceless pals of yours walking around are thoughts. The thing in—"

"Yep, I'm nuts."

"The big, shiny thing in the center is your focus and consciousness."

"All the people are heading toward it," Kevin said.

"Of course they are. A belief is a thought you make real. You have a body because you believe you do."

Kevin pulled down the vanity mirror and stared at his transparent face.

"That's not really a face you're looking at. You are still stuck believing in these limitations." The cabbie pulled out a knife from his boot. "I'll bet you think this is real."

"I think—"

The blade jammed through Kevin's throat and into the headrest.

Kevin jumped in his seat and pressed his arms against the dashboard. "Oh, fu—I'm sick of being screwed with," he said, rubbing his neck.

"Trust is wonderful, isn't it? I knew you would believe I'd never hurt you. Thus, you escape harm."

"I get screwed over by people I trust all the time. And it never works out that way."

"Not here. Not in this place. As you can see," the cabbie continued, pointing to the dashboard, "things are solid when you believe they are.

"Can you take a guess at what those fancy, colorful lads are coming out of the buildings?"

Kevin turned his head and looked exasperated. "Just who are you?" he asked, looking at his own bearded face sitting across from him.

The cabbie smiled. "That took a while. Who do you think I am?"

"I'm not playing."

"I'm you."

Kevin sighed. "No, you're not. I'm me."

"Quite right. I am not a projection of your mind like everything else you're seeing, but we're all connected. Think of the heart, the lungs, and the brain. They are all separate, but united in purpose. There is no real individuality, even though everyone believes they are apart from everyone, alone. We all stem from the same energy. Energy and thought are united even beyond this world, so in a sense, the land of the real is very much the same as this one.

"When you are ready, you will feel this connection. You will be able to communicate with reality itself, because you are a part of it, and it is a part of you."

"You haven't answered my question."

"I have gone by many names. The Holy Ghost, Azrael, the Spirit of Truth, or most commonly—"

Kevin was staring at a grimacing skull. "Death." Fear splashed over his face.

"Most people trust images of things older and weaker than them—you know, old men with really long white beards wearing nonthreatening white robes. I have not used this visage in hundreds of years. For some reason, it doesn't inspire cooperation," the cabbie said, clacking his bony teeth.

And with that, his face swirled back into Kevin's. "I knew that you were the only person you trusted; that's why I look like you."

"What you are, right now, is consciousness. Your spiritual essence."

"Your heart does not beat. You do not breathe. As far as the doctors of your time can tell, you have no brain waves; they are too low to detect. You live because your essence remains in your physical body. You live because at this moment you requested that I keep you alive, and I agreed."

Kevin was still staring out his window at the glowing rainbow silhouettes leaving their buildings. They resembled the faceless creatures, except with human arms, lips for a mouth, and slits for eyes.

They were each carrying a briefcase, divided vertically down the center. Half of the cases were shimmering white, half were coated in dark black swirling shadows. Each of the multicolored figures was standing in front of its plants at the base.

Kevin blinked. "What—what the hell are th—"

"Your past beliefs; that's why they carry those cases. The other faceless pale creatures roam this world as empty shells. Thoughts without information, without substance.

"A thought's purpose is to justify its own existence, to become real. Each thought connects itself with past beliefs, and each belief carries with it luggage of memories that have been assigned both a negative and positive emotional color."

Kevin watched the sequence as they roared down the road.

Tentacles burst from the foliage and whipped an empty shell creature into a building, filled it with color, then pulled it down to one of the more humanlike briefcase-carrying figures.

The hollowed-out fingers of the faceless beings pushed into the arms of the multihued, more human silhouettes.

A few moments later, they merged, half of them dragging a pale arm behind them and the other half holding the case.

Streams of energy rushed around them as the newly made beings walked toward the center of the city.

The cabbie popped a bubble. "Your power—all power—starts from within. You are going to have to learn to focus and control everything.

"It's quite easy to let the darkness in and remain negative. You must work at the positive. If you let even one bad thought fester unchecked . . . well, your savior days could be over. Neurons that fire together, wire together. The shadow is filled with the darkness and connected to every evil act. It is a demonic tree that everyone chooses to grow from birth, and it takes over their mind. You know right from wrong deep down, which means every evil act is self-deception."

Kevin pursed his lips. "The hell?"

The cabbie took another piece of gum out and added it to the already large wad in his mouth. "Emotions are linked to memories, and memories are linked to emotions. Think of times when you were angry. It is no coincidence that other memories stemming from anger come surging into your mind. The flooding emotions and bad memories stack on one another, and before you know it, you lash out; you act irrationally and make a choice. Sometimes you lose control though, because the shadow takes over. The darkness bleeds into your mind and treats you like its puppet. But only because you let it. Every choice someone makes is based on this universe, their biased worldview. Even an irrational act, in actuality, has a thought that preceded it."

Kevin could see the cabbie's cigarette-and-coffee-stained smile through his beard. "How do I defeat the shadow?"

"Recognition of its existence will only delay the inevitable. The shadow has its roots in hell. It transcends the mind and is propagated by sin and permeates the subconscious grown by self-deception, or lies. Repression only makes it stronger. The only way is to adopt the opposite, a transcendental light grown by truth.

You have to believe in a god. God is truth. You can't just say it, or pretend, because that would be dishonest."

"Can't I just be a good person?"

"Okay, so Stalin and Hitler. How many dead people do you need as evidence that a godless existence does not work? Soon it will be revealed that many priests have sexually abused young boys. Even they will fall to evil, but at least they are on the right road.

You want to go to the destination of the good when you aren't even going in the right direction? Good luck."

"Atheists can be good people too."

"They can perform good acts, but they will either die before their mind becomes like Stalin's or they will change. The shadow grows, and if not tended to will take over. They will become a bad tree out of their own choices and will be completely out of control."

The cabby pointed at him. "Don't be confused. Prisons will be filled with those who claim belief. Only one percent of all people can be correctly categorized as actually believing. Hypocrites everywhere."

"I can't just choose to believe in something."

"You are not your mind, and you can rewire your entire brain, including all preferences."

The car sped over the white transparent roads, which turned into a massive bridge. Coalescing from snaking streams of pulsating energy rising in the middle of the road was a demon's mouth. Kevin glanced at its teeth, then back at the cabbie, then back at the red tongue that flopped out. The cab rolled into a dimly lit tunnel. The walls appeared to be glass, and dark creatures pounded on the large tube.

Kevin's eyes widened as the cabbie shifted into a higher gear.

The creatures were mirrored copies of the faceless monsters he had just witnessed, except they were comprised of spiraling clouds and shadow and, of course, their foot-long crimson claws. The ones not pounding with their fists against the glass were frantically scraping away at the clear surface.

"Scary, aren't they?" The cabbie smiled.

Kevin grabbed the cabbie's knee, forcing his leg down on the gas pedal.

CHAPTER TWENTY-THREE

*"The self is not something ready-made, but something
in continuous formation through choice of action."*

—John Dewey

Y our fear causes us danger, not them," the cabbie said.

Cracks like growing spiderwebs spread through the passageway. As the fingernails pushed into the cracks, the cabbie grasped Kevin's shoulder. He pointed both fingers at his pupils. "Look at me. Focus on my eyes."

Kevin, almost in a state of hysteria, paused for a second and complied.

"Breathe," the cabbie said, placing a palm on Kevin's chest. "Calm. Slow down."

"What are those things?"

The cabbie grasped the wheel and dodged glass fragments that had fallen into the tunnel. He shook his head and *slap*—struck Kevin's forehead with an open palm. Kevin's head jerked back and hit the back of the seat. "Hey! Asshole!"

The growth of the cracks suddenly came to a halt.

Kevin grasped the cabbie's neck; the cabbie pointed one finger at the windshield. The glass of the passageway had turned to metal, and there was a glowing light at its end.

Kevin loosened his grip.

"Sometimes anger is more useful than fear."

Kevin folded his arms.

"Those were your dark, destructive thoughts. Not created by you, but placed there by another."

"A minister," Kevin said.

"He's trying to invade your mind."

Kevin placed his hands on the sides of his head. "What's the use of having that gun of yours if you don't use it to kill that guy?"

"That is beyond my power. I'm the counterbalance to the voice people hear in their head telling them to do something bad."

They exited the tunnel and were back on the transparent road, but this time it curved among giant multicolored trees in a vast forest.

Kevin raised his eyes and nodded. "So you manipulate people into doing what you want."

"Control is an illusion. Think of an average Joe. Suppose there was a million dollars sitting in his driveway. Suppose he won it in a contest, and he just needs to go pick it up. What do you think Joe does?"

"I don't get it," Kevin said.

"You think he says, 'I'll show 'em; I'll prove my free agency by burning that money'?"

Kevin laughed. "So we're not free?"

"Think of it this way," the cabbie said. "Joe walks outside to get the money. He could turn around, but why? He's already thinking about how to spend it. He doesn't even consider going back into the house. He's already made the choice: to pick up the money.

"The only problem with fate is when it's an undesirable outcome, something not chosen."

Kevin managed a deadpan expression. "Excuse me, Monsieur Death. What does this have to do with me?"

"To be free of a prison, one must first be aware of his shackles." The cabbie turned his head and stared at him. "Why do you think I'm here?"

"I'm really sick of these games," Kevin said.

"Your old beliefs, your old ways of thinking, must die. I'm here to kill your old self. You must go beyond the limits of your physical body."

"Ridiculous. I'll just sit here and let fate do all the work for me."

"You do what you want to do. That is the true essence of fate. Life is in the experience of the journey."

Kevin sat silently and, crossing his arms, stared at the transparent flowing foliage inches beyond the window. "Where are we now?"

"You tell me, we never left."

Kevin whipped his head around to the driver. "What?"

"You think we're moving, so we move. Your limiting beliefs are stuck three-dimensionally. The background changes while we remain stationary."

Kevin watched the trees pass by the window. "How can I deny my eyes?"

The cabbie smiled. "Think you're using your eyes right now?"

Kevin ran a finger over an eyelid.

"Are you familiar with lucid dreams?"

Kevin nodded. "You can control your dreams, and you know you're dreaming, yes?" He saw the trees begin to fade. "What's happening?"

"What would happen if someone in a dream told you that you were dreaming?"

Like pulling away a curtain, the background changed to an empty city complete with gray, nondescript buildings. The street was gray, the sky was gray, and even the windows were gray.

"This is where you doubt; where you still have questions. So fire away," the driver said.

"Is the Bible true?"

The cab driver rolled down his window. "No matter how many times I've been asked that question, I have still not come up with an easy way to answer it. Yes, it's true, but—" he spit out his gum onto the road and pulled out another pack.

Kevin raised his arms. "But what?"

Another gray building erupted from the ground in front of the cab. The brakes slammed, and Kevin's palms struck the dash.

The car was thrust into reverse. "The original Bible is the best source for truth, but even that is incomplete."

"Incomplete? What about what it says in Revelations about not adding stuff?"

"That was talking about Revelations, not about the Bible. And even with the first Bible, there are pages missing, and it tells you only what you need to know."

"I need to know the truth; that's what I need."

"It's not going to talk about aliens; it talks about only the things you need to know, so there are things you have to discover for yourself. Much like when you discovered 'thou shall not kill' was mistranslated from 'thou shall not murder.'"

"Why wouldn't God just make the Bible complete?"

The cabbie rolled his eyes. "You should have figured that out by now. Knowledge is a gift as well as a curse."

Driving down the gray path, Kevin saw the cracks along the foundation of the buildings begin to grow. "So the truth is out there; we just have to find it?"

The cabbie smiled. "Oh, it's out there, but for some, if they pray a hundred times, they'll still never get an answer."

"What!? That hardly seems fair."

"You forgot what Robert said?" The driver took off his thick glasses and began rubbing them on his stained shirt. "You cannot sarcastically pray. The truth will be revealed to those who really want it, who wanted it in the preexistence. God would not reveal the truth to someone if doing so damns them to misery, unless of course misery is what they wanted."

Kevin watched his hands phase through each other. "Who wants misery?"

"For the people who choose darkness, the light of heaven would be hell."

Far off on the horizon was a fiery pillar of light flowing from the ground and spiraling into the sky.

"So what about the Book of Job?"

"I'm so sick of being asked about that one. I mean, we named him 'job'!"

"That's not how you pronounce it, but what's employment have to do with it?"

"It's meant to be a hint. But I thought it was a good one. Look, you gain light only by earning it. Many sins are trying to get something for nothing, like rape, theft, gambling, and an attitude of entitlement. Job's journey was to show the world that you must earn your way, like a job. Faith without works is dead. You need both."

"Didn't God deceive him?"

"Like I said, God didn't tell him everything because Job didn't want him to. Yes, his family members choosing to die was part of the plan.

"He wanted nothing more than to have an audience with God and have eternal rewards in heaven. Personally, I think he got a great deal. He's a rock star up there who never retires and is forever loved. And even when he was on earth, God gave him a ton of stuff after he went through it."

The buildings exploded into bright energy. Liquescent colors fell on the car like rain.

Kevin closed his eyes.

"Think of something good," the cabbie said.

The fluid began to grow around the moving car, forming human figures. Kevin smiled brightly, mischievously, and then opened his eyes.

The driver gave him a look. "We don't have time for this."

Thousands of supermodels in bikinis scampered after the slowing car.

"Please have sex with me!" they screamed.

The cab slowed almost to a complete stop.

The string-bikinied, perfectly toned, big-breasted women were getting closer.

"This is not going to end well." The cabbie shook his head.

"What?"

"You'll see."

As the first women got a foot away from the cab, the ones behind them pulled on their hair, stopping them from grabbing the handle.

"No! He's having sex with me first!" those in the front yelled.

Then the slapping and scratching started.

Continuous screams of "He's mine!" could be heard from the erupting chaos that followed.

Slaps turned to punches and hair-pulling into neck-snapping.

"What the hell. Why?" Kevin screamed as the car started moving again.

"You want beautiful women, but you must believe you deserve it and can achieve it. Desire opens the door; you still got to walk through it."

The chaos of women crumbled into liquid colors as the car sped away.

"Great. So even my fantasies suck. It might as well be real."

"Who says the real world is different?"

"Um, everyone? I can't just will myself a pizza."

"People believe things are a certain way by default. To walk through walls, you have to believe that you can more than others believe you can't. This only opens communication to the wall, making it possible. You will be in control of all that is, but only because the intelligences within all matter will trust or have 'faith' in you."

They stopped in front of the giant pillar of fire erupting from what looked like a hundred-foot-wide hole in the ground. "What is this?" Kevin said, staring into the blazing inferno.

"Here we go!" The cabbie floored it.

Kevin's back slammed into his seat, his hand nearly gripping the leather off the door's armrest.

The fire engulfed the car, yet the cab did not burn. "You're gonna need to learn to loosen up there, buddy."

They tumbled down the chasm. "You assho—"

The car stopped and righted itself. "We're here," the cabbie said.

They hovered in front of a fiery ball a hundred stories high bursting with torrid storms of pillars. The pillars surged in all directions, making the chaos resemble a circulatory system.

"This is your spiritual heart."

They moved slowly, circling the ball and keeping their distance.

As they got closer to it, Kevin felt a glow, a warm tingle in his chest. The feeling moved through his body. He took a deep breath and relished the sensation.

He was glowing; light bounced off the mirrors. "I've never felt anything like this; this is incredible."

"That, right there, is the feeling of truth, of purity, of righteousness," the cabbie said.

Kevin pressed his hands to the glass. "This is pretty neat. But what is it exactly?"

"Have you ever not trusted someone and then trusted them later?"

"Your point?"

"Have you ever looked back on that and knew both choices were the right ones?"

"Yeah, but I—"

"You think believers in God just look in a book and say, 'Gee, murder is wrong. I think I'll stop doing that.'?"

Kevin smiled.

"This is the source of your power that allows you to see someone's true nature."

Kevin looked at the cab driver and saw a circular glow sparkle in his chest. "Oh, I get it, like if they're good or bad?" He could actually feel the warm tingle of his goodness.

"Everyone, of course, has this ability to discern good from evil. Some people choose to wash it in darkness, typically through backward rationale. But some people just like being jerks."

"Cool. Everyone can see shiny things in people's chests?"

"You're unique in that respect." The cabbie popped a bubble. "Your power is timeless; it can see the future outcome of who people will choose to be."

"Great. So I see a bad guy, know he's going to be bad, and take care of him. Easy."

"Not so fast. Some people are misguided and fall to temptation, but their spiritual heart is good, and because of this they will eventually choose the light. But, yes, some are just bad guys."

"So just forgive and forget?"

"It's up to the person to atone for the evil things he's done."

It was as if Kevin's mind was an eye and it had blinked. The cab was driving on streets once more, traveling through the endless plant life sprouting along the road.

Kevin's eyes dilated. "Whoa."

"What you do tomorrow," the cabbie said, "will profoundly affect the future of everyone, of all existence."

Kevin shook his head. "This is stupid. What if I make the wrong choice?"

"Every choice is the right one."

"And if people die because of my choice?"

The cabbie blew a big blue bubble, and it popped. "Then, they die. Mistakes are just an unforeseen outcome."

"Being the Holy Ghost, can't you see every possible outcome?" Kevin asked.

"I'm not God. It's hubris to think anyone can interfere with a plan created by an all-powerful being."

"You mean I have no choice but to be this"—Kevin gritted his teeth—"'savior'?"

"The cosmic plan is all-inclusive; it could be a part of that plan that you die and never save humanity."

"This is stupid. What does God do? Is he a part of this plan?"

"Certainly," the cabbie continued. "A god has to deal with the law of interference. In other words, how does one all-powerful being assist in the lives of his children while simultaneously giving them free will? What if his children cry out for help because they're about to die? Does he just make an exception?"

"Yes."

"So does he cure them if there's a widespread plague, an epidemic?"

"Sure." Kevin nodded.

"What about war? One country decides they want someone else's stuff. What does he do then for those who cry for help?"

Kevin hunted for a rebuttal but sat silent.

"Does he interfere?"

Kevin's face was vacant.

"It's simple," the cabbie continued. "He assists them before they were born. It can only be through someone with that much power, who can see every outcome and every decision and know you well enough to know what you want to help you choose your lives. This means every miracle that appears without reason was, in fact, patterned by an agreement with God. In other words, his actions with humanity are in accordance with the agreement, just like anyone else's."

"Okay, right. Whatever."

The cabbie slammed on the brakes; Kevin's head whipped forward.

"Look, pal, this is important. You must understand that every single word, every action in life is necessary. Life is a puzzle with no missing pieces; every word I am saying will guide you one way or the other. Each word out of my mouth is said because you and I wanted it to be said."

Just off in the distance, Kevin noticed a building—an actual hospital—that looked as real as any he had seen.

"Well, that's out of place," he said.

G.R. MORRIS

The cabbie dipped his hat. "Of course it is. I put it there."

As they pulled into the empty parking lot, Kevin saw images of normal people going about their day inside the building.

"Real people?"

"Indeed. A window into the real world," the cabbie said. "I influence the minds of every human being, just as Kain does."

"Sounds like a lot of work, even for both of you. Everyone?"

"The purpose of Kain and the darkness is to influence people into choosing evil, to offer an alternative to light. Without them, choice would certainly be limited."

"So I chose to have this minister inside me?"

The cabbie nodded.

"Okay, fine. Now, I choose for you to get it out of me."

"That's not what you wanted. You needed him in here so good can now be a part of you as well."

The cabbie got out of the car, and Kevin opened the passenger door.

"It's overlapping the data streams?" he said, looking down at solid pavement.

The large double doors to the hospital slid open to reveal rippling blue water blocking the path. The cabbie paused, smiled at Kevin, and walked into it. The water swallowed his body, leaving only fading ripples. Kevin stared into the blue of the shimmering aquatic vertical wall.

"Um. You may want to decide quickly. Turn around," he heard the cabbie say.

Kevin glanced back to find hundreds of the phantasmal thin blank creatures swarming a mere dozen feet away.

"Oh crap ," he said, closing his eyes. Stepping backward into the liquid, he could feel the cold of the water rush over him. When he opened his eyes, he was standing in the lobby of what appeared to be a Los Angeles hospital.

"Hey, I know this place!" he said, looking out into the now-crowded parking lot.

"We are no longer in your mind. We have projected ourselves into the real world." As Kevin turned toward the voice, he saw the forehead of a stranger less than an inch from his face.

Before he could move out of the way, the man passed right through him.

"Wow. Nothing. I felt nothing."

"You won't," the cabbie said, "until you believe you can. You're still a projection of your mind." The cab driver was leaning with an elbow on the clerk's white information desk.

Kevin looked around the hospital; it became obvious no one could see them. He pointed at the cabbie's elbow pushing against the desk. "How are you doing that? Why don't you just pass right through?"

"Why don't you just fall through the floor?" he replied, turning around. "Come. Follow me." He walked down the crowded hall.

As Kevin followed steps behind him, dodging the crowd of people, his eyes widened. There was something strange about the people in this world as well. "I thought you said we were in the real world." Kevin looked up and down at each person passing by.

The cabbie dragged his hand through the walls of the hallway. "I see you noticed the diamond walkers."

Every person in the hallway seemed to have a bright glow and a surging, diamond-crusted crystal at the center of his chest. Tubes of energy, like veins, spread through their bodies, extending to their skin, which was nothing but glowing white energy.

G.R. MORRIS

As Kevin looked at their eyes, it was as if he were staring into an abyss. Under a layer of white fluttering energy that displayed facial expressions was another face, a deadpan stare, an artificial shape formed by energy.

"These things are everywhere. So I'm trading one creepy existence for another?"

The cabbie pushed through double doors.

"Nursery?" Kevin said, looking at the markings on the wall.

The cabbie stood in a hall, pointing at the long window displaying the newborns. "You are as stubborn as they come. You still hold to belief in chance, in randomness."

Kevin smirked and placed his hands against the glass.

"More than one-third of the souls I come across in my job are what people call accidents," the cabbie continued. "But as you know, accidents are the result of ignorance—another gift of free will. They come from cheating wives, one-night stands, rape; they're just brought into the world unintentionally. If not for what you call accidents, they would never be born.

"These children would be luck, a series of chance encounters, and a multitude of amazing coincidences. Chance, much like randomness, is at its very essence unknown, unpredictable, and has no cause. They are without pattern, without purpose. With chance, it is impossible for anything to happen for a reason. Chance and randomness have no reason. Chance is illusion."

"But chance can have a pattern," Kevin argued.

"Wrong. If you see the pattern, you're not playing by chance; it becomes a certainty."

The Holy Ghost paced back and forth down the hall. He stopped and turned around, holding a glowing coin the size of a dollar. "Since you believe so much in chance, I'll give you that option," he said.

Kevin took the glimmering coin and examined it. One side was bright gold and showed the head of a white, glowing angel complete with shimmering halo. The other was black and appeared to be made of charcoal. This side had a devil's tail, dark and full of moving shadows of demons and spiraling mists.

"Neat coin. Can I keep it?"

"This is how you want to live your life? Flip the coin: Heads, you go to heaven, tails, you burn forever in hell."

Kevin's jaw dropped.

The cabbie smiled and opened his hand to Kevin. "Alternatively, you can simply pick which option you want. You can choose."

Kevin thought for a moment, glaring at the coin and putting it back in the cabbie's palm.

"Nobody ever chooses the coin. Why leave your life in the hands of something else instead of designing it yourself through your own choices?"

Kevin's entire body began to flutter. "What was that?"

"That little lightbulb above your head is starting to turn on. You see, Kevin, if everything is chance, then we only choose between things that happen to us based on coincidences, or good or bad luck.

"Either our choices are accidents, or they're not. If they're accidents—just chance that I did not choose otherwise—it's surely irrational to hold people responsible for choosing as they do." The cabbie turned around. "If it's not an accident that someone chooses one thing over another, well then . . ."

Kevin shook his head. "I don't like the idea that I can't change my mind."

"Is it better to hold a man responsible for actions that happen by chance or for ones that arise from a choice that challenges and grows his character?"

G.R. MORRIS

Kevin nodded.

"If something is undetermined, there is no cause, and hence, it's by accident. Obviously, if things just happen, they happen randomly. It's impossible for someone to be the source of his own behavior if choices are based on the arbitrary."

Kevin was interrupted by his body flickering and almost fading away. Pressing his hands against the wall, he composed himself. "Wh—what was that?"

"Good. We don't have much time. My purpose here is almost complete. Look again at the children."

The hospital's newborns were displayed in their plastic containers, all lined up on carts like a typical nursery.

Then he saw why he had been brought there. The babies were glowing; every one of them had diamonds in their chests.

"I don't understand. If diamond walkers aren't—"

"The walkers are increasing in number. They believe they are human. They give birth as humans do. They feel as humans do. They even appear to bleed as humans do. Do not be fooled; they are not human."

"Wouldn't people notice?" Kevin asked.

"They are replaced when time is stopped."

Kevin turned away from the window. "Why should I care?"

"Force is an element of evil. It feeds the darkness. The darkness is the enemy of life, of progression."

"Wha—" Kevin fell to his knees and gripped his skull with both hands. "What's happening to me?"

Kevin was swallowed by vertigo. Everything around him suddenly became a blur, and pain pulsed through his skull.

Kneeling on the ground, he moaned, "Help me!"

"Your worldview is shattering," the cabbie said, placing his hand on Kevin's shoulder.

The vibrations stopped; Kevin could see, and he stood up. "Send me back. What's going on?"

"How much confidence do you put in a leader who believes in luck? Imagine for a moment if during one of his inspirational speeches he says, 'We sure lucked out, and we're going to win only if we're lucky.'

"The savior must believe luck does not exist. Don't ignore that voice in your head that says you can't; instead, control it, and make it tell you that you can."

Death placed his hand on Kevin's forehead, and in a blink, he was sitting inside the cab once more.

"Why didn't we travel like that in the first place?" Kevin asked.

"Leaving the astral plane is different," the cabbie said, flooring the gas pedal.

They sped over the roads of flowing information and headed toward the diamond palace in the center of the world. The road behind them crumbled, breaking apart, tumbling down toward other levels of the city and quickly fading away.

The structures in front of them were flickering, the ones in the distance were collapsing, and some were exploding into light.

Kevin rolled down the window, stuck his head out into the roaring screams, and peered into the sky. Every branch of the lavish world was deteriorating. Debris from the city above them rained from the sky, only to disappear hundreds of feet from the ground.

The faceless creatures were suffering the same fate, and the survivors collected at a bright yellow force field that protected the center tower of the palace.

G.R. MORRIS

"When your worldview is tested, thoughts will flood into your beliefs, and your beliefs will strike back. This is why I call this place W.O.B.: the World of Bias. Your worldview—your bias and your beliefs—is dying."

Kevin pulled his head back in. "You did this!"

The cabbie pulled out another pack of gum. "Thousands of thoughts are born every day. There are always snakes in the garden of the mind."

When they reached the border, the car stopped. Kevin could see his reflection in the cabbie's thick glasses.

"Make no mistake: life is not about becoming the new you; it's about becoming the real you." The creatures were pounding their fists against the glimmering fence.

"This is your stop. Get out."

As Kevin unlocked his door, the cabbie grabbed his arm. "Don't trust Robert. He's been manipulating you your entire life."

"Wait. What?" Kevin said, turning back to the cabbie.

The deterioration of the world was closing in. The cabbie began talking more quickly and put yet another stick of gum in his mouth.

"Okay. This is going to have to be short . . . Look, this temporal existence you call life is a game. There is a great debate happening right now. Think of it like chess. You are the white king—the most important piece on the board. You are not alone."

Kevin rolled his hand, attempting to hurry the conversation. "Right. I have pawns, so—"

"Shut up for a second. We don't have time for a conversation. Just listen."

The cabbie put a hand over Kevin's mouth and looked out the back window.

"You must protect your queen by destroying hell's armies and defeating pretty much every alien race in existence."

The ground beneath them started to rumble, and Kevin opened the door. "At least I got the apple."

"Placebo." The cabbie winked.

"Oh. What the hell!"

"How else are you supposed to believe you can move mountains? He essentially just poisoned you."

Kevin slammed the door, the ground vibrating under his feet.

"Is there anything else I should know?"

The cabbie shrugged his shoulders. "I suppose I can tell you; after all, you won't remember any of this until the time is right.

"Everyone, including myself, knows only what he must know. Robert did not know about the apple's true effect on you. The truth is, every human has access to one hundred percent of his brain, but since the apple, it's mostly noise. Your brain, like everyone else's, was like a drunken animal locked in a cage. Partaking of the forbidden fruit has set it free, allowing you to do the impossible; it will work as it was designed.

"But it is also true that you would have never discovered that you had the power all along. Nor would you have grown from this experience and from what happens next."

"Next?"

"Eventually, the savior brings victory to the light by defeating the Dragon. Oh, and one more thing about Robert . . ." The Holy Ghost smirked. "This will blow your mind." The cab began fading away. "Robert's never lied to you."

Kevin's eyes rolled skyward. "Wait! What? I thought you said not to trust him!"

Kevin stepped backward and watched as the car with the cabbie inside changed. He sighed. "Oh brother. I chose all of this? I must be some kind of masochistic asshole. I suppose it's better than drawing a short straw."

The car was no more; instead, it was a crystalline white dove, and it was soaring away. He heard the cabbie's voice. "Become one with focus. Do not be a victim of your belief in chance."

Kevin ran toward the field. "The tower represents my focus. Okay, here goes." Leaping into the luminous border, he was enveloped by a thin coating of yellow. When his heels touched ground, he was no longer transparent, and in front of him was the massive tower.

"Wow," he said, as diamond steps began forming upward. Each step he took created another one before him. He peered up the stairs into the sky. It was endless. Looking down, it was bottomless. The staircase seemed to sprout from a vast pit.

The steps suddenly stopped.

As he stared down into the vast chasm, fear froze his legs. The tower was still out of reach.

He yelled into the sky, "Hey pal! What do I do now?"

No answer.

Kevin clenched his eyes.

"Okay, this isn't real; it's like a dream. I can do this," he mumbled.

The diamond steps continued coalescing, and he reached the tower. He placed a hand on it. Crystalline bolts shot out from his body like a Tesla coil, and, like lightning, it struck the palace.

The electricity passed over his body and sparked in his pupils; for a moment, he could not see.

Kevin opened his eyes and saw that he stood on a platform like a plank extending out from the diamond pillar. The structures were gone and the cities destroyed; his mind was a tree with no branches.

A dozen feet in front of him, he was surrounded by a yellow field separating a world submerged in pictures and flowing information.

"Whoa. I can feel everything." Everything around him felt like an extension of his body. He waved his hand to his right, and the diamond step in front of him followed.

Kevin smiled. "Neat."

Slender beasts with long arms and eight-inch claws rode a shadow in the distance that spread out like a liquid web.

The hair on Kevin's neck raised. "Great." Kevin looked down the hole and then back at the swarm of demons.

Works like lucid dreaming, huh?

"No . . ." Kevin slammed his eyes shut. "My mind. My rules!"

The darkness splattered on the yellow globe of energy like a bug. The millions of pictures, numbers, and symbols bumped, rubbed, and passed through the darkness. They continued, dulled and stained.

"That's got to be bad." Kevin leaped into the air.

The demons plunged through the yellow. Kevin dropped.

"Come on, work . . . work!"

Like static TV reception, dozens of bloodied eyes swam through the monsters' blurred, flickering bodies. He watched the swarm of arms like jagged branches reach for him.

Kevin took a nosedive. "Ahhhh!"

Waving his arms feebly in front of him, he clenched his eyes. "Come on!"

Kevin's body jolted. He tasted blood and opened his eyes to four three-inch-wide claws moving through his chest. He winced as the thick black veins grew from the wound. "This . . . is my mind!"

The claws vanished, Kevin's body flipped around, and a ring of white erupted from his pupils.

Kevin roared.

G.R. MORRIS

Red thread materialized down the back of his neck.

The demons screeched. Their shark-shaped mouths gaped with dozens of moving teeth like daggers.

Kevin saw his cape and smiled.

He flew like a bullet.

Every punch splashed through their bodies. Dark goo erupted from their carcasses, and they were shot out of the yellow sphere.

Blow after savage blow, he smiled. But they were relentless, coming at him from all sides.

"Yeah! Woooo!"

Too many; they came too fast. When the first monster crossed its arms over him, they piled on, enveloping him in a breathing, heaving globe of darkness.

Inside, the goo was pressing against his flesh. The demons struck again, and again hundreds of spikes battered his body, but none punctured the skin.

Kevin's pupils flared; rising from his eyes, white luminous steam burned. "This is my mind . . . ," he mumbled.

He spun in a blur, creating a whirlwind of black sludge within the globule. Pillars of light exploded from his corneas. The lasers, impelled by the motion of his body, cut through them in a vortex of brilliance.

"Heat vision!"

His gooey cage exploded, and its remnants floated away. He stopped spinning, and the yellow field was gone.

The darkness was everywhere, with countless demons swimming in its murk. Black lightning bolts of shadow and slime fired from the sea of evil above him. The quagmire plagued the images and symbols, drowning them in dark.

A horde of hellions surged toward him. He blasted them with his eyes.

There were too many.

"What do I do now?" Kevin's voice echoed.

He heard another voice, and this time it was different. It was the voice of a woman calling out to him. "Follow me."

Her voice was like being warmed by a blanket of love in a snowstorm of hate, and it came from down below.

Clenching his teeth, he zoomed down the tunnel.

"Come on. Gotta be faster!"

The darkness moved like a tidal wave at his feet. There were no sounds, no images, not even air rushing against his face.

And then the cabbie's whisper. "The role of savior must be earned."

CHAPTER TWENTY-FOUR

*"Experience: that most brutal of teachers. But
you learn, my God do you learn."*

—C. S. Lewis

December 28th, 1976

 few days after the last dark flame had flung the orphanage into hell, a figure lay in total darkness, the victim of an unyielding coma. The heartbeat of life from the savior, which for a year had been too soft to notice, was getting louder. T*hump, thump.*

A glowing light of consciousness was resurfacing. His body had lingered motionless during the coma, lying flat on his back in a place void of any kind of illumination.

Am I dead?

Though his body had atrophied, somehow life remained. Erupting from his mind, an electrical energy surged through his body, trailing over every bone and every nerve. The streaming power was mental self-resuscitation, and the growing consciousness, the first taste of his new abilities.

Robert. That snaky bastard!

His focus was lost.

The blood-pumping muscle started again, and stopped.

Dammit!

He knew that he had been out for a long time. He figured maybe a few weeks. It appeared his ears were working; but instead, a reptilian voice slithered into his mind like thought.

"Morning, hero." His scratchy, grumbling voice grated on Kevin's soul. "Lazy-ass! Tell the sandman to piss off. The world isn't going to save itself, you know." Robert chuckled.

His heart wasn't beating. Fear set in. *Oh God. If you're up there, one savior to another, please help me!*

His lungs had no strength; attempts to breathe proved futile. His frustration hit solid when he couldn't utter a single word: "Asshole."

Note to self: Don't trust crazy-looking snake monsters.

"Your limiting beliefs bind you. You need nothing—no heart to live and no mouth for speech. Push your mind beyond your physical shell."

Kevin's heartbeat again. *Thump, thump.*

"I can't move!" He swore he heard himself.

That was me. What the hell?

Kevin sensed his voice pulsate from his head and grow like a balloon as he willed the words into the room.

He heard Robert's voice again. "Your mouth is closed; so where do you suppose that came from?"

Kevin soaked up the question, and his heart stopped again. Lying in defeat, he listened to the voice of the alien whom he had trusted.

"Get up, oh great Chokin' One."

Impossible! What a dick.

G.R. MORRIS

"Stop telling yourself you need muscles to move. Those are shackles invented by the mind. Will yourself to live."

Kevin struggled to get his eyes open; dried tears crumbled down his face. He could faintly make out the blur of transparent, thin, white particles floating in the air.

There were other orbs, a multitude of elements in a myriad of color. Water in his eyes and mouth had left him, and opening his chapped lips to breathe caused painful cracks to drip blood, saturating his mouth. Moisture in his skin had evaporated, and his muscle strength was gone.

His heart did not beat.

Robert's voice resonated through the walls. "You are too dependent on the body. Your focus lies in the puppet when it should be on the puppeteer, dumbass. You are witnessing existence at a subatomic level. You struggle to breathe because the body still thinks it's alive."

Kevin's mouth trembled as he tried opening it to breathe. *Breathe, damn it. Breathe!*

"In order to be greater than the flesh," Robert said, "you must conquer the flesh. It has been prophesied that the savior shall transcend reality itself. The moment you ate that apple, you entered a world where anything you envision in your mind can come true. If you want your body to move, make it move."

Kevin's doubt was disappearing. He could not deny that he felt no heartbeat, yet he lived. As a consequence, his faith began to grow and, with it, the amount of energy surging through his body.

Okay, Don Roberto. Let's see what happens.

Closing his eyes, he began to focus. In his mind, Kevin saw energy in the form of thought; it was concentrated vitality pulsing under his skin. He attempted to make it grow and extend through his entire body.

Scattering through his chest, it moved like an explosion into his arms, his legs, and his torso. Thump, thump.

"Stop it! Don't make me go get another savior. Because you have the ability to do something doesn't mean you know how. Focus solely on your heart."

Kevin, believing Robert, peered deep within himself. He focused on pictures, images of hearts, and on every beat itself. He thought about blood in the heart being pumped to his body. His mind was engrossed in every ventricle, fixated on pushing blood through his veins.

Thump, thump. Thump, thump.

Kevin pulled air into his mouth.

"Good. You begin to understand."

As he exhaled, Kevin twitched.

"I had to teach you how to breathe?" Robert smiled. "Can you move now, save-y boy?"

Kevin growled since he knew his muscles were useless. He attempted the same process with the rest of his body. His arms and legs fluttering through spasms, Kevin sat up.

"Splendid! You have the capability of an infant."

He ran a hand over his face, and the shakes were gone.

"Remind me when I get my superpowers to kick your ass." Kevin pushed himself off the floor.

The hero had risen. He heard the sound of rushing water. Reaching out his arms in the near total darkness, Kevin traced along a curved wall, the way the blind paint a visual by touching the face of a stranger. Beads of sweat formed on his face and his heart thundered in his tightening chest. "Let me out! Let me out!"

Images of his stepfather locking him in the dark basement rose to the surface of his mind. He slapped his hands against his confinement.

G.R. MORRIS

The chamber was made of stone shaped like an immense egg. He estimated it was about seven feet tall. And he was standing in a puddle.

Something else was there—an evil like a screaming madness demanding attention. It felt like something was moving in his head; an itch too deep inside his skull to scratch. Nausea was setting in.

Within seconds, the water was up to his waist. Bending down, Kevin felt a circular crack where the water seemed to be coming from, but felt no other distinguishing marks.

Robert's chuckle echoed. "You've been in there for a year, but you've been asleep your whole life. Wake up! You have just tapped the surface. Witness reality for what it truly is. Let your claustrophobia go."

Kevin recalled the ticking time bomb on his wrist. "A year?"

The digital display was dead. "Great. I guess time's up." He took a deep breath.

Water covered his nose. "Get me out of here, ugly gecko!" Kevin gurgled. His cracked lips and dry skin were now soaking wet, but so was his hair; the water was over his head. Yelling underwater, he threw bubbles into the chamber.

Frantically, Kevin slapped his hands against the shell and let out a bubbling, gurgled scream. No answer.

Kevin's voice echoed in the room. "I'm going to pluck each one of those stupid scales off your stupid face!"

The motion of his arms underwater swirled glowing particles. Curious, he reached out, pinching at the microscopic luminous orbs. As bright as the spheres were, they did not illuminate anything around them.

"Yoo-hoo! Wasn't the anointed one supposed to be drowning?" Robert yelled.

Kevin's chest tightened; his lungs demanded oxygen. Those seconds turned to minutes. Kevin's heartbeat was slowing, and all of that work was seemingly for nothing.

He was suffering from asphyxia, which would worsen if he opened his mouth and let the water fill his lungs. Just before blacking out, he felt the perfectly audible, unruffled words of Robert pass through the water.

"What makes you think you need air to live when you were alive without your heart? Stop letting fear defeat you. Concentrate! Ugh."

Kevin focused on the glowing particles surrounding him. He watched the swirling swarms of glowing orbs enter his nose and mouth. *Oxygen?*

He concentrated on one of the elements and peered at its essence. Instantly, the glowing particle stopped.

Hey, this is awesome! He realized he was moving them toward his head. He could actually see air within the water and mentally gathered a pocket of the element, like a large, bubbly bag wrapped around his face.

With the same mental process he used to start his heart, he moved the orbs into his skin; watching the light of the spheres pierce every pore and travel to his lungs.

"Sure, that will work—for two seconds! Can your thinking be more inside the box?" Robert said.

Kevin could breathe. He put his whole body into a haymaker and struck the stone wall. Crack! His knuckles broke. He winced in pain, cradling his right hand.

"You're imagining a wall defeating you?" He could almost hear Robert's smile. "Break free of the shells of your physical limitations and your restrictive belief systems."

"Be like a baby chick, picking at the fixed limits of its world, breaking them away until it can stand and be free. The breaking of the shell builds strength, and without this strength, it cannot survive. If you help it, it dies. Witness beyond what is real. See the impossible."

Kevin sat in the water. Thinking.

"Okay. I'll do it your way." Then it dawned on him. The pain of his broken bones was lessening.

If I were only stronger.

His biceps were slightly larger, and the skin in his hands was thickening—or at least that's what he thought. He closed his eyes and began flexing his entire body.

One droplet at a time, he absorbed the water, changed it into proteins, and fed his muscles.

"This is kick-ass." He nodded.

The droplets turned to jetting streams and surged into his body.

So he continued with his focus, this time on the density of his bones. Water changed to calcium and phosphorous, and the bones in his hands hardened like metal.

And with one powerful strike, the egg burst, exploding with geysers of water—a stone eruption. When the rocky dust had cleared, Kevin's body dropped to the ground. His eyes clenched at the change in light that pierced them, and he picked himself up. The expression on Kevin's face was one of defilement, like the victim of some grisly crime.

A woman's computerized voice in an British accent echoed in the empty room. "Stage one: endurance complete." It was as if the room itself was talking.

Kevin turned around and looked at the holding cell, the egg that he had just hatched from, and the piles of fragmented gray stone surrounding it.

He felt under his shirt, touching his six-pack abs and toned muscles. "Nice."

The water had disappeared, except for a few droplets. Pulverized bits of the stone shell were everywhere on the white tile floor; inexplicably, they were melting.

Something was in the tiles; molecules bustling to the point of blur.

"Yes, Kevin, that's what's called dense matter. Typically, the faster they move, the denser the material."

The room had white, square-foot tiles on all walls, the floor, and the ceiling. If not for gravity, it would be difficult to know which way was up. There were no markings on any tile, nothing to distinguish a way out.

Kevin's entire body radiated with a new sense of awareness. His head throbbed pleasantly; he was conscious of every vein in his body. It felt as if his heart was pumping someone else's blood.

I should be hungry.

For a second, he heard his stomach growl. *I could go for a couple of steaks right about now.*

Right then his body experienced nourishment, even though food hadn't passed through him for over a year. Smiling, he was imbued by vigor, and his belch was satisfying.

His nostrils flared. Eww! What is that smell? As he looked down, he actually saw the stench of near death and feces that rose off his skin like steam.

Dark, misty orbs swirled like microscopic tornados that seemed to travel and stain the air, like a plague. It was a virus of brown and black odors, spreading like a net, attaching to and darkening the blue orbs of oxygen.

Um . . . right.

"Robert!! Where are you?" he yelled.

G.R. MORRIS

"I'm here." The reptilian voice bounced off the walls.

But Kevin did not see his trainer anywhere in the room. He could, however, see everything else.

Kevin's eyes flickered with light, and for a moment he could see more; he could see the nucleus groupings and the element of light itself. Small, circular particles vibrated, spinning and moving incredibly fast within a thin, glowing outline that comprised every surface. However, his periphery was completely normal.

Kevin sailed his arm through a thick mass of transparent particles.

"What is all of this? I can barely see anything but a huge mess of energy circles, like atoms or something. They're everywhere. It's all I can see."

"That is reality itself. On a submolecular level, you can sense every degree below and between it. The particles you are seeing are air, light, dust, and moisture. You are just beginning. Go deeper."

Kevin closed his eyes to try to refocus his mind.

"Choice is limitless. Choose to see something more. You may want to hurry."

Against the far wall, two LED screens displaying the number zero dropped into the room from openings that snapped closed in the ceiling.

"Stage two: speed initialized."

There's that electronic female voice again, Kevin thought.

The bright white tiles in the floor, the walls, and the ceiling parted in their center. Each tile now had a four-inch flat, dark, circular hole in the middle, leaving less room for solid footing.

From behind the walls came the sound of gears grinding.

"What's going on?" Kevin nervously took a few steps back.

Robert's voice echoed in the room. "The noncorporeal moves before the corporeal. Every time you throw a punch, the mind sends a signal to the arm to move. Even in the inanimate, there is information communicating between its atoms; it is the very code of reality.

"When something moves through the air, for example, molecules move in a causal domino effect. There are always metaphysical ripples in reality that move through existence, transferring information before any physical action takes place. How fast would a man be if he could see that information and intercept that signal?"

A spray of thin blue beams of light washed over Kevin's body from every wall.

"Variable scanned," the electronic voice said.

A hard plastic ball shot from a hole in front of him, smacking him in the nose—"Whoa!"—and then one hit him in the groin. His eyes watered and, leaning over, he heard Robert again.

"They're just going to get faster; you may want to start moving out of the way. Why don't you conjure yourself a protective cup, Merlin?"

Kevin grimaced. "Hey! Thi—"

Another ball nailed him on the left side of his head, almost knocking him off balance.

"This isn't funny!" As soon as he yelled, another two balls shot out, nailing him in the stomach and then in the lower back.

He heard Robert's maniacal, reptilian laughter. "Sorry. It's hilarious."

His laughter continued to echo during the crescendo of pain. The number of balls shooting out of the holes from every direction quickly increased.

Unbeknownst to Kevin, the inky Darkness moved into his heart. The cells in his body were turning black.

The room echoed with the thudding sounds of meat being pulverized. Hundreds of balls grew to thousands per second.

Kevin did not dodge a single sphere.

They stopped.

The savior was kneeling in the middle of the room, covering his head with his arms. He was painted in bruises.

"This is stupid! No one can dodge this," Kevin cried.

"I'm disappointed. It's like you didn't even try. Look at your speed, you tortoise," Robert said.

Kevin raised his head and looked at the LEDs. One of them was blank, and the other said 0 MPH.

"Stage two: paused," the room said.

Across the other side of the room, the border around the group of tiles melted away, forming a flat surface. The door opened, and there was Robert, chewing a cigar and holding a handgun.

Robert stood two feet away from Kevin; his proximity made it clear how much taller he was. "Round two. This time I won't even punch back, I promise. Go on, let me have it."

Kevin inhaled a deep breath and blew out slowly.

Robert took the cigar out of his mouth and leaning over, tapped his chin. "Well, go on."

Kevin's eyes narrowed to crinkled slits. "No problem." He threw a right hook toward Robert's cheek.

It connected.

Kevin doubled over; his shoulder hit the ground, and blood trickled down his lips.

Robert was as still as a sculpture.

"What the hell was that?" Kevin asked, catching the blood from his lips.

Lowering his hand to help him up, Robert smiled. "Nice punch."

"You didn't even flin—"

"Let me rephrase. Good punch, for a man without the power of light." Robert pulled Kevin to his feet.

"I didn't even see you hit me."

"Because I didn't."

"What the hell do you call this?" Kevin showed the puddle of blood in his hand.

"The mind's reaction."

"What?"

"It's technical. You see, I transferred the information of the punch and the pain from my brain, to you."

"Ass." Kevin threw a knuckle into Robert's shoulder, and immediately felt pain in his own.

"You could have warned me," Kevin said, rubbing his shoulder.

"It would not have helped. Besides, this way is more fun." Robert grinned, rolling his cigar between his fangs.

"Why don't you show me how you did that? Let's see how you like it!"

Robert raised an eyebrow and held out his gun, handle first. "Here. Shoot me."

Kevin paused for a second and frowned. "I get it. I shoot you, and I get a bullet to the head."

Robert laughed. "Weapons are different. As with hand-to-hand combat, the transfer of pain requires physical contact. At least, for me it does. Eventually, you will learn how to break every rule. Shoot me."

Kevin held the barrel of the gun next to his trainer's chest and pulled the trigger. The bullet moved through the air and bounced off the tile wall. Robert stood behind Kevin.

"How the heck did you . . . I was at point-blank range."

"I moved before the bullet entered the chamber."

G.R. MORRIS

Kevin was speechless, staring at the gun and then back at Robert. In a blur of fading energy, Robert was gone and so was the gun.

Kevin could see steam rise from the holes in the walls; he could see the heat.

"There is no failure. Learn," Robert said.

Light in the room slowed to a pulse. He could see into the wall, through the spinning atoms and particles. A metal ball in the wall moved into a tube.

What is this?

"Ahhhh!" Kevin screamed. A chrome ball the size of a basketball shattered his face. As Robert's laugh slowed down to a deep rumble, he heard the crawling grind of another orb. Kevin's eyes filled with water as his nose filled with blood. Light was slowing.

Engulfed in agony, pain was like a familiar friend, assisting his focus. Sound was a hum; illumination rippled like water.

Blinking, he saw where the orb was: hovering an inch from his face, slowly spinning to a stop through currents of light.

Stepping to the side, Kevin let out a gust of air from his lungs, and the ball struck the opposite wall.

"You mind lowering the difficulty level?"

"Sure. How's this?" Robert said.

Hundreds of holes opened in the walls and shot five-inch balls at him.

"You bastard!" Kevin yelled, leaping over the first barrage. He looked at the LED in the left corner that showed the speed of the balls: Mach 20.

Time appeared to slow. He was floating in the room. He was manipulating the particles to lift him off the ground. He twisted and contorted his body around every projectile as if bouncing off the air itself.

Seconds passed, the projectiles cleared, steam rose from the emptied holes, and Kevin landed on the ground. "I understand now," he said, raising his head.

"Only through adversity can one see the truth."

Robert looked up at the LED on the right that recorded Kevin's speed. It showed 186,282 miles per second. "The speed of light. Not bad for your first try," Robert said.

"Stage three: strength," the room said.

"Oh boy." He heard a clicking, grinding sound of gears. The wall in front of him and the wall behind him were coming together.

"What are you? An evil supervillain?"

The walls were mere feet from Kevin's outstretched arms. *Click, click, click, click!* The gears continued grinding.

The cold of the strange, flat metal slapped against his palms, unrelenting, like a giant vise closing in on his body. His muscles twitched as pressure built in his arms; the strain on his bones caused his hands to shake. He felt beads of sweat rolling down his face.

When the walls pushed his hands next to his shoulders, Kevin screamed. "Great, you're making a succulent savior sandwich, aren't you?"

As the pain of being crushed vibrated through his body, something snapped in his mind.

I think I can.

He heard the room speak. "Feedback pressure measurement: initialized."

Kevin's pupils burned; beams of light shot out the sides of his eyes. An eruption of pure white power grew like blinding steam from his sockets. Light rippled with particles of energy moving through the air like waves. A clustering of incandescent energy stacked on his biceps, and the muscles throughout his body pulsated.

G.R. MORRIS

The crushing impediment began to divide. As he pushed the walls from his body, he saw the LED display. The twinkling digital numbers were speedily increasing:

700 lbs.

800 lbs.

900 lbs . . . *Whoa! No way.*

700 lbs.

For a moment, the pressure was too much for him. "Believe," Robert said. His voice became a lighthouse guiding a lost ship about to crash against rocks on the beach.

Believe. The word echoed in Kevin's mind.

950 lbs.

"No. Not enough."

2,000 lbs.

Kevin's smile grew wider as the numbers grew larger.

3,000 lbs.

"You're getting all the typical attributes of a superhero: superspeed, superstrength, and sleeping with a nightlight," Robert said.

And then, Kevin's grin changed to a grimace.

The light in his eyes flared up. Beams of white energy flowed through the veins in his arms as Kevin screamed. Pain drilled in his skull; he sensed the minister hiding in his head.

Light beaming from his eyes stopped. The smell of sulfur filled the room as tears of neon blue spewed like a river from his eye sockets and down his cheeks.

"Ahhhh!" Kevin's face was melting, burning in blue flames as dark tar poured out his nose and ears. He dropped to the ground; the two walls immediately slammed his body.

Bursting from a door made of light, Robert screamed, "Oh my God. Pause!! Pause!!"

The walls skidded back into their original spots, and Robert's scaly hands pressed down on Kevin's broken body while radiant blue flames spread over him.

"Heal, damn you. Heal!" he said, pushing down on the savior's chest.

Kevin's body contorted and bones snapped as if something inside him was breaking them apart.

Dark energy swirled around Robert's hand as he began drawing smoke out of Kevin's chest.

"Dammit!" Robert said. The black cloud reversed back inside.

Robert removed a square device with a flat screen from his pocket. A transparent fluttering of multicolored energy eddied beneath Kevin, and Robert raised his hand from his chest. He clicked his scaly nails on the screen, his cigar hanging immobile in his mouth.

Whirling, flat, transparent disks shot energy around Kevin's body, lifting him upward and across the room toward the doorway.

"Come on, get in there," Robert said.

The instant his body hit the door of light, a flowing energy moved over Kevin's face. The wounds began to mend. Although his visage was being reconstructed, sulfur was still running out of Kevin's eyes and igniting into blue fire.

As Kevin's body landed on the hovering white porcelain table, there was a rumbling growl; a demonic roar, bouncing tools in their trays.

G.R. MORRIS

The unconscious savior was in an operating room complete with various alien technologies. A floating panel at the far end of the room was slowly projecting a three-dimensional image of Kevin's body as a white, glowing cylinder moved across the ceiling. As the green light completed scanning his body and the hologram was completed, the six screens on both sides of the gray walls displayed images of the injuries, one monitor per body part.

The monitors shook and flickered with static. Robert's eyes widened as he frantically looked about the room. "Oh no."

Kevin's body convulsed.

Three-inch, scaly, slimy black tubules like tentacles emerged from the blue flames surrounded by gray smoke, streamed through the air, and spattered against the ceiling.

A geyser of black phantasmal scum spewed from Kevin's gaping mouth, splashing against the walls, stretching out, and overlapping in a web. A gust of dark slime burst from Kevin's chest, scattering blood and bone in the air. The dark mass splashed against Robert, crashing his body to the wall in a thickening goo.

Robert forced his arms to start to grow.

Too late; the concentrated darkness wrapped around him up to his chin like a fiendish cocoon.

A human figure was forming at the head of Kevin's floating body.

A familiar voice pushed against the walls of the dimming room. "At last, my brothers, we have found it. The Defiance is ours!"

Kevin's eyes opened, and unlike before, when he realized he could become normal even with a nonbeating heart, this time he was broken. It was like being strapped down with heavy chains made of pain. A single attempt at motion pushed him into throes of agony. Focus was futile.

Aggh! I can't!

All he could do was watch in frustration as his horse-toothed former lawyer raised his arms in the air, and dozens of spiraling clouds of smoke appeared throughout the room. He could faintly hear the sounds of people being tortured in the distance.

The man in the black suit turned around to Robert. "Your precious sanctuary will be destroyed, along with your pathetic savior."

From the clouds of smoke emerged monsters—humanoid men with heads covered in spikes and skin coated in tattoos and piercings. The tattooed creatures arrived with their arms and legs crossed, hovering in the air with their heads down, proudly displaying their horned domes.

Each of them dropped from a growing charcoal cloud and landed on its feet, as if small holes were briefly opened that led to hell.

Demons dressed in bandages appeared wearing black cloaks. Dozens of humanoid creatures with six eyes and faces full of spikes that chomped together like swirling teeth followed behind them.

They were outfitted in narrow black chains coiling around every part of their bodies. Sparks flew in their wake as they scraped their four fingers, like three-foot swords, against the walls.

There came a booming sound at the end of the room, a warning of something more sinister.

The odor of brimstone and burning flesh stained the air.

The Coven had arrived.

———————

Looking down at Kevin, the lawyer grinned, showing his perfectly square large chompers. His cheeks began to crack, bleed, and then divide. The smile extended, pushing away parting flesh, and slowly revealed huge broken teeth from ear to ear.

"We win."

PART TEN

AND THEN THERE WAS KEVIN

"*We cannot teach people anything; we can only help them discover it for themselves.*"

—Galileo Galilei

CHAPTER TWENTY-FIVE

*"Through the actions of man evil will cover the Earth. They will
lie in a bed of darkness which they have made for themselves."*

—Raksasha

Kevin's nightmare began with demons.

"Believe, Kevin! Get up!" Robert's scream breathed ice
into the room.

Everlasting fire was bitterly close. The quagmire was cold. Light
fluttered, as if luminescence itself was struggling to remain present.

Ghoulish, skeletal fingers quivered through the floor. Then were
gone. Bleeding faces, broken fangs, and torn tongues grew from the
walls, then vanished.

The dark, gooey clouds violently splashed together. The
conglomerate of murky sludge splattered against the back of the
room. Peeking from its surface surged countless transparent images
of twisting, butchered bodies crying in agony.

The first four demons that exited from the vertical pit were
wrapped in chains. Thrusting their long, spear-like fingers into the
walls, they scattered into the facility.

Arms folded, the bandaged, black-cloaked figures stood in a line along the damaged walls. The hovering demonic monks covered in tattoos closed their eyes. Lowering their horned heads in unison, the inked wretches became transparent. They phased through the ceiling like phantoms.

The darkness spread like an infection, bringing with it all the sensations of the underworld. Wails and moans echoed everywhere, as if they had been transported to hell's inferno. They were as audible as screams, shaking the medical instruments from their trays and bouncing them to the ground.

Dark malevolence erupted from the portal, painted the floor and curdled into a pool—a red carpet for fellow demons yet to arrive. Two-foot-wide carmine-barbed tentacles splintered out in a web from the exterior of the black cavity. Their jagged crimson tips crashed through the walls, the floor, and the ceiling. Fleshy vines coiled around each of the tentacles and sprouted fluttering thorns.

The black bubbling affliction oozed through the holes like a pestilence.

Robert gritted his teeth. "Kevin! Don't let the Darkness take you!"

A crescendo of screams filled the air. The demonic spears sliced, disemboweled, and lacerated.

Brambles coiled around their victims, collecting their bodies as if for a hellish shish kebab. Small, dark perforations began breaking open on the minister's scarred face. "Time is your enemy." Dozens of red, inch-long, prickly spikes emerged.

Fingers materialized from the demonic deluge and surrounded Kevin.

"We see the weakness of your hero." The minister raised his face to Robert. "We feel his pathetic power."

Hands followed the fingers, then arms. They snaked up the side of Kevin's floating metal table. It shuddered. The goo was trying to jar the savior down into the sludge.

There was distress in Robert's eyes. "Damn it, Kevin, hurry up."

"Did you believe I was just hiding away to discover your base? Oh no. You could not keep this from us." He ran his pale finger across Kevin's forehead. "Not from in here." He tapped a red nail at the center of Kevin's skull.

The dark slime of the forsaken pressed Robert hard against the wall.

"And it shall pass that the knight shall be consumed by evil. The Darkness shall rule the earth!" the minister screamed.

"Nullados is wrong," Robert mumbled. Hell's venom had moved up to his neck.

The minister spun around and pointed his long claw at him. "In a few seconds, his prophecy will be fulfilled!"

Robert smiled.

The big-toothed demon pointed at the sludge surrounding Robert's body. "Delusional!" he said, moving his arms through the room. "You hope when it is hopeless!"

Liquefied hell moved over Kevin's legs and up to his chest. He could feel the evil, like millions of fingers tapping and clawing through his clothes. It covered him like a blanket, pulsating into the skin of his arms and up his face.

It moved over his mouth and coated his eyes. The minister looked down at Kevin, consumed in a womb of the afflicted. "He will not survive this. Your hero is . . . but a child. He is afraid"—he grinned— "of the dark."

Kevin found himself mentally struggling against the edges of shadow, an invisible boundary creating a personal cage: a tomb of fear.

His stomach rose and fell. His heart was a thunderous roar, pushing blood at an incredible rate.

There was nothing more frightening, nothing else that shook him to the core in those sixteen years of abuse, nothing worse than feeling alone in that infinite, unrelenting shadow.

Time stretched, distorted. Pain manifested as tears.

They turned to ice against his face, but he could not tell which direction they came from, which way was up or which was down.

Please, Robert. Somebody help me! His attempt at screaming was futile. Struggle as he might, Kevin lay motionless on the table, submerged by evil.

His heartbeat slowed. Vital signs dropped.

Primal fear was drowning him. Focus was impossible. The darkness poured down his throat, into his nose and his ears. It began coating his brain, and blackness bled into his fading consciousness.

Is this the end? I wasn't strong enough to save my mother. He remembered his mother's ultimate wish. "Be better than who you are. Be the best," she'd said.

Mom.

As Robert's body was gripped by the murk, he watched bodies of skeletal demons begin to coalesce upward like dark steam from the bubbling river on the floor. Horn-covered skulls, their red, glowing sockets illuminating slack jaws, their canine fangs, rose from the horrid fluid. Breaking through the surface of liquid sin, the creatures took shape.

Pushing their spiked, bony arms against the ground, they struggled against the current like a phoenix rising from its ashes. Their upper bodies, solidified into jagged ribs, were followed by long, serrated spines that moved like snakes.

Robert's gaze dropped to the blob surrounding Kevin.

The minister smiled. His amusement was cut short.

Six glowing red dots moved around his body.

Two neighboring multistoried gray buildings were evenly placed along all sides of the complex.

The minister saw the Thaylax penetrators. Mounted on a balcony on every floor were six-foot-long, three-foot-wide spinning cannons bursting their projectiles into the hospital. Three of the oversize, wide-mouthed guns were unloading into Kevin's operating room. The remaining dozens were taking aim at the tentacles crashing into the other floors.

Pushing itself through the blast holes and shattering windows, it made its way to the ground floor. The devil's corruption ripped through streetlamps and rolled over cars parked in the lot.

The soldiers, while running backward, unloaded gunfire into the bleak, churning fluid.

The minister turned away and tapped a claw on Robert's nose. "We commend your efforts, as pointless as they may be."

Black blood burst from the cloaked demons; their mummified bodies fell into the flowing darkness. The toothy lawyer smiled, turning his back to the gunfire.

"There is one thing about the light you can always count on"—he looked up at the ceiling and grinned—"its predictable weakness for the lives of the innocent."

The tentacles around the hellish portal that had crashed through the upper and lower floors began thrashing into doctors and patients.

Foot-long slits quickly expanded on the snakelike monsters, into hundreds of hissing mouths. Dark slime oozed from their lips. Thick, vein-covered flesh chunks mixed with steaming crimson, acidic venom expelled from the spitting apertures.

Doctors, with screaming patients still in their beds, were picked up, thrown against the walls, and plastered by a thin layer of dark red pulsating goo.

Human flesh burned, melted.

Several floors above the operating room, the hovering horned demons closed their eyes.

The monsters pressed their palms together and lowered their heads.

Terrified children, weeping mothers, and even wailing newborns still in the nursery began to rise in the air. Their bodies jolted, slammed against concrete, joining the legion of still-living victims lining every exterior wall like a massive human shield. Scores of red dots passed through the metal and stone. Like infrared laser sights from guns, they were moving across the victims clustered together as a living barrier protecting the demons ravaging through the hospital.

The minister turned back toward the chaos in the city. Cracks branched up his cheek when he smirked. "This is much more fun than I expected."

Across the street, the men were panicked. "But, sir. The children!" A soldier slammed his arms down against the gun mount. "My God! The people!" he cried, raising his head from the embedded targeting visor.

Robert's voice buzzed from hundreds of speakers touching every ear in the city. "This is an order!"

A glimmer of light moved over the retinas of every soldier as soon as Robert said the word.

The big-toothed lawyer spun his head around to face Robert. "No! You wouldn't dare!"

Robert smiled.

"Now?" Jason asked.

"Now," Robert whispered.

The first blast burst through the human wall was the beginning of a crimson river that would spill into the hospital. The children, mothers, daughters, and doctors plastered together were being shredded.

Soggy flesh exploded on the floor, and bloody mist filled the air. The gunfire breaking through the human shield stopped, halted in misty shadows.

The demonic monks hovered, arms folded, eyes closed. Dark pulsating energy swirled around their tattoo-covered skulls.

The bullets gathered and vibrated but remained hovering. A ring of light grew from the middle of each projectile, like an illuminated angel's halo. The bullets hummed and spun, shaking away the dark. The eyes of the monks opened in unison. "Kain, help us," they whimpered.

The massive collection of gunfire broke through the invisible force and continued on its original path. The bombardment struck the tattooed devils. Their black blood splattered; their bodies burst.

The blasts streamed through the demons, cutting into the gooey tentacles and breaking away dark flesh. They fluttered about in response to the pain. The bullet holes were closing.

"They're not dying!" a soldier yelled, staring through his turret.

The spiked tentacles thrashed through concrete, arching into the sky. The wriggling tendrils sprouting from the roof crashed into the streets, violently puking seeds of evil.

Bones began to coalesce from the torrential sludge; the skeletons of hundreds of giant demons.

"Fall back! Fall back!" a soldier ordered, peeking out from a hatch.

The tanks followed suit.

A dozen of the main guns on the treaded vehicles fired explosive shots into the massing liquid. The goo detonated, splattering the streaming evil back against the walls of the hospital.

"What is this stuff?" a soldier screamed. The goo simply rolled down the side of the building and rejoined with the rest, continuing its relentless attack.

Hundreds of large demons flowed in the ominous river, their torsos emerging from the muck. The monsters were layered; faces within faces.

The demons' heads were like cocoons, covered in dark green slime. Opening vertical mouths with fangs, they revealed their jagged skulls. Bullets bounced from their bones. Their rotten brown teeth clattered when they spoke in unison. "Soooouuulss!"

The hellion creatures were ten feet tall with swirling smoke rising from their eye sockets, their pointy teeth adorned with dark, leathery flesh. Their wide wings burst out from the sludge, spreading out like dead trees to either side.

Their wings and arms doubled the height of the flowing torsos; they worked ferociously at pulling themselves out of their gooey prison.

"Heaven help us!" Yellow ran down a soldier's leg.

The skeletons opened their rib cages like doors and revealed their blackened, spiny hearts. The organs swirled with ghostly human faces churning in dark clouds.

Launching their ribs, tarlike, wretched mire spurted from their ventricles, instantly reloading the cages by its fusing darkness. The projectiles blanketed the sky like arrows and rained down on them.

"Take cover!" a soldier screamed.

Bony spikes streaked like black lasers into a hundred of the soldiers' skulls. Tips of the demonic ribs erupted out of the backs of their heads, through the front of their mouths or under their chin.

Before their targets could fall to the ground, the projectiles liquefied, turning into dark crimson.

Fire erupted from the wounds. The acidic goo spread over their bodies; their flesh melting. The horrified men, still alive, screamed in agony.

The tide turned; a hundred of the army's fighting companions became the enemy.

This new army of undead creatures bit with tar-covered teeth. Their oozing embrace burned the fleeing human soldiers. Along with their bellowing moans came the random gurgling sounds of one word: "Taaaasssteeee."

Others, bubbling with red fire, moaned "Paaaain!"

Some became walking gore, a mesh of human skin in layers moving around their bodies and tightening like demonic boas. Gurgling and convulsing, they ran toward the living.

Dozens of tanks launched fire into the bony demons, shattering many of the monsters into dark goo.

As each one was destroyed, another took its place. Some soldiers gripped the sides of their white helmets, activating their communicators and giving instructions to their squads. Some were used out of terror. "Robert! Jason! Somebody, help us!"

The darkness spread through the city and slowly infected the dying army. The freezing cold was seeping into Kevin's pores; evil's bite was chilling his soul. Fear had taken root in his mind as his consciousness slipped deeper into hellish imagery.

A grumbling, crackling dark voice pounded through his skull.

"You are afraid."

Pain covered him. It pulsed up his arms; it radiated with every gush of damnation entering his veins.

The skeletons looked around, and Robert's fang-filled grin enlarged.

The horse-toothed minister's eyes widened. "This cannot be! No. This can't be!"

Sounds of rock and roll music mysteriously began coming from the hospital speakers. Robert nodded as if it were some kind of signal.

The shocked lawyer stepped backward and turned to Robert. "At the very least, I'm killing you!" he said, reaching out his hand to grip Robert's skull.

"That's funny," Robert said. "I'm not really here." His body flickered.

Just before the minister could grab him, thousands of squares of light moved over Robert's body. He began crumbling apart into microchips that fluttered into the darkness.

The gunfire into the room stopped.

CHAPTER TWENTY-SIX

*"Your pain is the breaking of the shell that
encloses your understanding."*

—Khalil Gibran

That must mean—" the lawyer turned his head to the destroyed wall.

"It's a trap!" Jason's fist crunched against the large-toothed face. The minister did not budge.

"Ahhhh!" Jason backed away, cradling his right hand.

Robert's voice bounced off the walls. "Arrogant bastard. Timing! I warned you. Put the suit on first."

Hands emerged from liquid evil. They splashed against a collection of glowing squares gathering at Jason's feet. Robert's deteriorated body was making its way around him.

The microchips began stacking up to his knees, parting the dark river. Shooting wires, they meshed together, becoming a shimmering empty humanoid shell.

The female British accent accompanied Jason in his room. "Armor creation ninety-nine percent complete."

"Eve! Now would be a good time!" Jason said, ducking and dodging attacks from the lawyer.

The minister smiled, opening his hands at his sides.

Long obsidian claws began pushing out of white flesh at the tips of his fingers. The four-inch jagged talons parted the human digits, tearing through skin, gushing red blood, and breaking away the human hands. Its tattered flesh dangled at its wrists.

The microchips began spiraling in the air, enveloping Jason in a glowing cocoon of energy. The minister shielded his eyes.

The light cleared. Jason was in a glimmering full bodysuit of diamond armor. Sparks burst from the claw strike across his chest, propelling him through the air a dozen yards and through the gun-blasted wall.

Jason fell ten stories before crashing against pavement.

Computer text moved across the screen in his helmet: [**Minor damage to front breastplate. Ten percent reduction. No other impairment of note.**]

Stacked letters, numbers, and symbols moved like thick fluid through the suit.

"Thanks, Eve. Begin repairs," Jason said as he watched the minister leap out of the building, bearing down on him.

Jason, not even fazed, got to his feet.

Four screens turned to six at each side of his face.

Below each display, rolling text described each of the scenes, including density, weapon damage, ammo, and the vital signs of himself and others. A numerical value of Skyviewer-synced chips showed at the top. Pulsing circular dotted lines indicated the source and direction of the gunfire above him.

It was coming from every surrounding building, shooting into the hospital.

It took inventory of the skeletal demons growing from the river of dark sludge that was pouring into the streets from the now numerous gaping holes in the hospital.

The minister landed in front of him, a mere ten feet away, looking as if the drop didn't physically register. "We will enjoy devouring your soul!" he said. His jaw cracked and began to elongate. The flesh in his face broke apart; the skin in his cheeks stretched and tore.

Jason raised his fist. Light sprung from its jagged diamond edges, projecting an image of a gun the size of a bazooka mounted to his arm. It took only a second to materialize. The minister cocked his head.

Glowing destructive orbs the size of fists, bright energy surrounded by rings of transparent swirling tubes filled with light, burst from the nozzle. The creature took off, speeding away from Jason's aim, leaving a trail of large exploding craters close behind him.

"Eve! Target lock! Where's your target lock?" Jason yelled.

"Velocity unregistered. Unable to comply. Manual targeting now engaged," Eve said.

Jason gritted his teeth. "Too fast for you? Impossible!"

The minister moved in a black blur. Jason directed the gun's barrel at the trail of shadows and fired wildly. A dark puff of smoke blossomed inches away from Jason's back.

The minister lunged. Jason spun around and ducked. Jagged diamond spikes materialized over his fist. Putting his legs into the strike, he launched a thrusting uppercut into the creature's throat, crashing into his bony chin.

The demonic lawyer's body arched backward, over a dozen feet in the air.

"Target locked," Eve said.

"Yes!" Jason said. Following up the strike, he leaped into the air.

Bursting from his gun, bright pulsing balls of energy thundered into the thing's body. The bombardment exploded into it, jettisoning the creature across the sky. The lawyer's body volleyed through one of the surrounding building's walls and crashed through the floor.

Jason clenched his fist. "Woooo!"

Jagged crystals on his right arm flickered and shifted. The gun vanished. "Engage boosters." Light energy expelling from the armor's feet and back rocketed him toward his target.

Meanwhile, the dark river, flowing like molasses, was making its way to the surrounding buildings. Hundreds of demons materialized along the way. The ooze crept forward, attempting to destroy the gun mounts and the new positions the army had retreated to.

The tanks rolled back, launching volleys. "We're running out of real estate here!" a soldier said, unloading his gun.

Dozens of swarming, sludge-covered, zombielike soldiers were breaking apart. Their bodies piled up.

"This is it, men! Your last fight—make it count!"

The ribs of the monsters snapped into metal; the tanks began to look like pincushions.

Robert stepped out of the shadows at the base of the building. "Time for me to end this."

A torrential strike of bony spikes rained down on him. Grinning, he raised his hand. The hundreds of jagged ribs instantly stopped a foot before landing on his green-scaled face.

Robert clenched a fist. The storm of bony spears coated in light energy shot down toward the winged, skeletal demons.

G.R. MORRIS

Every glowing spike expertly pierced the wailing demonic skulls, passing through their faces and exiting out their spines. The demons exploded into creamy marrow and cartilage splinters and plopped back into the dark river of evil. The crowds of mindless humanoid sludge creatures turned their heads toward Robert.

Small wisps of dark clouds swirled between his fingers. "Too easy," he said, thrusting an arm forward.

Several dozen closest to him launched into the air and flew hundreds of feet backward. Dark flesh chips and red goo splattered against the building. The fifty-five remaining men cheered as Robert clasped his hands together and closed his eyes.

The river of dark goo froze. They could hear his raspy, snakelike voice hum deeply.

The sludge began retreating, rolling under itself, churning, like an unseen force was pushing it back toward the hospital.

Meanwhile . . .

As the dark river was forced back into its abyss, Jason flew to the large crumbling hole where he had dispensed his target. Hovering in the dark building, the single slit across the eyes of Jason's diamond-covered helmet put a spotlight over the rubble. [**No life signs in structure**], his monitor told him. [**Switching to DNA targeting.**]

A deafening shriek came, like nails scraping down a chalkboard. The black-suited demon catapulted onto him from above. Its claws clamped on Jason's wrists.

"You cannot stop usss!" he screamed as they spun through the air.

Squirming to wrest his arms free, Jason kicked repeatedly. The minister's body shifted away. "Eve! Get this thing off me!"

The demon, lurching his head forward, elongated his facial spikes.

The serrated diamonds in the suit began to revolve, grinding into the dark flesh of the minister's hands. Twenty jagged, crystalline spikes burst from his armor's glistening shoulders, shot into the air, then zoomed into the earth.

Jason broke free. Kicking the creature with both legs and shooting him with his boot launchers, he backflipped away, propelling the minister toward the ground.

The demon landed in the trap, thudding on the blanket of projectiles laid out for him. When he hit, the spikes exploded in a blaze, launching the creature in the air once more.

Jason's feet struck the dirt. He pushed his hand forward and out from the armor's palm. A stream of concentrated blue-white light emerged. Like a tentacle, the glistening beam shot up, wrapping itself around the minister's body. Abruptly jerking his arm back, Jason threw the monster to the ground.

The demon slammed through dirt and rock, forging a deep crater.

Jason swapped out the energy beam for his gun and aimed for the pit.

"Unable to reestablish target lock."

"What th—?"

Claws burst from the ground beneath his feet. In an instant, dozens of strikes slashed in a fury against the diamond bodysuit.

"Error. Error. Massive damage. Attempting to compensate."

Jason stumbled, his targeting visor coated in static. The minister thrust his arm forward.

The ground beneath Jason's feet faded as its density thinned. He dropped up to his chin in transparent dirt. Before he could react, his surroundings hardened to something stronger than steel.

The density increased. Like a magical vise, it began crushing his armor.

"Eve! Get me out of here!"

The minister, leaning down, gripped his helmet.

His claws began to squeeze. His jaw elongated, and Jason heard—from deep in its bowels—the moans of the souls it had devoured.

"Emergency evacuation protocol initialized."

Light consumed the air and swirled around Jason's body. His armor shifted, and the jagged edges spun. Grinding out enough room for the suit to part down its center, it launched its passenger.

The armor exploded. Jason flipped, rolled into the air, and then both sneakers hit flat on the ground.

The minister smiled. "You've lost."

"I don't—"

A set of claws thrust toward Jason's stomach.

His block was fast enough, but the ghostly talons phased through his forearm into his gut. The monster was deep inside him, up to its wrist.

"Oh, fu—"

The minister solidified the strike while still inside him and, expanding his claws, ripped through Jason's insides, spilling his guts to the ground. Jason dropped to his knees, trying to pull his insides back. His vision blurring, he saw the minister standing over him.

"Your blood smells sweeeeet!" The demon's mouth grew large enough to cover Jason's entire body. As the fiend's head began to lower, Jason heard a familiar voice.

"Catch," Robert said.

The world blurred around him.

"Taste this!" With his last bit of strength, he shoved his arm deep into its giant mouth and down its throat.

He let go.

The minister stumbled backward in shock, and Jason's arm dropped out and away.

Falling backward, Jason fought to stay conscious. He heard the hum of the spinning orb.

The minister danced around, going in and out of phase. "No! No! Nooo!"

The orb phased with him, and thousands of energy blasts in all directions cut the lawyer from the inside.

Jason didn't have enough strength to smile, but he still enjoyed watching the minister expand like a fleshy balloon. No longer able to hold on, he slipped into unconsciousness.

The minister wailed in pain as his growing skin rippled. After inflating ten feet, it reached its breaking point.

The bubble burst, sending white spikes, dark goo, and meat chunks in every direction. Maggots swimming in green slime splattered everywhere. Silhouettes of tiny humanoids made of white energy erupted from the prison of the demon's parts. Their souls were free. Ghostly spirits swirled into the sky.

"Thaaaank yooooou!" they moaned in unison. And they were gone.

A few men rushed to Jason's aid. "Medic! Get a medic! Now!"

Robert leaned down to his comrade's body. "That won't be necessary. Nothing happens that I have not foreseen."

He placed his green-scaled hand on Jason's gore-covered stomach, and his flesh began to pull back in on itself.

Black stitching knit together the edges of the wound as clouds of dark energy spiraled around Robert's hand.

A stygian patch swirled across Jason's stomach, and as Robert looked into the sky and saw the mounted guns still firing into the hospital, he felt something. Something filled with such massive evil that it caused his eyes to widen and fear to erupt over his reptilian face.

"Kevin!" he yelled, getting to his feet. "Jason will be fine; take him upstairs. Protect him."

As a group of soldiers picked up Jason's unconscious body, they watched their master sprint toward the hospital.

"No! It's too soon! Too soon!"

Robert could see the building's structure transforming into architecture derived from hell. The once metal-and-stone walls were turning into frothing flesh. He could hear the sounds of misery as he sped to Kevin's rescue.

Human faces, writhing in agony, appeared throughout the assemblage.

At each floor, the flesh began to crack and bleed.

They're preparing for Kain's arrival, Robert thought.

The river of darkness, once halted and pushed back into the portal, now gushed back into the streets.

The harvested carcasses disgorged from the building and splattered into the tanks below. The roaring sludge amassed to a twenty-foot claw. It plunged toward Robert. He surged from the ground and soared into the black sky.

The rolling ungodliness collided with the surrounding buildings and pushed through the streets with a fervent force. A demon's cackle popped through bubbles at its surface as it smashed the walls to bits and swept through the foundations. The booming, cold, dark liquid bile brought down the neighboring buildings. The architecture crumbled, with some humans leaping to their deaths and others still inside, crushed by the descending debris.

Robert landed on the hospital's tenth floor.

He felt the coldness of death reach the rest of the human lives in the city. A dense bluish smoke rose from the burning sulfur covering the bodies of demons and humans piled in his way.

He stood on the sludge as if it were stone, stepping to the side of the bodies as they tumbled out of the building.

He looked up at the black, starless sky. The hospital's tenth floor was now the roof; below his feet he could see doctors, children, and nurses, all being pulled by the demonic sludge. All of them were reaching toward the surface but gripped by skeletal demons clawing and ripping at their flesh.

Robert heard a familiar voice coming from far behind a pile of debris. "Welcome, my old friend."

CHAPTER TWENTY-SEVEN

*"Whoever fights monsters should see to it that in the process
he does not become a monster. And if you gaze long enough
into an abyss, the abyss will gaze back into you."*

—Friedrich Nietzsche

Stepping into what was left of the operating room and blocking his path to Kevin were two fifteen-foot monstrosities shrouded in dark energy. Executioners. They were humanoids with coarse, rotting skin, concealing their heads in jagged bags made of warped and cooked human flesh, sewn together by bloody stitching. They wore hollowed out halved human skulls painted in blood for shoulder pads, and three-inch black chains wrapped around dark, burned demonic flesh fashioned into a butcher's coat.

Robert watched the monsters in front of him grip their black, blood-dripping, gauze-wrapped hands. "I already know the outcome of all of this," he said as they dragged out their thirteen foot long, double-bladed axes.

"You aren't going to be able to run this time," a voice said.

Robert heard that voice again come from far behind them, and watched as the massive tentacles sprouting from the portal began to surround him.

"Did you honestly think your little ambush stood a chance against us?"

It was Blackthorne, standing right next to the unconscious Kevin, who was still completely covered in the pulsating dark liquid. Just like Robert, Blackthorne and the two giants were standing, unmoved by the flowing river beneath their feet.

Blackthorne squinted; his smile cracking his crow's feet. "Your savior is lost, your sidekick killed, and your army is destroyed. Not even you can defeat executioners. What hope do you have?"

Blackthorne stepped to the side. Emerging from the dark portal were three ministers smiling at him with their horse teeth and all wearing that same black suit.

"Why hesitate to kill me if you've already won?" Robert said.

Inky shadows rose from Blackthorne's clenched fist. "You live in darkness already; you still taste its power. Come back to us."

"Why? I'm on the winning side."

"Your Timeweb toy must be faulty." Blackthorne snickered. He ran his withered old finger across the flowing black cocoon that housed Kevin.

Blackthorne raised his fists. "And it shall pass that the knight will be consumed by darkness and will deny the snake, forsaking the path of the savior!"

Robert lowered his eyes. "No. I was wrong. We were all wrong. The book of Nullados is false."

"You have let the dogma of the changelings pull you away from your own teachings." Blackthorne's head darted to Robert. "Your savior will join us, whether he wants to or not. Do you deny your eyes?"

Looking at the flowing tarry shell, Robert's face sagged into despair. "Come on, get out of there!"

"Light is bonded with truth," Blackthorne continued, "and since you now favor it, it is only fitting that your new apprentice knows the truth about you. I know you can hear me, boy," he said, tapping his broken yellow fingernail on the hardening goo.

"Your little reptilian sensei and I are old buddies; in fact, he is the one who trained me. He trained all of us. He was the beginning of the Coven. The founder."

Robert heard something behind him crawling up the side of the building. Skinless humans wrapped in churning barbed wire were breaking out of the flesh of the walls. Covered in blood, the tortured souls were missing eyes, and the hooks of the wire were constantly grinding into their muscles and organs.

Robert turned back around. "That was a long time ago. I've seen the truth. I've changed; you can change!"

"You know I can't. The changelings must pay."

Robert watched as the tentacles formed a surrounding wall behind him, and the three ministers moved next to the executioners—one on either side, and one in the middle. They stepped toward him.

"You told me once that Ellodion was a fraud," Blackthorne said. "That he created the Timeweb as another means of control. You see, Kevin, the only way to defeat the changelings was to gain a source of power far greater than their technology. Manipulating just about everyone, he became the leader of CID . . . He's been a great asset."

Robert stared at the swirling, black, ghostly goo in his claws. "That power corrupts; it poisons your essence. You become nothing. I was a desperate fool."

Robert watched the three ministers as they moved in unison, their fingers breaking away to reveal their long crimson claws.

Blackthorne turned back to Kevin and Robert. "Yes, trust this hypocrite. He's controlled you your whole life! Oh yes. Robert orchestrated your real father's death. He gave you your stepfather. And I'm the bad guy?"

"We do what we must," Robert nodded slightly.

Blackthorne smirked. "Precisely," he said as he snapped his fingers. "Gut him."

The giant demons crept forward and hoisted their axes. Robert's snakelike eyes opened wider, and he stepped backward. He lowered his head and glanced at the spiked boots of the towering demons.

"How delicious! Can it be? The great serpent is afraid! He's weakened! Strike him down—now!"

Time slowed to a crawl as Robert watched the blade of one axe shoot down toward his face and another come at him from the side. He saw the ministers charging at him with their claws drawn, ready to strike. The massive squirming tentacles joined together behind him, interlocking like fingers and blocking his escape. The skinless horrors were crawling over them.

Blackthorne steepled his fingers and brandished a pompous grin.

A rumbling of several demonic growls came from the dark portal. And then there was Kevin.

Robert knew that behind Kevin's eyes, buried deep beneath the skull, sat the invisible shard, a memory, a souvenir from a ghost and the twilight of his past.

The cocoon of darkness containing the savior began to ripple as Kevin's body twitched.

Robert thrust out both palms aimed at the ministers. He pulled back his clenched fists, and the minsters jerked forward through the air. Robert rolled between the executioners' legs, their axes still descending.

The black-suited, horse-toothed demons collided at the very spot

Robert had left, right into the path of the swinging axes. With their joined mouths gaping, they watched as the blade of the axes slashed into them. The edge of the weapons cut through, splattering dark goop and white flesh.

The blades did not stop. Parting the flowing darkness that coated the floor, they pierced the concrete, and the roof of the third floor collapsed, bringing with it the dark slime splashing down.

Robert reached into his trench coat as he fell toward the third floor and released two metal orbs into the air.

Laughing, Blackthorne lowered himself with Kevin's body, still in the cocoon, cradled by a pillar of darkness.

"Our creatures are limitless. Your powers are not."

The first metal ball spun, discharging hundreds of energy blasts per second at one of the plunging executioners. The second shot a shower of white tentacles that wrapped themselves around the other towering monster. The other giant landed, unfazed by the thousands of shots striking his body. The demon answered, its axe splitting down the orb's center. Popping in a cloud of sparks, the hovering globe vanished.

The encumbered executioner crashed to the floor on its back. Slowly, it pulled its arms apart. Shaking, the orb threw sparks, and the trembling tentacles began to fade.

Just as Robert raised his head from rolling out of this fall, his body erupted in fire. He saw bloody, skinless fingers grip his shoulders and felt them clutch at his arms.

He spun out of their grip and faced them.

The fire vanished.

Dozens of two-inch thick barbed wires, covered in gobbets of torn flesh, shot out and were now an inch from his face.

He threw himself on his back, the darting missiles shooting over him.

Robert thrust his arms out once more, slamming the dozens of blood-covered demons against the far wall.

Blackthorne raised an eyebrow, watching their bodies flatten and splatter into red goo.

Robert's back to the ground, the minister stood over him, showing him his transparent arms.

Robert's body flickered in and out of being. Robert caught the strike at the wrist and felt the heat from the ghostly claws. The minister cocked his head and pressed down, pinning the reptilian hero against the dark, sludge-coated floor.

"Your head will be the centerpiece of my collection," Blackthorne said as he watched one of the executioners raise his axe.

The demonic growl rumbling from inside the dark portal was growing louder.

A wall of light preventing memory dimmed and shattered like glass in Kevin's brain. Forbidden recollections bled back into his world, and he heard the last words of the Holy Ghost echoing in his skull: "Don't trust Robert. Become one with focus."

Kevin gripped the Superman emblem in his front pocket. This was the last gift Mom gave me. He rubbed it between his fingers.

Something warm stirred in his mind: a glow. Light exploded into a myriad of color, shooting streams throughout his head.

Kevin wasn't sure if the Holy Ghost saved him, or if it was hearing the truth about Robert's manipulation that centered him. He knew he had to save humanity. His voice boomed through the entire building, commanding attention like a god.

"STOP!"

CHAPTER TWENTY-EIGHT

*"It is better to conquer yourself than to win a thousand
battles. Then the victory is yours. It cannot be taken from
you, not by angels or by demons, heaven or hell."*

—Buddha

The hard, black cocoon around him thinned enough for Kevin
to watch it become a rapidly expanding bubble.

Hearing the thunder of Kevin's voice was so startling, the
executioner halted his strike three feet from Robert's neck. The minister
lost focus.

Robert thrust his arms forward and propelled the minister
backward with an invisible force. The blow launched the creature
upward into the blade of the axe.

Punctured through the chest, the demon ended in a burst of
light.

"I love these executioners," Robert said, leaping to his feet.

Blackthorne ground his teeth and turned his head to the side.
"You idiots! Kill him!"

He noticed the cocoon around Kevin expanding. "No, no, no,
no, no!"

The sludge bubble exploded, and blinding light burst in the room. The darkness on the floor and walls evaporated. The giant tentacles coming out of the portal withered into dark dust.

Kevin now appeared as an all-white silhouette. His clothing was glowing white, and so was his skin. The only thing that remained dark was his black hair. He was hovering in the center of the room, lying flat.

Bright steam rose from his fingertips, and the hospital shook.

He grinned.

Luminescence swirled around his body like water as sprites of light rose from its surface. The liquid, made of pure white energy, collected at Kevin's chest.

Blackthorne, turning away, shielded his face with his forearm. "No! A boy cannot stop me! You kill me, and you destroy all hope for humanity!"

Kevin's eyes opened. The rings of his cornea and iris were burning white fire surrounding the yellow intensity of his pupil, which was bright like the sun.

A pillar of the white energy burst from his chest and struck Blackthorne. "Ahhhh!" Blackthorne screamed.

He was lifted in the air, his body sprawled as if invisible ropes were pulling on his arms and legs. Kevin closed his eyes, and a glimmer of white light began passing over objects in the hospital.

"You'll kill us all!" Blackthorne trembled.

Swarms of syringes stuck in his face and surgical instruments stabbed his chest. Bedpans, defibrillators, monitors, and medical beds pounded his body.

After being sandwiched by a stack of vending machines, a ring of white light carried away his body, smashing through every wall in the complex.

Flying through plaster and concrete, every inanimate object—from pencils to thermometers—bounced off his withered old hide.

◆

Kevin's victim finally exited the building, his body splashing into the river of goo covering the city streets. His body, gripped in the dark liquid, slowly sank.

Kevin reopened his eyes.

"Apparently, he hasn't heard . . . I'm Kevin," he said, floating to his feet. His pupilless eyes were blazing, steaming with white fire.

Dozens of large chains erupted from an executioner's belt; the first three coiled around the hero's chest.

With one hand, Kevin clutched several of the chains, yanking them toward him.

Pulled off his feet by the immense force, the giant sped across the room, colliding with Kevin's glowing white fist. The strike slammed into the demon's stomach.

The monster's body rippled in cracks of white light and began breaking apart. The monster exploded, shooting his remains into the room.

"Kevin!" Robert screamed.

A white glow moved over the edge of the blade, stopping an inch from the back of Kevin's skull.

The axe jerked back. The demon was brought down by its own weapon, the other side of the blade splitting its head and erupting out its tailbone.

As the second executioner met his demise in a gooey black explosion, hundreds of skinless demons were punching and clawing through the walls.

Outside, Blackthorne's unconscious body was rising in the air; strands of sludge were snapping loose. Hundreds of snaking beams of dark energy shot out of the portal and streamed into him from all directions.

The growling from the portal changed to a roar. Kevin turned around to see a sludge-coated hellhound covered in a scaly, spiked exoskeleton.

"Hmm." Kevin slightly tilted his head.

The two-headed, four-legged beast rammed its red horns into Kevin's chest, knocking him through the far wall and out of the hospital. Its flailing tails left a trail of acid that burned holes in the floor.

Kevin fell; the monster's small-clawed arms growing out of its necks gripped his shoulders. Its multiple spiked tentacles sprouting from its back elongated and shot toward his body.

A few feet before he hit the ground, Kevin pulled the horns apart. The monster's body split in two, ripping down the center, bursting into fire and a fountain of red blood clusters.

When Kevin landed in the river of darkness, none of the bleakness touched him. Instead, he stood surrounded by a deep crater of dry land.

Streams of smoky white energy spiraled around his arms as Kevin's fists began to glow brighter.

"Wow . . . Cool." Kevin grinned.

He could see through the thirty-foot walls of darkness and into the city.

"Diamond walkers!" Kevin said, looking at the human remains in the building. In fact, even the buildings were fakes.

He could see beyond the city, to the sky. "No human lives were lost. Robert, you clever snake," he said, looking straight up.

The various demons were cutting through humans and the sludge kept growing. "Time to call for reinforcements." Kevin smiled and closed his luminous eyes.

A white celestial glow churned around his arm, then blazed from his fingertips.

The blinding pearly essence stopped behind the deluge of evil and split into three beams.

The particles in the beams hardened, fusing together and forming two portals.

Out from the first jumped the elderly crazy man in his straitjacket, clicking his heels together. "Hee heee!" The man twirled his legs, hopping around the tentacles trying to impale him.

From the second emerged two floating guns. "Let's see what some of your toys do, Mr. Robert," Kevin mumbled.

"Okay, gun number one." The switch marked PEOPLE GONNA DIE flipped up. The transparent rifle with a matte finish buzzed, the internal servos lit up. Gears clicked as wires fluttered inside and ghostly plasma churned in the dual spinning barrels at the base. The trigger pulled. The bursts were bright. Hundreds of demons splattered, their disintegrating parts sailing in the air and landing back into the sludge from whence they came.

Horned floating demons folded their arms and lowered their heads. A shadow washed over a few buildings.

Plaster, steel, and wood exploded from the structures and collected in a fifty-foot-thick mass in front of the discharging weapon. As the junk collided, the crazy old man rapidly kicked through the demonic horde. But for each monster his feet tore through, two more emerged from the lake of hell.

The transparent energy projectiles passed right through their shield and the demons raised their heads. Their eyes grew wide. In a panic, the monsters chucked human soldiers at the weapon. The human bodies burst into vanishing particles leaving their guns and clothes untouched.

Kevin shrugged. "A phase gun that only affects organics. Neat."

As the first gun continued to fire, a white glow washed over the second. "Okay, gun number two."

A small golden button on its side depressed.

The seven-foot-long chrome Gatling rail gun hummed as the holographic display marked every demon in red. "Targets acquired," the gun said.

A kaleidoscope of energy burst and coalesced into a portal in the large transparent dome-shaped magazine. Ammo dropped from the portal to a conveyance that fed into its chamber.

Kevin smiled and the trigger pulled.

Electricity stormed around the rotating barrel cluster as a torrent of five hundred projectiles per second burned through the air. Some of the thirty-inch projectiles popped the demons, leaving acid-drenched disintegrating gore. Others broke apart in midair; the middle chambers split, saturating the evil goo with acid, and the rear segments dropped off and drilled just beneath the ground. The land mines only detonated when one of the targets got in range. But all of them launched spiraling tips that opened and broke apart to reveal six-inch glimmering chrome robotic ninjas.

When the thousands of mini robots hit the ground, they raised their samurai swords and screamed. The metal army spun, kicked, punched and slashed their way through the monsters, more than half immediately exploding under a hail of spiked demon tentacles.

Kevin nodded. "A Gatling gun that shoots robo ninjas. Hmm."

The sludge surged. He felt the rage of hell grow and watched the goo pass over him, containing him in an air pocket.

Kevin was in a dome in the middle of the Sahara desert. The buildings, the city, the tanks, the soldiers, and the victims were all forgeries of reality.

He felt the evil in the monsters; the demons were very much real. It was not a simulation or a test. He was certain of it. Standing in the middle of the surging walls of darkness, he smiled.

Meanwhile, back in the building . . .

Robert darted around the room, ducking under barbed wire strikes and slashing through skinless bodies. He was fast, gutting groups of them per second. But there were too many. A few of them caught his arms, picked him up, and pinned him to the wall.

"He's mine," a voice boomed like an avalanche.

Outside, the dome began to shake. Sand trickled through, falling from the cracking exterior. The skinless, bloody figures dropped the trench-coat-wearing snake.

"Kain," Robert said, as he watched them slowly back away.

Blackthorne appeared before him in a puff of swirling darkness.

The old man's withered face was darker, transparent. Inside, his head was a swirling mesh of humanoid bodies, mangled and misshapen. Countless tormented souls burning in agony and swimming in a pool of darkness filled his body like water fills a glass.

"You aren't supposed to be here," Robert said.

"Breaking rules is in our nature." The voice of Kain coming from this mouth was like an echo of harmonized demons all talking at once.

Robert took a deep breath. "Don't you have a kingdom to rule?"

Kain stepped forward , pressing his arched nose against Robert's. "I know what you're going to do. Don't."

Robert lunged, extending his large hand around Kain's head, throwing his body backward and slamming him hard enough to explode plaster.

Kain's head crumbled, transforming into acidic maggots that bit through Robert's scales and burrowed into his skin.

Screaming in agony, Robert pulled his arm back and cradled his steaming hand. He stumbled backward, watching the worms squirm up to his wrist.

Kain's head returned, reformed by growing maggots from Blackthorne's shoulders. He opened his mouth, letting the larva drop from his lips.

"They will take over your mind, and you will be one of us again." Kain smiled, his teeth smudged by tar.

"No!" Robert screamed, burying claws into his own shoulder. Ripping through flesh, he tore his bubbling arm off. It flopped on the ground; he watched as it dissolved into black ooze.

"Fruitless." Kain raised his transparent, shadowy hand toward Robert; its yellow fingers and nails were dripping in blood.

Robert fell to his knees and began twitching. Black pulsating veins spread over his body. Vomit gushed through his fangs in the form of liquid darkness.

"I wi—will . . . n . . . n . . . n—never!"

G.R. MORRIS

Meanwhile, at the bottom of the hospital, a rumbling of voices bubbled in the walls around Kevin. "Kill the light bringer!"

Kevin lowered his head and closed his eyes.

Dozens, then hundreds of demons splashed out from all sides of the darkness blob. Long-clawed monsters of various shapes and sizes slashed at the savior's body.

Kevin stood still.

The fiends cut and stabbed the hero. They hit him with thousands of strikes, but no wounds were made and no blood was spilt.

Until after Kevin raised his head with a cocky smile.

Demon bodies exploded. They were slashed, stabbed, and cut in the exact way they hit him. Hundreds screeched as they burst into goo and then evaporated.

Kevin remained still. He slapped his hands together and slowly pulled them apart. Streams of white energy swirled through the river of darkness as they parted.

"Moses, this one's for you."

Crouching on one knee, Kevin launched himself into the air. He saw Robert on his knees, surrounded by hundreds of skinless demons. To get to him, Kevin had to get past the demons first. Landing, Kevin lowered his head, put out his arms, and curled his fingers into his palms.

"Come and get me." He grinned slyly.

Hundreds of barbs shot from the bloody creatures, then froze. Thrusting his arms out, he sent sparkling clusters of pure white energy into every corner. Streaming from the clusters, luminescence thundered into the monsters all at once. Their bloodied bodies burst, disintegrating by the hundreds.

The demons were gone. The darkness was retreating back into the portal.

Kain snarled and, turning his attention to Kevin, dropped Robert's body to the ground.

"Run! You are not ready!" Robert cried.

"He's right, you know," Kain said. "You are in good fortune this night. I did not come here to kill you."

"Good," Kevin smirked. "Then that will make this easy." He jumped forward at the speed of light, throwing a fist toward Kain's face.

Blocked. "The speed of darkness is faster than the speed of light." Kain smiled.

Kevin screamed, throwing a series of strikes at the monster. None landed. Frustrated, he paused. Closing his eyes, he clenched his fists; white light coated his body.

"I have come to offer you a de—" the blinding luminescence caused Kain to stumble backward.

"No. It's not possible," Kain said, throwing up a dark barrier. Squinting, the wrinkly demon curled his fingers. From his palms emerged a swirling pillar filled with vileness—the essence of evil. Thrown from his hand, the concentrated darkness burned through the air.

Like a living Tesla coil, energy erupted as bolts of lightning from Kevin's body. Striking through the floor, his illumination spread to all the corners of the dome.

In a blink, a small wall of white light took shape in front of Kevin's arm. The beam of darkness poured into the field, pressing Kevin backward. Glimmering platelets appeared on his feet and moved up his body.

"The White King," Robert said.

The heels of his knight's armor scraped across the floor.

"Focus!" Robert yelled.

Lowering his head, Kevin thrust his shield forward. A burst of white energy expelled from its center, blasting a beam of purity.

Both beams collided in the middle of the room. Slivers of darkness splintered, and white energy broke into sizzling sparkles. Neither was giving way.

"It cannot be! It cannot be!" Kain screamed as more bile pushed from his fingertips into the stream. The beam was thicker, darker.

Robert winced as he felt anger, sorrow, pain, greed, and suffering radiate into the room. Grabbing the side of his head with his remaining arm, he knelt down, nearly drowning in the negative energy.

The light was being pushed back.

Kevin turned his head and looked down at Robert's quivering body. He pressed his other hand into the back of the shield. A second burst of light pushed through the shield, merging with the first. The beam thickened and became brighter.

The darkness fluttered. Pockets of sludge sizzled and popped.

"I am not afraid of the dark!" Kevin screamed.

A massive explosion of the two opposing forces caused Kevin and Kain to rocket thousands of feet backward.

"Take that, you ass!" Robert yelled, holding the stub of his arm. He watched the image of Blackthorne get smaller and smaller as it spun down into the chasm.

"This isn't oveeerrr!" Kain yelled.

Kevin's body crashed through the dome's exterior, plowing into the side of a sand dune.

G.R. MORRIS

CHAPTER TWENTY-NINE

*"We can easily forgive a child who is afraid of the dark; the
real tragedy of life is when men are afraid of the light."*

—Plato

S tanding in the steady sandstorm, Kevin slapped the sides of
his hands together. Sprites of energy burst from the corners
of his armor. A pillar of light formed between his fists.

"Hero!" Robert yelled, running away. "Kill that thing!"

Kevin paused to behold the immensely bright seven-foot-long
double-bladed Zweihander. The white light of the blades seemed to
extend forever. Jagged angel wings like daggers moved and fluttered
about at the hilt and shielded his hands. He marveled at the halos
overlapping and swirling in the hilt.

"I'm going home," Kevin said, leaping from the dune. He sped
through the air.

The gloppy creature swatted at him like a bothersome fly.

Kevin's blade slashed down into the center of the beast's forehead.
He crashed inside the monster. He fell down a gut filled with boiling
brimstone and sizzling sin.

The esophagus was a dark ocean swell, thickly rippling with screaming skinless human torsos growing out from an undulating well of red-scaled demonic arms. Thousands of claws reached for him.

The tip of his blade extended, cutting through demonic flesh and exploding darkness into glimmering flashes of light. Hundreds of halos in Kevin's hilt spun out like growing shuriken with minds of their own. Slashing and dismembering, they disintegrated dozens of victims per second.

The blades shaped as wings covering his hands grew. Branching out, hacking and slicing, they slowed his drop. At the heart of his weapon, a luminous salvo of white beams surged through the monster's hide.

Wailing in agony, the creature split in two. Its body exploded in quick, brilliant bursts, ending in a hail of sparks.

Landing on the ground, Kevin whirled his sword in the air and thrust it toward the portal. Crackling energy dispersed, and the sounds of the tormented souls stopped. Like a closing eye, it shrank to a slit and disappeared.

Kevin dropped his sword and his shield; his armor vanished. His pupils returned, and he was now wearing jeans and a T-shirt.

Robert was patching his missing arm with green goop when Kevin walked up to him. "I'm done with this," he said.

"What?"

"All of it."

"Time to leave," Robert said.

A puddle of energy appeared on the sand dune in front of him. It was a doorway into another place, a wavy hole that resembled a reflection in water on the ground.

Kevin, brow furrowed, peered down and saw a padded white room. "Where is this?"

G.R. MORRIS

"Fine. Stay here and die of thirst," Robert said, and he dropped inside.

Kevin looked around at the burning sky and then back at the puddle. The portal was closing.

"I should so kill you right now." Kevin followed him. He landed surrounded by dozens of hovering orbs, all of which had an optical lens in its center.

Layers of colors inside bars of light shot out of them and pressed through their bodies as Kevin looked about the room.

Robert was in the middle of a conversation, staring up at the corner of a wall at a black oval camera.

Kevin cocked his head back at the puddle.

Diamond-tipped tubes along the sides of the walls were protecting the portal.

Robert pointed at the camera. "I want to remind you that you have other people in Africa to bring in."

"Okay, boss. Is that the savior?"

"Shut up. Keep pretending you have work to do."

The portal above closed, the energy subsided, and the pillars retracted. The white padded walls in front of them slid away, revealing a circular door that began to twist open. "This is air lock station one. Don't mind the security," Robert said over the sound of metal gears. "If we weren't who we appeared to be, those other padded walls would slide open and fill this whole tube with acid while shooting us full of holes, and then we'd get sucked out into space."

"Space?" Kevin said, walking behind him down the tunnel.

The door opened, and like a liquid blanket, a flowing field of energy covered a white passage with white steps going up. Robert walked through the field and continued up the stairs.

He could see the stars. He felt the lack of oxygen, and then he saw Earth floating far off in the sky.

"We're on the moon?"

"You have a better place where the Skyviewers can't see us?" Robert said as he typed on a panel of keys.

Kevin hurried up the stairs. "What happened to Africa?"

Robert just looked down at the stub of his right arm. The green goo had regenerated a bicep and was working its way to his elbow.

As soon as there was enough room for his body, Robert stepped past the parting doors. "There have been no plans to use the Skyviewer to monitor anything except earthly events."

They stepped into a long, white hallway with two ten-foot windows on either side. "Africa was home. This is where I work," Robert said, pointing to the window. "Welcome to Defiance."

As Kevin followed Robert down the hall, he turned his head and surveyed the base through the window. That room was massive; its length spanned three football fields, and its height was double its width. The storage warehouse near the window had hundreds of three-foot gray metal boxes marked HANDLE WITH CARE: REVNIC PLASMA ROUNDS.

Behind the thick glass, the place was bustling.

Hundreds of men and women in white military uniforms were stacking products and marking boxes, while dozens of forklifts were coming in and out of another room, unloading supplies. Tanks were stacked in levels, displayed in transparent boxes on shelves like giant vending machines being sorted by a retractable mechanical arm.

Still walking, Kevin turned his head to the other window—even the window was slightly tinted white.

That room was just as large. Millions of boxes of M16s, handguns, and even alien weaponry were piled on countless shelves throughout the area.

"Planning an invasion?" Kevin said as they reached the end of the hall.

A thick steel door slid open vertically, revealing a transparent tube with a keypad on the side. They both entered the elevator, and Kevin looked up and down the shaft. The floors seemed to go on forever.

The tubes above and below were lit up like Christmas and scrolling information in multiple languages down its walls.

"Construction of this place was started roughly a thousand years ago," Robert said, pressing a button to close the sliding doors.

"Specify floor," a voice said.

"Subbasement ten. Authorization: Robert Alpha One. Speed nominal."

Kevin looked at the keypad and the LED that said 200 MPH.

The tube descended on a pillar of yellow energy surrounded by twisting columns of whites and greens.

"You've been quiet. I figured you would be screaming at me by now," Robert said. They moved down through the living quarters, millions of housing developments layered one on top of another.

Kevin turned away. "I just can't believe what you did. You poisoned me, basically killed me, killed my father, and you're the leader of the demons from hell. You put this asshole stepfather in my life and took away any ounce of a regular life I might have had. You should be thankful I don't kill you right here."

The elevator elongated after colliding with another energy pillar and shot down a path, moving horizontally.

Kevin turned around and stared into Robert's reptilian eyes.

"I have to know. Is it all true?"

"Don't you know? Can't you feel it?"

"I need to hear it from you."

"Forgive me. I do what I must," Robert said.

Kevin, grinding his teeth, threw out a hand, and a blast of white energy slammed Robert against the wall. "Wrong savior. Christ forgives."

Robert, rubbing his back and shaking his head, slowly brought himself to his feet. They moved past training grounds. There were hundreds of vast rooms echoing with a cascade of heavy, continual weapons fire, scattered single shots, and some short bursts. Towering mechs and giant humanoid robotic suits were launching missiles into transparent holograms of weapon-yielding monsters.

They continued past giant rooms full of these machines conducting various training sessions. They were twenty-foot-tall mechanized armored fighting vehicles shaped as suits. They appeared to have spring-loaded lower leg mechanisms that resembled an animal standing on its back legs. The bodies tapered out into a broad chest section that opened up to contain the pilot. Some had miniguns mounted on the sides of their forearms and boxes mounted on their shoulders containing rows of missiles.

"You obviously don't need me if you have all of this," Kevin said, watching some of the humanoid vehicles cloak and de-cloak themselves.

"The Coven took a serious blow today, thanks to you. But what you witnessed is nothing compared to what's to come. Kain will be back. All of this by itself will fail without you. You have a responsibility to the people of Earth." Robert rubbed his fully reconstructed arm.

Kevin turned and pointed his finger an inch from Robert's nose. "Don't you dare talk to me about what's right and wrong!"

"But the—"

"Shut. Up. I'm done with your speeches."

The elevator stopped, the doors opened, and Robert walked into the room beyond.

Inside was a giant device resembling a syringe covered in blinking lights and hardware. A metal reclining chair blanketed in hundreds of thick spikes was right below it.

"I told you a long time ago that the path of the savior must be chosen; it cannot be forced."

Kevin stepped into the cold, sterilized room that had reflective square tiles on the floor and ceiling. Alien machines were on tables and against every wall. Flowing from each one of them were pipes of fluid and tubes of energy that segmented together, running to the silver chair in the middle of the room.

They connected to its base and ran along the ceiling, pushing swirling, multicolored contents into the chair and a large device mounted on rails just above it. At the front of it, facing the head of the seat, were hundreds of points like syringes collected in a group.

"I offer you a choice: the option to change your mind."

Kevin stood still.

"You are free and in control of your own life. You can return with me," Robert said, pointing to the door they had come from. "Or you can sit in that chair, and I will take everything away. Your memories will be blocked. Your appearance will be altered, and this version of you will be gone. This savior path will be over. You will live an ordinary life; you will be normal."

Kevin could feel by the warm glow in his chest that Robert was telling the truth. He took a step toward the chair.

"I warn you. All of your powers will be gone," Robert said, "But remember, sometimes the process repeats itself."

Kevin paused and then sat in the chair, and like being in an iron maiden, the spikes dug into his back.

He knew what Robert was referring to: the idea that before he was born, he was shown his path, then his mind was wiped. "I will not force you." He recalled Robert's words: "This decision to continue must be yours. You have already noticed that the only fair choice is an informed one."

He remembered standing in front of two doors and picking the one with the cab being chased by supermodels in bikinis. He remembered experiencing that same thing in his mind.

Kevin could see his face reflected in the machine and watched as his long black hair fell out. Strands of blond hair sprouted immediately.

"Just wondering what you are going to look like with blond hair." The memory of Robert's words echoed in his mind.

He planned this whole thing?

He could feel the power in his veins, and something deep inside said to him that his abilities would always be there. He wasn't giving those up. There was a memory in the back of his mind sticking him like a thorn. It was of the woman in the brown cloak. Just who was she? His heart was still emotionally bruised at the thought of his dead mother. He felt betrayed; ostracized by the entire world. Robert was the catalyst for his decision to have a life of acceptance, of friends, and of trust.

"Are you sure about this? There is no going back, not from this."

There was one thing that stuck in his head: the idea that there is no such thing as failure because it's all part of a plan.

For a second, Kevin laughed. He no longer doubted the supernatural—or God, for that matter. But most importantly, he knew this was the right thing to do.

"Goodbye." Kevin smiled and closed his eyes.

CHAPTER THIRTY

*"Fate is nothing but the deeds committed
in a prior state of existence."*

—Ralph Waldo Emerson

Robert pressed a large red button, "Well, Blackthorne. Kain. You got what you wanted." A light smile moved over his fangs. Robert remembered the Nullados prophecy: Knight will be consumed by darkness, will deny the snake and forsake the path of the savior.

Spikes shot up into Kevin's back, impaling him with hundreds of needles. He screamed in pain. His bones snapped and then instantly healed as white fluid poured into his skeleton.

The machine above dropped to an inch above his face. Wire straps wrapped around his body, mummifying him in technology. Metallic braces snapped over his wrists and around his ankles and began to move and stretch his body. An energy stream burst from the device's tip and struck his forehead.

Then he saw something; he felt something that put his pain at ease. He felt the goodness in Robert's heart, and he saw the glow. He pieced together the cabbie's words: "Don't trust Robert," and, "Each word from my lips is said because you and I wanted it to be said."

The savior's screams stopped.

Jason glared at the date above the monitor and watched Kevin's new life unfold.

September 2, 1985

A buzzing alarm woke a fat blond boy from his slumber.

"Eric! Time to get ready for school!"

"I'm up! I'm up!" he said, rubbing his eyes.

You could not find a place to stand in the boy's room without stepping on something: dirty clothes, socks, Pepsi cans, or comic books. There was one math book in particular that stood out among the candy bar wrappers covering his desk. It was marked Property of Kamilo High School.

He stood up in his Superman boxers, his medium-length hair disheveled, and looked in the mirror to see his face full of zits and a mouth lined with braces, and sighed.

"Picture day. Ugh. Can my life be any worse?"

At the front of his lawn, a mailman was pulling letters from his bag, brushing his hand against the black silencer of a handgun. He waved to Eric's mother, her blonde hair still in curlers, drinking coffee while she looked out through her screen door.

"Good morning, Alice!" he said, closing the mailbox.

He turned his back to her and smiled, revealing unusually large square teeth. The sides of his cheeks began to crack.

Mrs. Soterios put down her coffee, "What a nice man." As she walked out the door, the mailman, still with his back to her, stepped into his company car and drove away.

High in the dawn-lit sky, stars were disappearing. A rumble in space vibrated the surface of the moon, shaking the gray dust from its craters. It was a deep, demonic growl spreading across all existence as countless screams of living creatures cried out. Entire galaxies were being exterminated.

The Dragon was coming.

———◆———

Meanwhile, hundreds of miles away near the moon's core . . .

Jason walked into the room where Kevin had changed and looked at Robert. "Is this part of your brilliant plan?"

"It took hundreds of years to get this machine just right. And all of that for just a one-time use."

Robert was typing rapidly on keys, watching his newly blond protégé in the bathroom brushing his teeth.

"Have faith."

Jason moved his eyes over the room, admiring it almost as if it were a well-designed painting. "I don't believe in your religion. I never have."

"Your belief is not required for it to be true." Robert smiled. "The path of the savior must be chosen. It cannot be given. A perfect plan considers all contingencies, every permutation, including people who change their mind."

Jason walked over to the empty chair where the savior once sat. "I can't believe he's gone," he said, covering his eyes with his hand.

"You do not listen. Why do you suppose this room has been locked until today?"

"Do you honestly believe that a machine could completely wipe out his abilities?"

"But you said—"

"You've come far, but learned so little. Kevin would sense dishonesty. Once someone makes any decision, it is over. It cannot be undone. This path of the savior is over. He will be ordinary. He will have a normal life. Until he is ready, his powers will be dormant, waiting for him to believe he made a mistake."

Jason shook his head. "Then what was the point of all of this?"

"Have you forgotten? There are no mistakes. In order for a sacrifice to have meaning, it must have value.

"He must freely give away a normal life to solidify his commitment to the plan of our salvation. Once he makes that decision, the memories of this life, of this path, will return. The savior will return."

Jason paused and looked down at Robert clicking his green-scaled nails over tons of sliding screens and buttons.

"Please tell me you moved the halo to his new home," Jason said.

"I did. He'll be fine."

"The halo can't just follow him around. Why not just make the halo a ring and give it to him?"

"He'll be fine."

"You know, if you had given him the ring before all of this, maybe he wouldn't have left us."

"He's not ready."

"What if you're wrong?"

Robert's nails stopped for a moment as if he were in deep thought. "There is not a man, woman, child, alien, or living thing of any kind that can resist the beauty of the changeling god. I am still in awe of her. Amazingly, she even affects blades of grass. Daren is the key to bringing him back."

Above Robert was a repeating image of Kevin's face being shifted into that of Tom Bane. "He doesn't look exactly like Tom; do you think it's close enough?" Jason asked.

Robert smirked. "It just needs to spark her interest."

On a computer screen next to the one showing Kevin was an image of Daren. The beautiful girl was brushing her hair in front of a mirror. On her desk was a textbook labeled Property of Kamilo High School.

"You let all of those awful things happen to her in the orphanage, didn't you?"

"Planned would be more accurate."

"How could you do that?"

"It is my purpose, and her suffering was part of hers. It was the only way to ensure her strong feelings for Bane."

Robert pointed at Kevin's shifting face nearly resembling Tom Bane. "Men fall in love with that which they are attracted to." Robert then pointed to Daren.

"Women are attracted to that which they fall in love with; they won't be able to resist each other. The story has just begun."

"Our savior is a fatty. How can you be so sure?" Jason asked.

Light burst from the ceiling and took the shape of a bird. A ghostly crystalline white dove fluttered its wings and landed on Robert's shoulder.

"Because it's what we chose; it's what we all wanted."

CHAPTER THIRTY-ONE

"Behold, The Dragon, the great serpent that will kill them
wherever he finds them. His power is ever growing, yet
unmatched, and the violence he brings to the universe
is a righteous cleansing. Hail the black king."

—Nullados

Near to present day...

Kain's voice rumbled in the darkness of hell. "Our savior draws near."

Something darker than space spiraled through the universe, and as it did, stars began to vanish. In a peaceful corner of the galaxy, a flourishing green planet spun serenely in its orbit, vivid in the light of its own sun. Of the billions of organic worlds in the universe, this was the last. Life there was bountiful to the point of crowding, in spite of it being larger than Jupiter.

"Mommy, Mommy! What is that?" A small alien child with hair of green tentacles pulled on the glistening, golden skirt of her mother and pointed to the sky.

A rumble in the dark of space appeared as a growing eclipse. Yet its citizens were blissfully unaware of the horrible fate they were about to suffer.

"Another passing meteor," Jaradrax said, putting a beaker on a shelf.

One of the scientists looked through the window and ran his green leathery hands through his glowing yellow hair. "That dot was a lot smaller a second ago." He squinted nervously, his white pupilless eyes nearly closed. "If that's a meteor, then I'm Emperor Slopack!"

A dark globe half the size of the living world itself was slowly growing; streams of immense black tentacles spiraled out of it. Its mandible and fangs spread out like a giant hand, abruptly stopping the planet's rotation.

The beaker shuffled and fell to the ground, shattering. It was a quake, something the people of Exorac had never experienced in the history of the planet. In some sections, the world was experiencing a shudder so violent that it would have rivaled a scale of eight on earth's Richter scale. Jaradrax was experiencing a level three, and even that was terrifying.

"What's happening?" Jaradrax screamed.

Jaradrax held on to his precious shelves of science, stabilizing himself with his reptilian tail. The planet was bleeding, crumbling, and in pain.

A deep rumble vibrated and the living world spoke.

"The Darkness . . ."

From the blackness of the cloud came its teeth. Thousands of bodies shaken from windows plunged to the ground, only to be drawn into the atmosphere with the debris. A dark hole in the sky appeared to be digesting them and everything on the surface.

It was the mouth of a demon.

G.R. MORRIS

Billions of the planet's inhabitants joined hands and knelt down and hummed in unity, "Help us! We pray to you, Lord Exorac! Deliver us from this evil!"

Craters opened like giant volcanoes as oval spores the size of continents rocketed into the atmosphere. The spores breached orbit, blanketing nearly the entire sky, each one unleashing the force to obliterate life and eradicate a small moon. An incandescent series of deafening explosions larger than any nuclear clouds made by man brought about seconds of hope as the remaining dying aliens shielded their eyes.

Unfortunately, no damage was done to the monster. Its meal was not even interrupted. It didn't even notice. The villain no longer paid any attention to its victims' efforts.

It was made beyond caring hundreds of years ago. It had grown too powerful.

In a cacophony of explosions, the planet crumbled as the immense teeth chewed and devoured what was left of Exorac.

With a savage fury unequaled in the entire known universe, within minutes, the immense beast known as The Dragon brought the planet's life to a torrid and merciless end.

Another light in the darkness of space was eliminated. A monster once bigger than worlds returned to its preferred size of ten feet. The creature surveyed space, looking for its next meal.

It sensed something. Something that made it feel like a child opening his first present on Christmas day. Something that would finally satiate its hunger permanently. A power that would rival its own. Living on a little blue world.

The Dragon growled.

"Earth."

G.R. MORRIS

65 million B.C...

hen ya said we were going to get here a little early, I didn't think you meant this," Wildfire said.

She looked around at the world: the lush greens, the swarms of insects, the giant trees, and the bright blue sky.

Earth was full of life. Wildfire shook her head and pinched her nose. "Disgusting."

Nightstalker snapped the neck of a velociraptor with one hand. "These things keep bothering us. You're going to have to take care of them."

"God, I love you." Wildfire smiled and pulled her long samurai sword from her back.

The ground began to shake. The giant lizards scattered, and speckles of ash touched her face. "Earthquake?"

About thirty feet away, a figure in a black leather trench coat walked up from behind some trees. "Not exactly," Robert said, pointing to the sky.

The immense spaceship was like a flattened metropolis blanketing the atmosphere. Hundreds of metallic tentacles launched from multiple orifices, plucking the lizards from the surface.

Wildfire cut the air with her blade. "Slavers."

Strolling toward them, Robert pulled his cigar out of his mouth and smiled at Nightstalker. "Hello, *hero*."

"Don't call me that."

Robert pointed his cigar at him. "Perhaps you would prefer I call you Kevin."

Robert's body slammed against a tree as Nightstalker's hands clasped around his throat. "Don't make me kill you, old man."

Robert vanished. Nightstalker quickly turned around, and there he stood. "I'm here to help."

Lasers rained down from the sky, and the forest around them caught fire. None of them cared.

Nightstalker twirled a hand. "The great Robert cannot be surprised. *He knows everything!* Hmm. Which means you know what I plan to do."

Robert smiled. "You plan to become the head of the HPA, and you're going to make me your assistant—or that's not going to happen. So, are you going to let me help you or not?"

Nightstalker shook his head. "No."

Robert turned around.

"Since you know my plans, I obviously can't accept."

"Sounds like you figured it all out." Robert started walking away.

"Wait," Nightstalker said, rubbing his chin. "But you've also seen everything happen, so you know what I'm going to say."

Robert stopped and turned back around.

Nightstalker started pacing. "You would have come here deliberately, knowing, which means you wouldn't have wasted your time coming. That means I'm going to say yes. If that's true, then that means I'm making the wrong choice."

Robert folded his arms and looked around at the dinosaurs bursting into ash.

Nightstalker raised an eyebrow and pointed at him. "You would have counted on me saying that as well."

"Let me help you noodle this through. If you say no, you will not only fail to become the head of the HPA, but you will never see Daren again. She dies before she becomes Raksasha."

"So, I don't really have a choice. I never did," Nightstalker said.

"You've already made your choice. What do you think it was?" Robert smiled.

A metallic thunder boomed in the sky. Multiple segments of the massive ship began opening like a hand.

"Wildfire, you got one shot before they see us," Nightstalker said, nodding yes to Robert.

She pointed her six-foot gun at the sky. Marked in red on its side was the word SPARKY.

"That's all I need."